REASONS AND
KNOWLEDGE

REASONS AND KNOWLEDGE

MARSHALL SWAIN

Cornell University Press

ITHACA AND LONDON

First published 1981 by Cornell University Press.
Published in the United Kingdom by Cornell University Press Ltd., Ely House 37 Dover Street, London W1X 4HQ.

International Standard Book Number 0-8014-1378-8
Library of Congress Catalog Card Number 80-69825
Printed in the United States of America
Librarians: Library of Congress cataloging information appears on the last page of the book.

*For Connie, without whose loving attention
I probably would have completed this book
at least a year sooner.*

CONTENTS

CONTENTS

ACKNOWLEDGMENTS

While I was working out the views presented in this book, I received valuable philosophical advice and criticism from students and colleagues, for which I express my gratitude. Two of my teachers, Keith Lehrer and the late James W. Cornman, gave me constant encouragement. William Lycan read the entire manuscript, and I have benefited greatly from his comments. I have also profited from the suggestions made by three anonymous referees for Cornell University Press. In addition, my thinking on the topics examined in this book has been greatly influenced by discussions and correspondence with David Annis, John Barker, Fred Dretske, Robert Ennis, Alvin Goldman, George S. Pappas, Mark Pastin, Thomas D. Paxson, Jr., John Pollock, Ernest Sosa, Irving Thalberg, and Joseph Tolliver. Despite all this help, I fear that many mistakes remain; for these, I am solely responsible.

I have received financial aid at various times from The National Science Foundation, The National Endowment for the Humanities, and the College of Humanities of The Ohio State University. The Ohio State University has also provided me with intervals of released time for research. I am grateful to these institutions for their encouragement and support.

Portions of Chapter Two are taken from my paper "A Counterfactual Analysis of Event Causation," *Philosophical Studies*, 34 (1978), 1–19. Other portions of that chapter appeared in "Causation and Distinct Events," in Peter van Inwagen, ed., *Time and Cause*, copyright © 1980 by D. Reidel Publishing Company, Dordrecht, Holland, pp. 155–169; Chapter Three is based on "Justification and the Basis of Belief," in George S. Pappas, ed., *Justification and Knowledge: New Essays in Epistemology*, copyright © 1979 by D. Reidel Publishing Company, pp. 25–49; these passages are used by permission of the publisher. Chapter Four contains material from "Epistemic Defeasibility," *The American Philosophical Quarterly*, 11 (1974), 15–25. Chapter Five is partly derived from "Reasons, Causes, and Knowledge," *The Journal of Philosophy*, 75 (May, 1978) 229–249. The material from these papers is incorporated into this book with the permission of the respective publishers.

   I wish, finally, to express my gratitude to Bernhard Kendler of Cornell University Press for his help and encouragement, and to Mary Lee Raines, who did all the typing with unwavering expertise.

MARSHALL SWAIN

Columbus, Ohio

REASONS AND
KNOWLEDGE

INTRODUCTION

During the past fifteen years, interest in the problem of defining knowledge has mushroomed. The topic has become a central matter of concern among epistemologists in the United States and, to a lesser degree, in other countries. The phenomenon began with the publication in 1963 of a brief paper by Edmund Gettier ("Is Justified True Belief Knowledge?," *Analysis* 23.6 (1963), 121–123) in which it was argued that a traditional conception of the nature of knowledge is inadequate. The traditional conception is the view that knowledge is justified true belief. The early reactions to Gettier's arguments consisted largely of efforts either to show that his arguments did not succeed or to modify the traditional conception of knowledge in such a way as to avoid Gettier's objections. These early reactions led to new questions, and it became clear that many difficulties would have to be resolved before an adequate account of the nature of knowledge itself could be given. The most recalcitrant of these is the problem of justification, which itself has many facets. Thus, in the effort to devise an adequate account of the nature of knowledge, activity in this area of epistemology has expanded considerably beyond the specific difficulties raised by Gettier; the questions he brought forward are among those that require solution, but they are no longer the only, or even the primary, focus of attention.

When I was taking graduate courses at the University of Rochester from 1963 to 1966, it was my good fortune to be a participant in some seminars on the analysis of knowledge conducted by Keith Lehrer. This was a time when epistemologists were just beginning to deal with the Gettier arguments, and the lines of battle were barely formed. Lehrer has continued to be one of the most active participants in the debate and is now regarded as one of its leading figures. He is also a brilliant teacher, and those early seminars were gems of exciting philosophical dialectic. My interest in these problems was born at that time, and over the years I have closely followed the literature, contributing an occasional paper to the continuing debate. My purpose in this book is to present what I believe to be a reasonable set of suggestions concerning the central problems involved in the analysis of knowledge and justification.

I have found that attempting to write a book on this subject is a difficult business, not only because the issues are complex, but also because new work by good philosophers is constantly appearing. Even so, the general lines of approach to defining these concepts are now fairly well established, and I believe one can in good conscience take a definite stand. Mine constitutes a defense of what has come to be known as the *defeasibility analysis* of knowledge, which is the view that knowledge is indefeasibly justified true belief. I defend a *causal* version of the defeasibility analysis of knowledge. According to this version, the character of the causal processes by which one comes to have beliefs is vital to the question whether those beliefs are instances of knowledge. I also defend a *reliability* theory of justified belief.

The book opens with a discussion of the requirements associated with the traditional analysis of knowledge which were initially criticized by Gettier. One of these requirements I take to be uncontroversial, namely, that a person can be said to know that h only if h. Another of the requirements is more controversial, namely, the requirement that one must believe that h if one is to know that h. Some philosophers have argued that this requirement is mistaken; I defend the requirement against some of the arguments that have been leveled against it. The third traditional requirement is the one that really interests me, however, and the major part of the first chapter is devoted to developing a precise initial formulation of that requirement. This requirement is often expressed thus: a person, S, can know that h only if S's belief that h is epistemically justified. This expression of the requirement, however, disguises a number of often overlooked but important considerations. In attempting to formulate the justification requirement adequately, I introduce the notion of *reason-*

based belief. This concept plays a central role in the account of knowledge developed in the remainder of the book. No effort is made at this early stage to define either this notion or the concept of epistemic justification. At the end of Chapter One, I suggest an incomplete definition of knowledge, my version of the traditional analysis. The requirements embodied in this definition are necessary, but not sufficient, conditions for knowledge.

In Chapter Three I present a theory of reason-based belief. This presentation has two parts. First, I characterize the class of states of a person that can be reasons upon which some belief is based. According to the view that I develop, beliefs may be based not only upon other beliefs, but also upon nonbelief states, such as sensation states and perceptual states. Second, I provide an analysis of the basing relation. The account that I give is a causal one; that is, the basing relation is defined in terms of several kinds of causal relations. Because these causal relations are of central importance not only to this account of the basing relation but also to my causal version of the defeasibility analysis of knowledge, I devote Chapter Two to an analysis of the relevant causal concepts.

Once the concept of reason-based belief is defined, the question remains under which conditions such a belief is epistemically justified (that is, justified in a way appropriate for knowledge). Chapter Four is devoted to analysis of the difficult concept of epistemic justification. Most well-developed accounts of epistemic justification define the notion in terms of a family of concepts which includes the concepts of evidence, having evidence, and evidential support. It is fashionable to classify theories of justification either as foundational or as nonfoundational, according to the kind of structural dependency required within the corpus of a person's justified beliefs, and also according to the degree to which evidentially basic beliefs play a role in the structure of justification. The theory of justification that I develop is similar to many other theories in that it employs some members of the family of concepts mentioned above, primarily the concept of evidential support. The structure imposed here on the corpus of a person's justified beliefs is reminiscent of foundational theories (I am not convinced, however, that the distinction between foundational and nonfoundational theories is ultimately of any very great philosophical importance). I call my view the *probabilistic-reliability model* of epistemic justification. The leading intuitive idea behind this view is that people are, in many respects, analogous to barometers. As a result of causal interaction with the world around them, people come to have beliefs both about specific events and about general features of the world. These beliefs are to the way the world is as the point readings on a barometer are to the atmospheric pressure. But, of course, neither barometers nor people are totally reliable indicators of the way things are. Our belief-forming mechanisms are subject to bias and prejudice. There are many respects in which we may be defective as information-gathering devices, and many ways in which we can be poorly situated for information gathering. If, however, a believer has appropriate reliability-making characteristics, and if the belief is based upon the right kinds of reasons in a given situation, then the very fact that the person in question has the belief may render it much more probable than not that the belief is correct. When this is so, then, on the view that I defend, the belief is epistemically justified. Needless to say, this rough, intuitive picture needs to be replaced with a precise one; this is what I endeavor to do in Chapter Four.

Up to this point in the book, concern has centered on understanding the concepts employed in the requirements associated with the traditional analysis of knowledge, especially the concept of justified reason-based belief. In Chapter Five, I consider the ways in which the traditional analysis is defective, beginning with the examples that Gettier originally proposed. These are examples in which a person has an epistemically justified true belief but in which it is clear that knowledge is lacking. I argue that the problem may be expressed by saying that the subject's belief is defectively justified, from the point of view of knowing, and my main task is to provide an account of the notion of defectively justified belief. I consider a variety of proposals made in the literature and show that each is subject to difficulty. These proposals are discussed in an order that leads naturally to the concept of defeasibly justified belief, a concept that I develop at length. Defectively justified belief is analyzed in terms of the concept of defeasibly justified belief, leading to the general defeasibility analysis of knowledge, which is presented in the last section of Chapter Five.

I argue that the general defeasibility analysis of knowledge is correct. This analysis, however, does not provide any particular insight into two important questions. First, there is the question of the origins of knowledge. In constructing my account of reason-based belief and justification, I take seriously the fact that people are information-gathering and -processing entities. Beliefs are based upon reasons, and reasons arise as the result of causal input, most of which is traceable in one way or another to the external world. My approach assumes that the nature of this causal input is relevant to whether the resulting beliefs are defectively or nondefectively justified, and hence relevant to knowledge. Although the general defeasibility analysis of knowledge is sensitive to such matters, the conditions given in Chapter Five do not provide any clear indication of *how* the causal ancestries of reasons and beliefs are thus relevant to knowledge. In Chapter Six I develop an alternative account of knowledge, which focuses on the kinds of causal ancestries that reasons typically have, and attempts to account for the distinction between defectively and nondefectively justified belief in terms of a related distinction between defective and nondefective causal ancestries. Second, the general defeasibility analysis in Chapter Five provides no insight into the structure of knowledge. It is clear, however, that knowledge does have a structure; some instances of knowledge are dependent upon others. In an effort to clarify the nature of this dependency-determined structure I distinguish between two kinds of knowledge which I call *primary* and *secondary* knowledge. Roughly defined, primary knowledge is knowledge of specific spatiotemporally located events and states of affairs, whereas secondary knowledge includes such areas as knowledge of general features of the world around us. I provide separate analyses of these two kinds of knowledge and argue, with a number of examples, that all instances of secondary knowledge are dependent upon instances of primary knowledge.

These six chapters provide a detailed philosophical analysis of reason-based justification and knowledge. They do not, and are not intended to, provide a comprehensive epistemology. Although the issues dealt with are central ones and I believe that such a system of definitions is essential to any adequate comprehensive epistemology, many traditional problems remain outside the scope of these pages. First, I take no stand here on whether skepticism of any form is correct or incorrect (although, of course, I believe that many forms of skepticism are false). I do not take it to be the business of an analysis of knowledge or justification to settle skeptical questions. The analysis of knowledge and justification is, however, relevant to skeptical challenges, for the skeptic and the nonskeptic must agree antecedently about the nature of knowledge and justification if they are to argue meaningfully whether there are any instances of either. Second, I confine myself to the analysis of propositional knowledge and justified belief; that is, I am concerned with defining knowledge (or justified belief) that h, where 'h' may be replaced with any truth-valued sentence. In doing so, I ignore what may be other independent kinds of knowledge, such as knowing *how* to do something. Third, although a variety of examples of knowledge and justified belief are used throughout the book, no concerted effort is made to distinguish between knowledge of the external and internal worlds, the past, the future, and other minds. Nor do I give much special attention to perceptual knowledge, memory, a priori and a posteriori knowledge, mathematical knowledge, or scientific knowledge. To be sure, each of these kinds of knowledge has its special problems; I believe, moreover, that these problems can be handled within the general analysis of knowledge and justification developed in this book. Suppose, for instance, that one is concerned with knowledge of other minds. On my causal account of knowledge, this will be accounted for in terms of appropriate causal connections, reasons, and the reliability of one's beliefs about another person's mental states. The special problems involved with knowledge of other minds can be formulated in terms of the kinds of reasons involved and the kinds of causal connections that would be appropriate. Similarly, suppose one is concerned with memory of past events (presumably events that one has experienced). According to my causal account, any knowledge of past events requires an appropriate causal connection between the event about which one has knowledge and the reasons upon which one's belief is based. Memory of past events will be a special case of this, and the interesting question would be one of determining what sorts of causal connections and reasons distinguish cases of past-event memory from other cases of knowledge of the past.

Having indicated the main features of my project and noted its limitations, I turn to the details of the analysis of knowledge and justified belief.

CHAPTER ONE

TRADITIONAL REQUIREMENTS

1. *Factual Knowledge Is Factual*

Suppose Fred's employer tells him he will be promoted to the vice-presidency of the company. The employer is a generally reliable fellow, and so Fred has excellent reason to believe that he will be the next vice-president. But the employer has made an unfortunate slip; it is actually George, who looks very much like Fred, who is to be promoted. Hardly anyone will say that Fred has knowledge here. He believes that he will be the vice-president, and he has excellent reasons for this belief, but he will not in fact be the vice-president, and so he is wrong. In general, a person knows that *h*, where '*h*' stands for any factual sentence, only if *h*. Fred knows that he will be the vice-president only if he will be the vice-president. This is one of the requirements for factual knowledge. It is a simple requirement, indeed almost a trivial one. As we shall see, it is probably the only requirement that virtually everyone agrees upon.

But even this simple requirement leaves room for misunderstanding and confusion. One source of confusion stems from the fact that we sometimes say things that appear to violate it; for example: 'Scientific knowledge in the seventeenth century was expressed in theories that we now know to be false'. If we take this sentence to imply that scientists in the seventeeth century knew some things that we now know to be false, then, if what we are saying is true, the factual requirement would appear to be violated. The appropriate way to deal with such examples is to draw a distinction between the strict and philosophical sense of 'know' and various loose and popular senses of 'know'. In the strict and philosophical sense, one cannot know something that is not the case. But in a loose and popular sense, we may speak of scientific knowledge in the seventeenth century; and when we do so, what we are really saying may be expressed in this way: 'Scientists in the seventeenth century were fully justified in believing certain theories that we now know to be false'. This sentence, we may suppose, is true. But, there is no conflict between what it expresses and the factual requirement for knowledge.

There are other loose and popular senses of 'know' in addition to the one above. I suggest that, for each of these, there is a way of paraphrasing the assertions in question so that there is no conflict with the strict and philosophical sense of 'know'.

2. *Belief*

We can discover yet another requirement for factual knowledge by considering the following situation. Suppose Sam and Alfred both come to have precisely the same reasons for believing that Smith killed Jones. Moreover, suppose that Smith did kill Jones, and that the reasons for believing this are virtually impeccable (perhaps there are several highly reliable eye witnesses). Sam comes to believe that Smith killed Jones, whereas Alfred does not come to have this belief. Alfred, let us suppose, is a good friend of Smith's and, despite his good reasons, simply does not believe that Smith did such a thing. Sam knows that Smith killed Jones, but Alfred does not, even though Alfred has all the reasons that Sam has. This points to another requirement for factual knowledge, namely, that a person can be said to know that *h* only if the person believes that *h*.

We must be careful not to confuse Alfred's situation with the following very similar one. Suppose Leonard, another friend of Smith's, also comes to have excellent reasons for believing that Smith killed Jones. Leonard recognizes that his reasons are impeccable and admits that Smith must have done it. Yet, being a friend of Smith's, he finds it extremely *difficult* to believe that Smith has killed Jones. We might even suppose he finds it so difficult to believe that he suppresses the belief and cannot get himself to admit, at the conscious level, that Smith has killed Jones. Even so, there is a vast difference between Alfred's situation and Leonard's, for Alfred does not believe, either consciously or unconsciously, that Smith has killed Jones, whereas Leonard has come to have the belief, even if only at the unconscious level. We may say of Leonard that he, like Sam, knows that Smith killed Jones. This shows us that we can have knowledge even though we find it all but impossible to believe the thing in question. Finding it very difficult to believe something is different from being unable to believe it.

These considerations naturally raise the question: What does believing consist in? In this essay, I intend to remain as neutral as possible concerning the empirical nature of mental events and processes, although it is impossible to remain entirely neutral. An explication or analysis of the concept of belief is beyond the scope of this book; however, a number of assumptions about belief are pertinent to the following pages and require discussion at the outset.

One assumption is that a certain view about belief is false. According to this view, whenever a person can be said to believe something, there is a state of mind that the person is in of which the person is aware, and when this state of mind ceases then the belief in question ceases. For example, it might be held that when a person, S, believes that h, then S is consciously entertaining the proposition that h and is entertaining it with an affirmative attitude.[1] We might grant that sometimes, when S believes that h, it is also the case that S is consciously entertaining the proposition that h with an affirmative attitude. But it would be a mistake to suppose that consciously entertaining the proposition that h with an affirmative attitude is either necessary or sufficient for belief that h. To see that it is not necessary, we may note that we often ascribe beliefs to people at times when they are not consciously entertaining the proposition in question. Most normal adults, for example, can be said to believe at any given time that two plus two equals four, but no normal person entertains that

---

1. In *The Analysis of Mind* (London: Macmillan, 1921), Bertrand Russell defends a view of this sort. On page 250, for example, he says, "It seems to me that there are at least three kinds of belief, namely, memory, expectation, and bare assent. Each of these I regard as constituted by a certain feeling or complex of sensations, attached to the content [i.e., proposition] believed." On the next page he characterizes this feeling as "the feeling of assent." In later writings Russell abandons this view.

proposition all the time. Concerning sufficiency, we may consider the fact that people often entertain things affirmatively even though their actions make it clear that they do not believe the thing in question. Some persons, for example, exhibit an affirmative attitude, even inwardly, toward the proposition that women are as capable as men of holding executive positions, but the sum of their actions indicates that they do not really believe this at all. There are other conscious states that might be identified with believing, but similar objections will apply to all of them. Perhaps the best we can say is that sometimes, when we believe that h, we are in some conscious occurrent state, but that being in such a state is neither necessary nor sufficient for belief that h. Such states are, perhaps, occasional concomitants of belief.

Beliefs are states of a person, but they should not be identified with occurrent conscious states. Some philosophers have suggested that belief states are sui generis: they cannot be analyzed and cannot be reduced to other states. Other philosophers have attempted to reduce belief to some other sort of state. According to one popular view, beliefs are to be identified with dispositional states; to have a belief is to have a complex set of dispositions to behave in appropriate ways given appropriate stimuli.[2] Another view is that beliefs are functional, or logical, states of a person.[3] Yet another is that beliefs are brain states or some other sort of physical state.[4] Each of these propos-

2. In *The Concept of Mind* (New York: Barnes and Noble, 1949), Gilbert Ryle defends this view. On page 134 he says, "To believe that the ice is dangerously thin is to be unhesitant in telling oneself and others that it is thin, in acquiescing in other people's assertions to that effect, in objecting to statements to the contrary.... It is also to be prone to skate warily.... It is a propensity not only to make certain theoretical moves, but also to make certain executive and imaginative moves, as well as to have certain feelings." For some of the standard criticisms of this view, see Roderick Chisholm, *Perceiving: A Philosophical Study* (Ithaca: Cornell University Press, 1957), pp. 168–185; and Jerry A. Fodor, *Psychological Explanation: An Introduction to the Philosophy of Psychology* (New York: Random House, 1968), chapter 2.
3. See Hilary Putnam, "Psychological Predicates," in W. H. Capitan and D. D. Merrill, eds., *Art, Mind, and Religion* (Pittsburgh: University of Pittsburgh Press, 1967), and other writings. See also Gilbert Harman, *Thought* (Princeton: Princeton University Press, 1973), and Fodor, *Psychological Explanation*.
4. See, for example, David Armstrong, *A Materialist Theory of Mind* (London: Routledge, 1969), and *Belief, Truth and Knowledge* (Cambridge: Cambridge University Press, 1973), part I.

als has received considerable discussion, but there is no general agreement about which is closest to the truth.

Without settling the main question ("What are belief states?"), we may distinguish two kinds of views about belief. Let us use 'X-state' as a variable for which we can substitute names of types of states that a person can be in. The substituends may designate types of mental states or physical states. Then, one kind of view about beliefs may be partially expressed as follows:

(1.1)   For any h, there is some X-state P such that, for every person S, S believes that h at t if and only if S is in X-state P at t.

According to this view any specific belief, such as the belief that the sun will rise tomorrow, will always be manifested by the same specific X-state P. If Smith and Jones both believe that the sun is shining, then Smith and Jones must both be in X-state P. If they are not both in X-state P, then their beliefs must be different.

Another kind of view may be partially expressed in the following way:

(1.2)   For any h, and for any person S, there is some X-state P such that S believes that h at t if and only if S is in X-state P at t.

This view requires only that S be in some X-state or other if S believes that h, but does not require of any specified state that S be in *that* state if S is to believe that h. Thus, Jones and Smith may both believe that the sun is shining even though they are in different X-states. Moreover, Jones could believe on both Friday and Saturday that the sun is shining, even though she is in different X-states on these two days.

If we adopt the view that beliefs are sui generis, unanalyzable and nonreducible, states of a person, then (1.1) and (1.2) amount to the same thing. (1.1) will simply say that for any h, there is some belief state, P, namely, the (unanalyzable) state of believing that h, such that for any person, S, S believes that h if and only if S is in belief state P. Similarly, (1.2) is trivially satisfied on this view. The distinction does not apply here.

If we adopt a reductionist view, the distinction between (1.1) and (1.2) becomes interesting. Suppose we take the view that beliefs are to be identified with brain states. In (1.1) and (1.2) we would substitute 'brain state' for 'X-state'. (1.1) would then tell us that, for any h, S believes that h if and only if S is in the specific brain state P. (1.2), however, would require only that S be in some brain state or other in order that S believe h, but would not require the same brain state for each person.[5]

I shall only *assume* that some version of the kind of view expressed in (1.2) is correct. I do not thereby deny that the kind of view expressed in (1.1) is correct. That issue could be settled only by further specification of the type, or types, of X-states that beliefs are to be identified with, and by empirical investigation.

In addition to assuming that beliefs are states of a person, I assume that belief states are causally efficacious; that is, beliefs are states that a person can be caused to be in, and can in turn cause other states (including other belief states). This assumption is of particular importance for the theory of knowledge to be developed in later chapters. For now, we need note only two things concerning this assumption. First, it excludes any view which holds that belief states are only epiphenomenal; that is, that beliefs are caused by other states but are not themselves causally efficacious. This stipulation establishes belief states as full-fledged members of our causal ontology. Second, this assumption excludes any view which holds that there is an unbridgeable causal gulf between mental states (including belief states) and nonmental states. Thus, the event of a gun's being fired can be a cause of my believing that a gun has been fired; and on the other side, my believing that a gun should be fired can be among the causes of a particular gun's being fired.

I assume also that belief states have objects. In expressions of the form 'S believes that h', it is natural to suppose that the object of the belief designated by such an expression is the proposition that h, and that is how I shall understand the objects of such beliefs. A belief that has a proposition as its object is a belief *de dicto*. In addition, we often ascribe beliefs to people by using expressions that seem to indicate that the object of the belief is something other than a proposition. Consider these examples:

5. For a similar distinction and a helpful discussion of functionalism, see William Lycan, "Mental States and Putnam's Functionalist Hypothesis," *Australasian Journal of Philosophy* 52(1974):48–62.

'Smith believes, of Jones, that he is evil'; 'Sammy believes, of Santa Claus, that he knows whether you are sleeping'; and 'Abernathy believes, of the null set, that it is essential to his theory'. In the first example, the object of Smith's belief would appear to be a person, namely Jones. In the second, the object of Sammy's belief would appear to be a fictional creature. And in the third, the object of Abernathy's belief would appear to be an abstract object. Let us say that beliefs that have things other than propositions as their objects are beliefs *de re*.[6]

The distinction between *de dicto* and *de re* belief has been the subject of considerable recent philosophical controversy. Not wishing to include concrete things, fictional entities, abstract objects, and the like among the objects of belief, some philosophers have attempted to show, for example, that all *de re* constructions can be replaced by, or defined in terms of, *de dicto* constructions.[7] Although the arguments concerning such issues are both interesting and important, it is not necessary for the purposes of this essay to take a definite stand on such questions. I shall simply assume that there are beliefs *de dicto* and beliefs *de re*. There are, however, two considerations concerning this assumption which must be noted.

First, the distinction between *de dicto* and *de re* belief is not a clear one. Consider this example: 'Smith believes, of the proposition that *h*, that it is true'. Is this belief *de dicto* or belief *de re?* Consider also this: 'Jones believes that this table is brown'. Is this a belief *de dicto* or a belief *de re?* Perhaps the answer is that some beliefs can be both *de dicto* and *de re*.

Second, just as our manner of speaking seems to point to a distinction between *de dicto* and *de re* beliefs, it also seems to point to a distinction between *de dicto* and *de re* knowledge. We may say, 'Smith knows that it is raining', and we may also say 'Jones knows, of Smith, that he believes that it is raining'. The first

6. In allowing such things as fictional creatures and abstract objects to be the objects of *de re* beliefs, I differ from some other philosophers who will allow only existent, concrete entities to be the objects of *de re* beliefs. For my purposes here, it is not necessary to restrict the class of objects of *de re* belief in this manner.

7. See David Kaplan, "Quantifying In," in Donald Davidson and Jaakko Hintikka, eds., *Words and Objections* (Dordrecht: Reidel, 1969); and Roderick Chisholm, *Person and Object* (LaSalle, Ill., Open Court, 1976), appendix C. For arguments against this reduction see Tyler Burge, "Belief *De Re*," *Journal of Philosophy* 74 (June 1977): 338–362.

expression seems to indicate that a proposition is known by Smith, and the second seems to indicate that the object of Jones's knowledge is Smith. As with belief, let us assume that both kinds of knowledge ascriptions are legitimate. From this point on, however, the primary concern will be *propositional* knowledge, that is, knowledge *de dicto*.[8] Nevertheless, the various definitions that I shall give have analogues in *de re* constructions. To illustrate, let us consider the two requirements for knowledge that have been advanced thus far. If we are talking about propositional knowledge, we may express these requirements in the following way:[9]

(1.3) A person, S, knows that h at t only if (1) h; and (2) S believes that h at t.

The *de re* analogue would be:

(1.4) At t S knows, of a, that it is F only if (1) a is F; and (2) at t S believes, of a, that it is F.

In the following discussion we shall pause to consider *de re* analogues to the conditions for propositional knowledge only if it seems important to do so.

3. *Some Arguments against the Belief Requirement*

Some philosophers have argued that believing that h is not a requirement for knowing that h. These arguments fall into two main groups. First, there are arguments based upon facts about our usage of terms such as 'know' and 'believe'. Second, there are arguments based upon examples involving persons who appear to know without believing. Let us consider a few representatives from each group.

One fairly typical linguistic usage argument runs as follows.[10]

8. In this regard I am in the company of most epistemologists who have discussed the analysis of knowing in recent years.

9. In the formulation of these conditions I include reference to a time, t, at which S believes, etc. In some cases this explicit reference will be suppressed, but it should always be assumed that there is such reference.

10. As Keith Lehrer notes in his discussion of this kind of argument, the origins of the argument are not at all clear, despite the fact that it is often brought forth as a standard line of objection to the belief requirement. See Lehrer, *Knowledge* (Oxford: Oxford University Press, 1974), p. 49.

When I say that I believe something, I usually imply that I am not absolutely certain. For example, when asked where John is, I might reply, "I believe that he is upstairs, but you had better check for yourself." In saying I believe that John is upstairs, rather than simply saying that he is upstairs, I am implying that I do not know with certainty where he is. From these facts it is concluded that my believing consists in my not being quite sure where John is; for if I were quite sure (and if John were where I am quite sure that he is), then I would *know* where he is, not merely believe that he is there. Thus, believing implies not knowing, and by elementary inference we conclude that knowing implies not believing. It is clear that this conclusion is in conflict with the requirement that knowing implies believing.

Two responses are appropriate. First, it is a mistake to claim that 'I believe' is *always* used in such a way that uttering it implies one is not quite sure about what one believes. Even though we often use 'I believe' with this force, we sometimes do not. Suppose I am visiting a friend in Alaska, and one day he tells me that there is a palm tree growing in the park nearby. When I express serious doubt about this, he takes me to the park and shows me the tree. Having seen many palm trees, I am easily able to tell that it is indeed a palm tree. I might very well remark to my friend, "All right, now I believe you!" In making this remark I am saying that I have been convinced there is a palm tree in the park. I am *not* saying that I do not know with certainty whether there is, nor am I implying any such thing; instead, I imply that I do know that a palm tree is there. In other words, my saying I believe something does not always imply that I do not know whether what I believe is true.

Second, this linguistic argument seems to involve the following premise: 'If, when I say "I believe that h" I imply that I do not know that h, then when I believe that h, I do not know that h'. Even if the linguistic generalization in the antecedent of this were true (contrary to the example above), this premise is based on a fallacy, which rests on a failure to distinguish between what a speaker implies by uttering a certain expression and what the expression that the speaker utters implies. If I say "This painting is beautiful," then I imply that I find the painting to be beautiful, but the sentence that I have uttered does not imply this. Similarly, even if it is true that when I say "I believe that h" I imply I do not know with certainty whether h is true, it does not follow that the sentence I have uttered implies this; hence, it does not follow that if I believe that h, then I do not know with certainty whether h is true.

Another type of linguistic usage argument against the belief requirement is based on some observations of J. L. Austin's concerning the way in which we use expressions containing the word 'know'. When a person says "I know that h," is that person describing some condition he is in, or is he using the expression in some other way? Austin argued that when 'I know' is used in the first-person singular, present indicative, it is not being used to describe a state of the person who utters it. Rather, it is being used in a way that is analogous to the use of the expression 'I promise'. This use of expressions such as 'I promise' is what Austin calls *performative*. If I say "I promise," then in uttering those words I have *promised*, I "have bound myself to others, and staked my reputation."[11] According to Austin, it is a mistake to conclude that I am, in addition, describing something I am doing. Specifically, when I say "I promise," I am not thereby describing my act of promising. As Austin puts it, "If I say 'I promise,' I don't say I *say* I promise, I *promise*, just as if he says he promises, he promises.... I *describe* his promising, but I *do* my own promising."[12] To suppose that one is describing in addition to promising when one says "I promise," is to commit what Austin calls the *descriptive fallacy*.

Just as 'I promise' is not used to describe something that I am doing, we can, according to Austin, also see that 'I know' is not used to describe some condition of myself. As Austin says, when I say "I know" I am "*not* saying 'I have performed a specially striking feat of cognition' ... [rather] when I say 'I know' I give others my word: I give others my authority for saying that 'S is P'."[13] Hence, when I say that I know something, I am not describing my cognitive state nor am I saying that I am giving my

11. J. L. Austin, "Other Minds," in *Philosophical Papers*, G. J. Warnock and J. O. Urmson, eds. (Oxford: Oxford University Press, 1961), p. 67. This essay originally appeared in *Proceedings of the Aristotelian Society*, Supplementary Volume 20, 1946.
12. Ibid.
13. Ibid.

authority; I am, simply, giving my authority. By analogy with the case of 'I promise', to suppose that one is also describing himself when he thus gives his authority is to commit the descriptive fallacy.

What do these various observations have to do with the question of whether knowing implies believing? Although Austin did not go on to argue in this fashion, some philosophers have based roughly the following argument on Austin's remarks.[14] Because 'I know' is not used descriptively, knowing does not consist in some state of the person who knows. Moreover, because it is clear that believing is a state of a person, we can conclude that believing is not part of what is involved in knowing; hence, knowing does not imply believing. Let us consider this argument, as well as Austin's observations.

What can we say about Austin's suggested analogy between 'I know' and 'I promise'? Even though there may be some interesting analogies between first-person uses of these expressions, there are also serious disanalogies. The most serious one is also the most obvious. If I say "I promise to pay you back tomorrow," then I have thereby promised to pay you back tomorrow. However, if I say "I know that I will pay you back tomorrow," it cannot be said that I thereby know I will pay you back tomorrow. Saying "I know" does not guarantee that I know, whereas saying "I promise" guarantees (under normal circumstances) that I have promised. It is clear that if there is a performative aspect to utterances of 'I know', it is different in character from the performative aspect of 'I promise'.

In a critique of Austin's writings, Roderick Chisholm notes the disanalogy above and suggests that 'I know' is more analogous to expressions such as 'I want' than it is to 'I promise'.[15] If I say "I

14. In *Theory of Knowledge*, 2d ed. (Englewood Cliffs, N.J.: Prentice-Hall, 1977), and in "J. L. Austin's Philosophical Papers," *Mind* 73 (1964): 1–26, Roderick Chisholm traces this line of argument back to Austin. In "Parenthetical Verbs," to be found in A. G. N. Flew, ed., *Essays in Conceptual Analysis* (New York: St. Martin's Press, 1956), J. O. Urmson defends this line of argument. There is a fine discussion of these matters in Jonathan Harrison, "Knowing and Promising," *Mind* 71 (1962), reprinted in A. Phillips Griffiths, ed., *Knowledge and Belief* (Oxford: Oxford University Press, 1967). The arguments are also clearly presented in Lehrer, *Knowledge*, pp. 52–55.

15. Chisholm, "J. L. Austin's Philosophical Papers," and *Theory of Knowledge*.

want you to do this," then I am thereby requesting that you do it; I am not thereby wanting. If I say "I know that it is raining," I am thereby giving you my word, etc., but not thereby knowing. Chisholm suggests that 'I want' is performative only in an extended sense, and that expressions used in this extended performative way do describe some condition of the person who utters them. When I say "I want you to do this," I am not only requesting that you do it, but also saying, of myself, that I want you to do it. By analogy, when I say "I know that it is raining," I am thereby giving you my word, and also saying, of myself, that I know it is raining. According to Chisholm, Austin was mistaken in the claim that every performative use of an expression is non-descriptive. Those expressions that are used performatively in the extended sense are also used descriptively.

Even if Austin were correct in claiming that 'I know' is not used descriptively, this claim would not support an argument to the conclusion that knowing is not a state of a person. To suggest that 'I know' is not used descriptively is only to make a claim about the illocutionary force of that expression; it is not to make a claim about knowledge itself, and no conclusions about knowledge can be drawn from it. More important, even if knowledge is *not* a state of a person, it does not follow that knowing does not imply believing. Many things that are true of people do not consist of some special state that they are in, but rather imply, of some specific state, that they are in that state. For example, one's obligation to pay a debt does not consist of some special state that the person is in, but being so obligated surely implies that one is in (for example) the state of being alive.

The second type of argument against the view that knowing implies believing is based upon attempts to provide examples in which someone can be said to know something although the person does not believe the thing in question. Before considering such examples, however, we must pause to consider the conditions under which we can say that someone does not believe something. There are three distinct sorts of situations in which we can say that a person does not believe that *h*, but only one is prima facie a source of counterexamples to the claim that knowing implies believing.

Sometimes we can say that a person does not believe that h because, as a matter of fact, that person believes the denial of h. For example, if a person, S, believes that it is not raining, then, assuming S's beliefs to be consistent, we can say that S does not believe that it is raining. It is clear, I think, that when S does not believe that h because, as a matter of fact, S believes not-h, then S cannot be said to know that h. No counterexamples to the thesis that knowing implies believing could be constructed in which S knows that h but believes that not-h. A person cannot know something and also believe it to be false.[16]

Another sort of situation in which we can say that S does not believe something is the situation in which the matter has never entered S's mind. Most people, for example, have never entertained the question whether or not there is a three-ton boulder precisely one mile below the Empire State Building. Of people who have never entertained this question, we may say that they do not believe that there is such a boulder; of course, we must also say they do not believe that there is no such boulder. In short, such people have no beliefs whatever about the matter. It is again clear, I think, that this kind of situation cannot provide any counterexamples to our thesis that knowing implies believing. One cannot know something that has never entered one's mind, something about which one has no beliefs whatever.

The third way in which it can be true that S does not believe something is the situation in which S withholds belief both from the proposition in question and from its denial. If people were to be asked whether there is a three-ton boulder exactly one mile below the Empire State Building, most would reply, "I really hadn't thought about that, but now that you mention it I guess I do not know what to think about the matter." Such a response indicates suspension of belief, or the withholding of belief. If there is to be a counterexample to our thesis, it will have to be one that involves this kind of situation.

The following sort of example has been suggested by Colin Radford in support of the claim that knowing does not imply

16. This would hold even if S's beliefs were inconsistent and S also believed h. But such a situation would not be eligible to begin with as a counterexample of the kind we are looking for.

believing.[17] Suppose at some point in his life Jean learned a fair amount of English history; however, he has forgotten when he learned these things and even doubts whether he ever did learn any English history. Someone asks him whether he knows English history, and he replies that he is not really sure whether he does. He is asked some questions about events in English history and is somewhat surprised to discover that he is able to produce quite a few correct answers. For any given question, however, he is uncertain of his answer until its correctness is verified by an encyclopedia. He is asked to give the date of Elizabeth I's death, and after some hesitation says "1603." Until the date is checked in a book, he is not at all sure that his answer is correct. It seems that Jean does not believe his answer to be correct at the time that he gives it, but neither does he believe that it is incorrect. May we say that he *knows* the date of Elizabeth I's death to be 1603? We may say that he is in a position to give the correct answer to the question. It is also true that he once learned the date of Elizabeth's death, even though he has now forgotten whether or when he learned it. But does he *know*?

Keith Lehrer has argued that we should not say Jean knows the answer even though he is able to give the correct answer.[18] Lehrer points out that Jean does not know whether the answer that he is giving is the correct one. He does not believe that his answer is correct (that is, he is unsure), nor does he believe that he knows the correct answer. These facts, Lehrer suggests, are sufficient to support a proof that Jean does not know the date of Elizabeth's death. The proof is constructed by Lehrer as follows, where 'h' stands for 'Elizabeth died in 1603':

(1.5a) If Jean does not believe that h, then Jean does not believe that he knows that h.

(1.5b) If Jean does not believe that he knows that h, then, even though Jean correctly says that h and knows that he has said that h, Jean does not know that he correctly says that h.

17. Colin Radford, "Knowledge—by Examples," *Analysis* 27 (1966): 1–11, reprinted in Michael Roth and Leon Galis, eds., *Knowing: Essays in the Analysis of Knowledge* (New York: Random House, 1970).
18. Keith Lehrer, "Belief and Knowledge," *Philosophical Review* 77 (1968): 498; and *Knowledge*.

(1.5c) If, even though Jean correctly says that *h* and knows he has said that *h*, Jean does not know that he correctly says that *h*, then Jean does not know that *h*.

(1.5d) If Jean does not believe that *h*, then Jean does not know that *h* (that is, if Jean knows that *h*, then Jean believes that *h*).

This argument, although it is prima facie convincing, is not likely to convince those who deny that knowing implies believing. Premise (1.5c) of the argument begs the question concerning knowledge and belief. In the example, Jean correctly says that Elizabeth died in 1603, knows that he has said this, but does not know that what he has said is correct. According to (1.5c), he does not know that Elizabeth died in 1603. In support of this premise Lehrer says: "If Jean does not know that he is correct about this, then he does not know that Elizabeth died in 1603. For that is all he would need to know in order to know that he is correct."[19] But whether that is indeed all he would need to know in order to know that his answer is correct is the very question at issue in the example. Also involved in saying Jean does not believe that Elizabeth died in 1603 is the fact that he is not sure (and hence does not know) whether his answer is correct. The issue is whether these facts are compatible with the claim that he does, indeed, know that Elizabeth died in 1603. Simply denying that these claims are compatible does not suffice to show that they are not.

What shall we say, then, about the example at hand? We have noted that Jean is able to provide the correct answer to the question, and we can see why he is able to provide it. He has once learned the answer. Does he know without believing? Here it would be helpful to distinguish between the ability to recollect a fact once learned and knowledge through memory of that fact. We can say of Jean that he has the ability to recollect the date of Elizabeth's death, but not that he has memorial knowledge of that fact. It is initially tempting to look upon Jean as having knowledge, for typically when one has knowledge through memory one is also able to recollect the remembered fact. What the example

19. Lehrer, "Belief and Knowledge," p. 498.

shows is that the converse is not true; given that one is able to recollect a fact once learned, it does not follow that one knows that fact through memory. We can conclude from the example that it is possible for a person to have the ability to recollect something even though that person is unsure that what is recollected is correct. But, given the suggested distinction, we cannot conclude that a person can know something without believing it.

This brief survey of arguments against the view that knowing implies believing is by no means complete; however, I do not know of any arguments or examples that are better than these.[20] Consequently, I shall continue to assume that belief is one of the requirements of factual knowledge.

4. *Reasons and Justification*

From the preceding examples we have seen that S can be said to have factual knowledge that h only if h and only if S believes that h. The satisfaction of these two requirements does not guarantee knowledge, however, for they can also be satisfied if a person makes a lucky guess. Because lucky guesses do not constitute factual knowledge, philosophers traditionally have imposed yet another requirement, which says that S can know that h only if S's belief that h is justified. In situations in which a lucky guess is made, the very fact that it is a guess precludes our saying that it is an instance of justified belief. Chapter Four presents in detail the conditions under which a person's belief can be said to be justified. The remainder of this chapter is devoted to complications involved in the initial formulation of the justification requirement. These complications are important in their own right, and a discussion of them is essential preparation for consideration of the nature of justified belief.

According to the justification requirement, S knows that h only if S's belief that h is justified. Whether S's belief that h is justified depends upon the reasons for which S believes that h. The reasons for which a person believes something consist of those rea-

---

20. The debate between Lehrer and Radford has expanded considerably since this chapter was written. The details can be found in Lehrer, *Knowledge,* pp. 55–69. Nothing in the extended arguments substantially changes my view about this kind of example.

sons upon which that person's belief is based. Chapter Three specifies the conditions under which a person's belief can be said to be based upon a set of reasons; for now we shall take the notion of basing as given. The present concern is to emphasize an important distinction between the reasons upon which a person's belief that h is based and other reasons a person may have which are relevant to justifiably believing that h.[21] It often happens that S's belief that h is based upon a set of reasons, R, even when believing that h on the basis of R is not justified for S. This can happen even though S has some other set of reasons, R', such that if S's belief that h had been based upon those reasons, then S's belief that h would have been justified. When this happens, S's belief that h is not justified and S does not have knowledge. Let us consider an example.

Suppose that Frank and Laura are tellers in a large bank. Each of them is efficient, responsible, knowledgeable about banking transactions, and well liked by fellow employees. It is the stated policy of the bank that such employees can expect to be promoted to higher positions in due time. So, Frank and Laura each have reasons upon which a belief that they will be promoted would be justified. Let us suppose, moreover, that each of them does expect to be promoted. Frank, however, suffers from the illusion that the president of the bank, who happens to be his uncle, will do anything to keep him on thè premises in order to maintain peace in the family. His belief that he will be promoted is based on these reasons. Secretly he believes that efficiency, responsibility, and such things have nothing to do with promotional decisions. Laura, on the other hand, is also related to an officer of the bank but believes correctly that such facts do not influence her employers' promotional decisions. Laura's belief that she will be promoted is based upon her belief that she is efficient and responsible as well as upon beliefs about the bank's policy. We may say of Laura that she knows she will be promoted, but we may not say this of Frank. The reasons for which Laura believes she will be promoted are also reasons upon which that belief is justified. Frank's belief, however, is based upon something other than those reasons that would justify his belief.

21. The concept of having reasons will be explicated in Chapter Three.

These considerations suggest that the justification requirement should be stated somewhat more precisely, as follows:

(1.6) A person, S, has knowledge that h at t only if there is some set of reasons, R, such that (1) S's belief that h is based upon R at t; and (2) S's believing that h on the basis of R is justified at t.

In the example involving Frank and Laura, Frank's belief that he will be promoted satisfies condition (1) but not condition (2), whereas Laura's belief satisfies both conditions. However, although the conditions in (1.6) are a necessary part of the justification requirement, they are not alone sufficient for an adequate formulation of that requirement. It is possible, indeed quite common, for a person to have a set of reasons that are relevant to justifiably believing that h such that some subset, R, taken by itself, is a set of reasons upon which belief that h would be justified, but such that believing that h on the basis of the entire set (of which R is a subset) would not be justified. In such a case, the person cannot be said to have knowledge, even though conditions (1) and (2) above are satisfied (and assuming that the basic requirements of previous sections are also met). As an example, suppose Abigail believes that Rudolph loves her. He calls her every evening, brings her flowers, is always polite and affectionate. Her belief is based upon these reasons, and her belief is correct, for Rudolph loves Abigail. A friend of Abigail's, however, has irrationally come to believe that Rudolph does not love Abigail. This friend is normally reliable and sensible, but this time she has gone off on the wrong track. Hoping to convince Abigail that Rudolph does not love her, she deceitfully tells Abigail that she has overheard Rudolph saying that he is only interested in Abigail's money. This testimony, though false and ungrounded, constitutes a set of reasons which is relevant to Abigail's justifiably believing that Rudolph loves her; in this case, the reasons are negatively relevant. Abigail ignores the testimony, however, and persists in her belief that Rudolph loves her. Because she has reasons that are negatively relevant to justifiably believing that Rudolph loves her, she cannot be said to know that he does. The justification requirement, as formulated thus far, is satisfied. Abigail does have a set of reasons, R, such that conditions (1) and

[38]

(2) are satisfied. Moreover, these are the reasons upon which her belief that Rudolph loves her is based. The problem is that Abigail has some additional, negatively relevant, reasons.

It is tempting to respond to this example by suggesting that S can have knowledge that h only if S has no reasons that are negatively relevant to justifiably holding that belief. This reaction would be too strong. For almost any belief we have, we will have at least some reasons that are negatively relevant to justifiably holding that belief. For one thing, there is the statistical fact that in the past some of our beliefs, no matter how well justified, have turned out to be false. This statistical fact provides a reason that is relevant to justifiably believing that at least some of our current justified beliefs are false. For another thing, there are situations in which a specific belief is justified even though the person has some reasons that are negatively relevant to justifiably holding that belief. For example, suppose we modify the case involving Abigail and Rudolph by supposing Abigail somehow learns that her friend has only made up the story about Rudolph's remark. If so, then Abigail's belief that Rudolph loves her is once again justified, even though she has some reasons (namely, the testimony) that, taken alone, are negatively relevant to justifiably holding that belief.

A more appropriate response is to recognize that a person may have reasons that are negatively relevant to justifiably holding a belief but may still be justified in that belief, provided that the union of the person's reasons constitutes a set of reasons upon which the belief would be justified. We can allow for this by adding another condition to (1.6):

(3)   If, at t, S has any other reasons, R', that are relevant to whether S is justified in believing that h, then S would be justified in believing that h on the basis of $R \cup R'$ at t.

In the original case involving Abigail and Rudolph, conditions (1) and (2) are satisfied but condition (3) is not met. Abigail does have some reasons R'—the testimony of her normally reliable friend—such that believing that Rudolph loves her on the basis of the union of her reasons R with R' would not be justified. In the modified example, however, the additional set of reasons, R', also contains information that counterbalances the negative testimony of Abigail's friend, and as a consequence condition (3) is satisfied.

Conditions (1), (2), and (3) of (1.6) constitute my formulation of the justification requirement for knowledge. As with the belief requirement considered in the previous sections, not all philosophers have agreed that the justification requirement is necessary. Opposition to this requirement, however, is not nearly as strong as the opposition to the belief requirement, nor are the arguments against it particularly convincing. The next section briefly considers some arguments against the justification requirement.

5. *Arguments against the Justification Requirement*

One line of argument against the justification requirement is embodied in an example suggested by Peter Unger. We are to suppose that a certain gypsy has been raised by the family to believe the reports of their crystal ball. As it happens, the crystal ball is always correct in its reports, although this accuracy is due to mysterious forces of nature which no one understands. The gypsy's parents have checked on the reports of the ball and know it to be accurate, but the gypsy himself has never bothered to check on a single report of the ball; he simply accepts what the ball reports. Moreover, the gypsy has been well educated and has come to believe that crystal balls are in general unreliable guides. Indeed, he believes that acceptance of the reports of the crystal ball is irrational and unjustified, but because of his upbringing he cannot help but believe what the ball reports. According to Unger, we should say that the gypsy knows what the ball reports: "This gypsy, though he is only unreasonable in believing that *p*, knows that *p*, where the report that *p* is a report of the ball that the gypsy accepts. Though our gypsy does not satisfy the justification requirement, he does have factual knowledge."[22]

It is difficult to see in this example why Unger thinks that the gypsy has factual knowledge. Presumably it is because the crystal ball is a highly reliable source of information about the world. But having access to a highly reliable source of information hardly

22. Peter Unger, "An Analysis of Factual Knowledge," *Journal of Philosophy* 65 (1968): 164, reprinted in Roth and Galis, *Knowing*.

seems sufficient for knowledge unless one also has some reason to think that the source is reliable. It is not clear in Unger's example whether the gypsy has any reason to believe this. If the gypsy's upbringing included testimony from his parents about the infallibility of the ball or some other indication of its reliability, then we might suppose that the gypsy has reason to think that the ball is an infallible source of information. But then there is no harm in saying that the justification requirement is satisfied with respect to the gypsy's belief in what the ball reports, and no harm in saying that he has factual knowledge of what the ball reports. But if the gypsy has no reason for thinking that the ball is a reliable guide to the world, then he is no better off than someone who has infallible extrasensory perception of the mental life of another person without being aware of his gift. We can say of Unger's example either that the gypsy's beliefs satisfy the justification requirement and thus he has knowledge, or that they do not satisfy it and he does not have knowledge. Either way, the example fails to be convincing.

In Section 3 above we considered an example proposed by Colin Radford as a counterexample to the belief requirement. This was the example involving Jean, who has the ability to recollect certain facts about English history. Radford also proposes this as a counterexample to the justification requirement. Taking the example involving Jean to be an instance of knowledge, he summarizes his conclusions as follows: "Neither believing that *p* nor, *a fortiori,* being confident, sure, quite sure, or certain that *p* is a necessary condition of knowing that *p*. Nor is it a necessary condition of knowing that *p* that one should have the right to be, or be justified in being, or have adequate grounds for being sure that *p*."[23] Because Radford's example is not an example of factual knowledge, however, it fails to show either that the belief requirement does not hold or that the justification requirement does not hold.

In addition to trying to find counterexamples to the justification requirement, some philosophers have endeavored to construct theories of knowledge which do not explicitly include a justification requirement. The most prominent theory of this sort is the

23. Radford, "Knowledge—by Examples," p. 185.

reliability theory of knowledge, exemplified in the writings of Alvin Goldman and D. M. Armstrong.[24] According to Goldman, a person has factual knowledge just in case that person's belief has been formed as a result of a reliable cognitive mechanism. According to Armstrong, one has knowledge if one's belief is a completely reliable sign of the truth of the proposition believed. In presenting their detailed definitions of knowledge, neither philosopher employs any explicit notion of justification or of justified belief, so that some students of the literature conclude that reliability theories of knowledge are antijustificationist and that proponents of such theories have rejected the claim that knowledge requires justification. In my opinion, however, this conclusion is unsupported by the writings of these reliability theorists.

Consider Goldman's account of knowledge. In "Discrimination and Perceptual Knowledge," Goldman explicitly rejects a particular kind of view about justification and argues that justification of that kind is not required for knowledge.[25] The kind of view that he rejects, called 'Cartesianism', is the view that a belief is justified only if it is either self-justified or is justified relative to beliefs that are self-justified. (Such a view is a version of what is generally called 'foundationalism'). Obviously, however, it is possible to reject the view that knowledge requires a specific kind of justification without thereby rejecting the justification requirement. In "Discrimination and Perceptual Knowledge," Goldman says:

> If one wishes, one can so employ the term "justification" that belief causation of this kind [the reliable kind] counts as justification. In this sense, of course, my theory does require justification. But this is entirely different from the sort of justification demanded by Cartesianism.[26]

24. See Armstrong, *Belief, Truth and Knowledge,* and Alvin Goldman, "A Causal Theory of Knowing," *Journal of Philosophy* 64 (1967): 355–372; and "Discrimination and Perceptual Knowledge," *Journal of Philosophy* 73 (1976): 771–791, both reprinted in George S. Pappas and Marshall Swain, eds., *Essays on Knowledge and Justification* (Ithaca: Cornell University Press, 1978).
25. Ibid., especially pp. 790–791.
26. Ibid., p. 790.

In a later paper, "What Is Justified Belief?", Goldman develops a reliability theory of justification and remarks:

> In previous papers on knowledge, I have denied that justification is necessary for knowing, but there I had in mind "Cartesian" accounts of justification. On the account of justified belief suggested here, it *is* necessary for knowing, and closely related to it.[27]

These remarks make it clear that Goldman's epistemological program is not antijustificationist.

Concerning Armstrong's reliability theory, similar observations are in order. In *Belief, Truth, and Knowledge,* for example, Armstrong provides a definition of noninferential knowledge (that is, knowledge that is not based upon reasons). This definition does not explicitly include any condition concerning justification.[28] His definition requires only that the subject have some appropriate complex property, H, such that, given that the subject has H, the subject's belief is a completely reliable sign of the truth of the thing believed. It is clear, however, that Armstrong does not exclude the notion of justified belief, for he says: "The subject's belief is not based upon reasons [in a case of noninferential knowledge], but it might be said to be reasonable (justifiable) because it is a sign, a completely reliable sign, that the situation believed to exist does in fact exist."[29] As with Goldman's view, there is no reason to think that Armstrong's account of knowledge is antijustificationist. In one respect, however, Armstrong's account of noninferential knowledge appears to conflict with my formulation of the justification requirement. According to my formulation of the requirement, *all* instances of knowledge are instances of reason-based belief, whereas Armstrong's account of noninferential knowledge assumes that some instances of knowledge are not instances of reason-based belief. As we shall see in Chapters Three and Four, my account of reason-based belief is

27. Alvin Goldman, "What Is Justified Belief?", in George S. Pappas, ed., *Justification and Knowledge: New Essays in Epistemology* (Dordrecht: Reidel, 1979).
28. See, for example, p. 182.
29. Ibid., p. 183.

different from Armstrong's, and the apparent conflict can be reconciled.

6. *Summary and Concluding Remarks*

In this chapter we have considered three basic requirements for factual knowledge. The results of this discussion can be formulated as an incomplete definition in the following way:

(IDK) A person, *S*, has factual knowledge that *h* at *t* if and only if:
  (1) *h;* and
  (2) *S* believes that *h* at *t;* and
  (3) there is some set of reasons *R* such that
      (a) *S*'s belief that *h* is based upon *R* at *t;* and
      (b) *S*'s believing that *h* on the basis of *R* is justified at *t;* and
      (c) if, at *t, S* has any other reasons, *R'*, that are relevant to whether *S* is justified in believing that *h*, then *S* would be justified in believing that *h* on the basis of *R* ∪ *R'*.

The conditions in (IDK) constitute a version of what has come to be known as the *traditional* definition of knowledge.[30] It is inadequate as a definition, and in later chapters we shall investigate its inadequacies in considerable detail. Before that, however, I shall turn to a detailed consideration of the concepts used in formulating condition (3), the justification condition. There are two reasons for considering the concept of justification in detail. First, the notion has considerable intrinsic interest of its own and figures in many epistemological contexts other than the analysis of knowledge. Second, virtually all the interesting problems and inadequacies of the traditional analysis of knowledge center in one way or another on the justification condition. In order to deal with these problems it is essential to arrive at a clear understand-

---

30. Some philosophers find this kind of definition in Plato's *Theaetetus,* but that is disputed. It is more clearly found in Russell's *Problems of Philosophy* (1912; reprinted in New York: Galaxy Books, 1959), p. 139; in Chisholm's *Perceiving: A Philosophical Study,* p. 16; and in A. J. Ayer's *The Problem of Knowledge* (London: Macmillan, 1956), p. 34.

ing of the family of concepts employed in the formulation of that requirement.

Discussion of the justification requirement is found in Chapters Three and Four. Chapter Two is a consideration of the concept of causation. This discussion may appear to be distinctly out of place, and so some explanation of this shift of subject matter is in order. The leading ideas of the account of reasons, justified belief, and knowledge that are developed in later chapters involve liberal reliance upon certain centrally important causal notions. According to the view I want to develop, beliefs are states of a person, and every belief state has a causal ancestry. The causal ancestry of a given belief will contain other states of the person who has the belief, and often some of these other states will themselves be belief states. The reasons upon which a given belief is based are, in my view, to be found among other states of the person which are causally connected in appropriate ways with the belief in question. Moreover, whether or not a person has knowledge on a given occasion is a function of considerations concerning the causal ancestry of the reasons upon which that person's belief is based. Because causation plays such an important part in the epistemological views I want to develop, it seems appropriate to indicate my interpretation of the relevant causal concepts. The reader who is not interested in these metaphysical matters may move directly to Chapter Three, where the epistemological discussion is resumed.

CHAPTER TWO

CAUSATION

This chapter provides definitions of causal concepts that will figure prominently in the epistemological theory to be developed in later chapters. My primary concern is to provide an explication of the locution '*c* is a cause of *e*', where '*c*' and '*e*' stand for names (or descriptions) of specific events that occurred, and where the kind of causation involved is what we typically call efficient causation. Thus, I am concerned primarily with *event* causation. In the course of this discussion other important causal concepts and locutions will be brought to attention and explicated. Chief among these are the notion of a *causal chain* of events and the notion of *causal overdetermination*. There are, however, many important causal concepts that I am not concerned with in this chapter. For example, I am not concerned to provide an explication of agent causation, as expressed in locutions such as 'Jones was a cause of my becoming angry'. I am also not concerned to provide an explication of locutions such as '*c* is *the* cause of *e*' or '*c* is the precipitating cause of *e*' or any other locution that implies that *c* is unique in the specified causal role with respect to *e*. Nor am I concerned to provide an explication of causal generalizations about types of events, such as 'Heavy drinking causes liver ailments'. Even though I am not concerned here to provide explications of these concepts, I believe that the causal concepts I shall be concerned with are essential to an adequate theory of these, and indeed all other, causal concepts and expressions.

Throughout this discussion, I shall use the term 'event' to designate states of affairs in addition to events. This does not mean that I consider states of affairs to *be* events; to the contrary, there are some good philosophical reasons for distinguishing the one from the other. But, for my purposes, it does not seem necessary to worry about this distinction. I shall, however, assume a rather controversial position concerning the nature of events, namely, that events are spatiotemporally located particulars. In support of this assumption is the fact that we speak of events in ways analogous to the ways in which we speak of persons, tables, and trees. We locate events spatially ('The murder of Smith occurred in the park') and temporally ('The picnic lasted from one o'clock to five o'clock'), and we even give names to some ('World War II', 'Hurricane Mabel'). On the negative side is the fact that at least some events seem to be repeatable, such as the event of John's running. That event, it would seem, can occur on Monday and again on Tuesday. As a result some philosophers have argued that events should be considered abstract objects, akin more to properties, propositions, and numbers than to persons, tables, and trees. It is a consequence of the particularistic view of events that events are *not* literally repeatable. If John runs on Monday and again on Tuesday, then two distinct events have occurred neither of which is a repetition of the other. Each is, we might suppose, a unique exemplification of something that *is* repeatable, perhaps the property of running or the event type of John's running.[1]

1. *Causal Dependence and Causal Chains*

There are a variety of definitions of causation available in the metaphysical marketplace. Among the more frequently purchased are those that define causation in terms of necessary and sufficient conditions, laws of nature, natural necessity, and ma-

1. In assuming that events and states of affairs are spatiotemporally located, nonrepeatable particulars, I oppose the view recommended by Roderick Chisholm in *Person and Object* (LaSalle, Ill.: Open Court, 1976), chapter 4. He views events as a subspecies of states of affairs and regards states of affairs as abstract entities that may be repeatedly concretized by things at times and places. I feel more comfortable with views such as those expressed by Jaegwon Kim in "Causation, Nomic Subsumption, and the Concept of an Event," *Journal of Philosophy* 70 (1973): 217–236, and other writings; or by Myles Brand in "Identity Conditions for Events," *American Philosophical Quarterly* 14 (1977): 329–337.

nipulability.[2] Although some of these have reached levels of considerable sophistication, each of them faces relatively well-known problems. Because this is not a treatise on causation, it is not my purpose to review these accounts of causation or their difficulties, nor even to reject any of these approaches out of hand. Rather, I want to pursue and develop a type of theory which has only recently begun to attract serious attention, namely, the counterfactual theory of causation.[3] The intuitive idea behind this approach is fairly simple: To say that event c is a cause of event e is to say that the occurrence of event e depended in some way on the occurrence of event c. According to the counterfactual theory, the nature of this dependence can be understood by considering various counterfactual truths. For example, if a person turns on a light by flipping a switch we would want to say that the flipping of the switch was a cause of the light's going on, and in a normal setting the dependency involved is captured (at least partly) by the true counterfactual conditional, 'If the switch had not been flipped, then the light would not have gone on'. But there are complex problems facing this approach to the analysis of causation. The more difficult ones concern the asymmetry of the causal relation and the situations in which an event is causally overdetermined. These are problems that have plagued virtually every theory of causation. In addition, the counterfactual approach faces special problems, for not all instances of counterfactual dependence are also instances of causal dependence, and not

2. The amount of literature on this topic is staggering. Three recent anthologies provide a fairly balanced picture of the varieties of views on causation: Myles Brand, ed., *The Nature of Causation* (Urbana: University of Illinois Press, 1976); Tom L. Beauchamp, ed., *Philosophical Problems of Causation* (Belmont, Calif.: Dickenson, 1974); and Ernest Sosa, ed., *Causation and Conditionals* (Oxford: Oxford University Press, 1975). In addition, John L. Mackie's *The Cement of the Universe: A Study of Causation* (Oxford: Oxford University Press, 1974), provides an interesting discussion of many of the major views, as well as a sophisticated defense of a conditions view.

3. Recent formulations of counterfactual analyses of causation can be found in Aardon Lyon, "Causality," *British Journal of Philosophy of Science* 18 (May 1967): 1–20; David Lewis, "Causation," *Journal of Philosophy* 70 (1973): 556–567, reprinted in Sosa, *Causation and Conditionals;* and Marshall Swain, "A Counterfactual Analysis of Event Causation," *Philosophical Studies* 34 (1978): 1–19. Lewis points out in his article that there is a hint of a counterfactual analysis in David Hume's *An Inquiry Concerning Human Understanding,* section VII.

all instances of causal dependence are also instances of counterfactual dependence.

This section presents a preliminary definition of the locution 'c is a cause of e' which will be modified in later sections to avoid these problems. In presenting this definition I shall use counterfactual expressions. I shall assume that some version of the possible worlds approach to the theory of counterfactuals is correct, although I do not assume that the success or failure of the counterfactual analysis of causation ultimately depends on the success or failure of that approach to counterfactuals.[4] The possible worlds approach to counterfactuals has considerable intuitive appeal and is of heuristic value when talking about causation.

For the purposes of this chapter, I shall take the three-place relation expressed by

(2.1)   World w_1 is closer to world w than is world w_2

as undefined, or 'primitive'. This relation is at the heart of the possible worlds approach to counterfactuals and ultimately requires specification of criteria in accordance with which judgments about closeness are to be rendered. According to David Lewis, for example, a world w_1 is closer to a world w than is the world w_2 if w_1 resembles w in respect of overall comparative similarity more than w_2 resembles w.[5] This particular suggestion faces difficult problems, and viable competitors are available.[6] Even with (2.1) taken as unanalyzed, however, we can state intuitively natural and appealing truth conditions for counterfactual expressions. Following Lewis, where A and C are any two prop-

4. The possible worlds approach to counterfactuals is represented in David Lewis, *Counterfactuals* (Cambridge, Mass.: Harvard University Press, 1973); John Pollock, *Subjunctive Reasoning* (Dordrecht: Reidel, 1976); and Robert Stalnaker, "A Theory of Conditionals," *American Philosophical Quarterly*, Monograph Series 2 (1968), pp. 98–112, reprinted in Sosa, *Causation and Conditionals*. The other main approach to counterfactuals (the 'linguistic' or 'metalinguistic' approach) is represented in Roderick Chisholm, "Law Statements and Counterfactual Inference," *Analysis* 15 (1955): 97–105, also reprinted in Sosa, *Causation and Conditionals*.

5. Lewis, "Causation," p. 559.

6. For some of the problems and a competitor, see John L. Pollock, "The 'Possible Worlds' Analysis of Counterfactuals," *Philosophical Studies* 29 (1976): 469–476; and *Subjunctive Reasoning*.

ositions, and where A-worlds and C-worlds are worlds in which A and C hold respectively, let us say that

(DST) The proposition that if A were true, then C would be true is true at a world w iff:

either (1) there are no possible A-worlds

or (2) some A-world where C holds is closer to w than is any A-world where C does not hold.[7]

(DST) is formulated in such a way that the world w, as well as the A-worlds and C-worlds considered, need not be identical with our actual world. From this point on, unless otherwise specified or indicated by context, the counterfactuals used are evaluated at the actual world. The world w will be the actual world.

An important relation is the relation of *counterfactual dependence* between two propositions. Intuitively, a proposition, C, depends counterfactually on a proposition, A, if the question whether C is true or not depends upon whether A is true. More formally, we may say:

(DCfDp) C depends counterfactually on A iff:

(1) if A were true, then C would be true; and

(2) if A were not true, then C would not be true.

Now I shall assume that if A and C are both false, then the counterfactual (2) in (DCfDp) is automatically true; in that case, the counterfactual dependence of C on A reduces to the truth of counterfactual (1) of (D2).[8] Similarly, if A and C are both true, then counterfactual (1) of (DCfDp) is automatically true; in that case, the counterfactual dependence of C on A reduces to the truth of counterfactual (2).

Counterfactual dependence is a relation that holds, as defined, between propositions. We can also introduce a relation of counterfactual dependence among *events*. To say that event e is counterfactually dependent upon event c is to say the proposition that e occurs is counterfactually dependent upon the proposition that c occurs. Because I will normally be concerned only with *occurrent* events, the proposition that e occurs and the proposition that

7. See Lewis, *Counterfactuals,* p. 16.

8. This is tantamount to assuming that w is the, or a, closest world to itself.

c occurs will both be true. Hence, we can use (DCfDp) and the considerations of the preceding paragraph to get the following:

(DCfDe) Where c and e are occurrent events, e depends counterfactually on c iff: if c had not occurred, then e
would not have occurred.

It is tempting to think that if an event e is counterfactually dependent upon an event c, then e is *causally* dependent upon c. Although this is often the case, exceptions must be accounted for. The most obvious problem is that nothing in (DCfDe) tells us that c and e cannot be the same event. Moreover, it seems trivially clear that if c and e are identical, e depends counterfactually on c. So, if we were to take counterfactual dependence to be suffi-cient for causal dependence, we would get the unhappy result that every occurrent event is causally dependent upon itself. There is a generally agreed-upon requirement that if one event is to be a cause of another, the two events must be distinct. The same requirement holds for causal dependence. We can therefore transform (DCfDe) into a definition of *causal* dependence by add-ing a requirement to the effect that events c and e are *distinct* events. But then we are faced with the question, when are two events distinct? If our only motivation is to avoid the obvious problem above, then the answer seems easy enough:

(IDD) Two events, c and e, are distinct iff c and e are not identical events.

I shall provisionally assume (IDD), although, as we shall see, this definition needs modification.

To be of any service, (IDD) requires some criterion for the identity of events. Providing a criterion is one of the knottiest of problems. There are two main approaches. One of these results in what Alvin Goldman calls a "fine-grained" view of events, and we may take the other to be the coarse-grained view.[9] Perhaps an

9. Goldman uses this term in *Human Action* (Prentice-Hall, 1970; reprint, Princeton: Princeton University Press, 1976), p. 8. In his discussion Goldman is concerned with rival theories of *action* identity. I am taking the liberty of extending his term to the problem of event identity in general, on the ground that actions are events. Goldman suggests this himself in a footnote on page 3 of his book.

example will help make the difference clear. Consider the following two events, which happen to be actions of a person S:[10]

   (a1) S's turning on the light
   (a2) S's alerting the prowler

According to a fine-grained view, these events are not identical; according to a coarse-grained view, they are. There are powerful arguments against the coarse-grained view, many of which Goldman has presented with admirable clarity.[11] I shall not repeat those arguments here, but I assume that some version of a fine-grained view is to be preferred. This means, among other things, that our criterion for event identity should yield the result that *a1* and *a2,* and similar pairs, are nonidentical events.

What shall our criterion for event identity be? Many suggestions have been made. Some of them, though interesting, would not serve my purpose. One might provide a criterion for event identity in terms of cause and effect: two events are identical, we might say, just in case they have precisely the same causes and effects.[12] It is not clear, however, that this approach will yield a fine-grained view. Even more important, to adopt such a criterion in the present context would be to use the notion of causation in analyzing a central factor in the analysis of causation, and thus the analysis would be circular. From among the many possibilities for a criterion of event identity, I adopt the following:[13]

(DIe)   Two events, c and $e,$ are identical iff, necessarily, c occurs if and only if e occurs.

10. Throughout this chapter I shall use expressions such as 'S's turning on the light' as descriptions of events, each of which will be associated with an abbreviated name of that event, such as '*a1*'.
11. Goldman, *Human Action* pp. 1–8. The coarse-grained view has had its most powerful defense in the writings of Donald Davidson; see, for example, "Actions, Reasons, and Causes," *Journal of Philosophy* 60 (1963): 685–700; "The Logical Form of Action Sentences," in Nicholas Rescher, ed., *The Logic of Decision and Action* (Pittsburgh: University of Pittsburgh Press, 1967), pp. 81–96; and "The Individuation of Events," in Nicholas Rescher, et al., eds., *Essays in Honor of Carl G. Hempel* (Dordrecht: Reidel, 1970), pp. 216–234.
12. This view is suggested by Davidson in the writings cited in note 11.
13. For a helpful and precise survey of theories of event identity and a sophisticated proposal, see Brand, "Identity Conditions for Events." My definition is in the spirit of the one proposed by Brand, but his involves several complications the inclusion of which do not seem necessary for my purposes here.

The kind of necessity conveyed in (DIe) is logical necessity. If we adopt a possible worlds semantics for this modal notion, this criterion says that two events are identical if and only if they occur in the same possible worlds. Thus, two events will be nonidentical just in case there is at least one possible world in which one of them occurs and the other does not. We can see that this criterion yields the nonidentity of *a1* and *a2,* for there are possible worlds in which *S* turns on the light without alerting the prowler and possible worlds in which *S* alerts the prowler without turning on the light.[14] In general, and I think this is intuitively clear, our criterion will yield a very fine-grained inventory of events.

I have provisionally characterized distinctness of events in terms of their nonidentity and have suggested the definition (DIe) for identity of events. Let us now see how these notions relate to the counterfactual analysis of causation. As indicated above, to obtain causal dependence from counterfactual dependence we must restrict the events involved to those that are distinct. Assuming for now that the notion of distinctness provided in (IDD) is adequate, we may define causal dependence in the following straightforward way:

(DCD) Where *c* and *e* are occurrent events, *e* depends causally on *c* iff:
  (1) *c* and *e* are distinct events; and
  (2) if *c* had not occurred, then *e* would not have occurred.

Let us turn now from the notion of causal dependence to the notion of causation.

If *e* is causally dependent upon *c*, then we may say that *c* is a cause of *e;* however, from the fact that *c* is a cause of *e* we may not conclude that *e* is causally dependent upon *c*. Often one event is a cause of another because there is a *causal chain* of

14. The second of these modal claims is less clear than the first. Is it logically possible for event *a2* to have occurred without event *a1*'s occurring? Obviously, it is possible (logically) for *S* to have alerted the prowler in a different way. But then, wouldn't that necessarily be a different (i.e., ≠ *a2*) prowler-alerting? The answer depends upon considerations concerning event construction that I am not prepared to answer. Fortunately, all we need is the logical possibility of *a1*'s occurring without *a2*, which I think is relatively uncontroversial.

events linking them. Suppose c and e are the first and last members of a chain of events, $c, d, e,$ such that c is a cause of d and d is a cause of e. Suppose, moreover, that d is causally dependent upon c and e is causally dependent upon d. We would then want to say that c is also a cause of e—this relation is transitive—but we are not entitled to say that e is causally dependent upon c, for that relation is not transitive.

To see that the relation of causal dependence is not transitive, consider this example. Suppose I am a heavy sleeper and have two unusual alarm clocks. One of them is equipped with a photo-electric cell that makes it go off when the sun rises. The other is so constituted that it goes off at the same time provided that it is still dark at that time. On a given day, the sun rises (let this be event c). The sun's rising is a cause of the photosensitive clock's going off (let this be event d). This clock's going off is in turn a cause of my awakening at 6:30 that day (let this be event e). Now we may note that d is causally dependent upon c. If the sun had not risen on this morning, my photosensitive clock would not have gone off, and they are distinct events. Moreover, event e is causally dependent upon event d. If my photosensitive clock had not gone off, I would not have awakened (for I am a heavy sleeper), and these events are distinct. You might ask whether the other clock would have awakened me in this case, and the answer is that it would not; for the *closest* worlds in which my photosensitive clock fails to go off would not also be worlds in which it remains dark. Even though these causal dependencies hold, however, event e is not causally dependent upon event c. They are distinct events, to be sure, but the requisite counterfactual is false. That is, it is false that if the sun had not risen this morning, then I would not have awakened at 6:30, for in that case my alternate clock *would* have awakened me. Transitivity of the causal dependence relation fails in this case because the closest worlds in which event c does not occur are farther away from the actual world than are the closest worlds in which event d does not occur.[15]

These considerations show that causation between events cannot be defined simply as causal dependence between those

---

15. For further discussion of the failure of transitivity for counterfactuals, see Lewis, *Counterfactuals,* pp. 32–35.

events. To define causation, we need the notion of a causal chain. This is easily constructed as follows:

(DCC) Where $c, d_1, d_2, \ldots, d_n, e$ is a sequence of occurrent events (but not necessarily a temporal sequence, and where c and e may be the only members), this sequence is a *causal chain* iff:

    (1) d_1 depends causally on c; and
    (2) d_2 depends causally on d_1; and

           . . .

    (n) d_n depends causally on d_{n-1}; and
    (n+1) e depends causally on d_n.

Given this notion of a causal chain, we may express the following incomplete definition of causation:[16]

(IDC) Where c and e are specific events that occurred, c is a cause of e iff there is a causal chain of occurrent events from c to e.

In (IDC) we have the core of the counterfactual theory of event causation. The definition is inadequate, however, and the remaining sections of this chapter investigate these inadequacies and offer some proposals for improvement. The first major problem concerns the account of distinct events. I have tentatively assumed that distinctness of events can be defined solely in terms of their nonidentity, as in (IDD). There are, however, difficult examples that show this conception of distinctness to be too narrow for our purpose of defining causal concepts. In the next section I consider such examples and argue that we must adopt a broader notion of distinctness of events.

2. *Compound Events*

As noted at the beginning of this chapter, there are strong analogies to be made between events and physical objects.[17] For example, we say of physical objects that they occupy space-time regions. It is natural to say the same thing about events. We give

---

16. This definition, as well as the definition (DDC) of a causal chain, is essentially the same as the view suggested by Lewis in "Causation," p. 563.
17. This is emphasized by Brand in "Identity Conditions for Events," p. 329.

names to physical objects, and we also give names to events. One very important analogy leads to the first of our troublesome cases for the counterfactual definition (IDC). Many physical objects (indeed, virtually all of those with which we are perceptually acquainted) are compound objects having other physical objects as their components. A brick wall is a physical object whose components are each of its bricks and bits of mortar. Each brick and each bit of mortar is in turn a physical object, and each is in its turn a compound physical object. It is notoriously difficult to say what distinguishes collections of physical objects that are compound objects from other collections of physical objects that are not compound objects. If you put all the bricks and mortar together in the right way, then you have a new physical object, the brick wall. But if you put those bricks and the mortar out in the yard helter-skelter, you have a collection of physical objects but no compound physical object. Similar things may be said about events. Many events (again, virtually all of those with which we are perceptually acquainted) are compound events having other events as (or among) their components. As with physical objects, it is difficult to say what the difference is between a collection of events which is a compound event and a collection of events which is not. Suppose, for example, I type the word 'Larry'.[18] This action is a compound event having among its component events the event (action) of my typing the letter 'r' twice in succession. Similarly, suppose my Christmas tree is rigged with a device that flashes the lights on and off every so often. Consider a given flashing of the lights on the tree. This is a compound event (in this case not an action) that has among its component events the individual flashings of each bulb on the tree. Now imagine that while I am typing the word 'Larry' the lights on my tree happen to flash. These events, it seems, do not together form a compound event. They are contemporaneous, and perhaps they could arbitrarily be labeled a conjunctive event. But if they were to be considered a compound event, we would be led to the conclusion that *any* two or more events form a compound event. Although this conclusion is not obviously absurd, it appears to be counterintuitive.

18. This example (and several of those to follow) is suggested by Jaegwon Kim in "Causes and Counterfactuals," *Journal of Philosophy* 70 (1973): 570–572, as counterexample to Lewis's counterfactual analysis of causation.

I do not know of any satisfactory way of providing conditions that will distinguish collections of events that form a compound event from those that do not form a compound event. It is not necessary for my purposes to provide such a criterion, however, for it is the relation between a compound event and its component events that leads to trouble for the definition (IDC). Compound events are such that they are counterfactually dependent upon at least some of their component events. Consider this example again:

(e1) S's typing the word 'Larry'
(e2) S's typing the letter 'r' twice in succession.

Given (IDC), we get the result that the event $e2$ is a cause of the event $e1$. First, it is clear that $e1$ and $e2$ are not identical according to our criterion (DIe): there are possible worlds in which S types the letter 'r' twice in succession without typing the word 'Larry'. Given that these events are not identical, it follows that they are distinct, in accordance with our assumed definition of distinctness (IDD). Third, in accordance with (DCD), we get the result that $e1$ depends causally on $e2$; this follows from the two considerations just mentioned. Fourth, in accordance with (DCC), there is a causal chain from $e2$ to $e1$. In this instance there are only two 'links' in the causal chain; no intermediate 'links' are involved. Finally, from all this we get the result that $e2$ is a cause of $e1$ in accordance with (IDC). Unfortunately, all these results concerning causal dependence, causal chains, and causation are mistaken. There is *no* causal connection between $e2$ and $e1$.[19]

A related problem for the definition (IDC) concerns events that overlap. As a simple example, consider a stretch of wire with four points along it, as follows:

$$p_1 \qquad p_2 \qquad p_3 \qquad p_4$$

Now suppose electricity passes through the wire from p_1 to p_4. If we consider events e_1 (=the current's passing through the segment p_1–p_2), e_2 (=the current's passing through the segment

19. I base this claim on another that I take to be obvious, namely, that the parts of a thing do not, in the efficient sense, cause the thing of which they are parts.

p_2–p_3), and so forth, these events form a straightforward causal chain. However, consider these two events: e_x (=the current's passing through the segment p_1 –p_3) and e_y (=the current's passing through the segment p_2–p_4). These two events overlap but are not related as compound to component. They have in common the event of the current's passing through the segment p_2–p_3. As with examples involving compound events and their components, this example presents a problem for (IDC), for event e_y is counterfactually dependent upon event e_x, and yet e_y is not caused by e_x. Nevertheless, the definitions considered above yield the result that e_x is a cause of e_y.

These counterexamples to (IDC) can be avoided if we adopt a broader notion of the distinctness of events than the one expressed in (IDD). I suggest replacing (IDD) with

(DD) Two events, c and e, are distinct iff:
    (1) c and e are not identical; and
    (2)   neither event is a compound event of which the other is a component; and
    (3)   the two events do not overlap.

Then, given that distinctness of the events involved is a necessary condition for causal dependence and that the latter is a necessary condition for the presence of a causal chain, the definition (IDC) is rendered immune to at least the problems considered above.

Up to this point I have been concerned to show that adoption of the broad notion of distinctness of events embodied in (DD) provides an intuitively natural way of interpreting the distinctness condition in the counterfactual analysis of causation. The class of examples that the distinctness requirement is designed to handle does not, however, exhaust the problems facing our account of causation. Indeed, the problems that remain are in some ways even more formidable.

3. *The Direction of Causation*

In this section I attempt to deal with a problem that has proved recalcitrant throughout the literature on causation, namely, the problem of guaranteeing directionality for the causal relation.[20]

20. For helpful discussion of this problem and further references, see David H. Sanford, "The Direction of Causation and the Direction of Conditionship," *Journal of Philosophy* 73 (1976): 193–207.

Briefly put, the problem is this. Suppose we say that some event, c, is a cause of another event, e. Then, we do not also want to say that the event e is a cause of the event c.[21] We want the relation is-a-cause-of to be asymmetrical. It would be simple to guarantee the asymmetry of this relation if causes always preceded their effects in time, for we could add a clause to (IDC) requiring that event c occur prior to event e. But there are convincing examples in which cause and effect appear to be simultaneous,[22] and there are arguments in the literature (not quite so convincing) that some causes may occur after their effects.[23] To avoid begging the question about such examples, it is best to find a way of establishing asymmetry which does not require temporal priority.

Let us first satisfy ourselves that the definition (IDC) does not guarantee the asymmetry of our causal relation. Consider a simple example.

Case 1. A light bulb is wired to a pushbutton that is wired in turn to a live electrical source. Suppose someone pushes the button; let this be event c. And suppose the light goes on; let this be event e.

It seems clear that c was a cause of e, and equally clear that e was not a cause of c. Moreover, the conditions in (IDC) appear to give the correct result that c was a cause of e. The events in question occurred, and there was a causal chain of distinct occurrent events from c to e. Even though the example is a simple one, however, the causal chain involved is complex. To simplify discussion, let us regard all the events between c and e in this chain as a single event and designate it with 'b'. Then, to say that c was a cause of e is to assert the joint truth of the following counterfactuals:

(2.2)   If the button had not been pushed, then event b would not have occurred, and if event b had not occurred, then the light would not have gone on.

---

21. Not everyone will agree that the relation is asymmetric. For an interesting example, see Pollock, *Subjunctive Reasoning*, p. 173.

22. For example, suppose a book is resting on a table from time t_1 to time t_2. Let e_1 be the event of the book's remaining unmoved from t_1 to t_2, and let e_2 be the event of the table's remaining unmoved from t_1 to t_2. Then, it would seem, e_2 is a cause of e_1, but they are simultaneous.

23. See J. L. Mackie, *The Cement of the Universe*, pp. 161–162, for some examples and references.

Moreover, the counterfactuals asserted in (2.2) seem to be true. The problem is that there *also* appears to be a causal chain from e to c. That is, the following counterfactuals also seem to be true:

(2.3) If the light had not gone on, then event b would not have occurred, and if event b had not occurred, then the button would not have been pushed.

It is only for purposes of simplicity that I am considering the complex of events in the chain from c to e as the single event b. It is obvious that we could make the joint counterfactual assertions in (2.2) and (2.3) as complicated as we like, depending upon how we subdivide the chain of events in question. Now, if the counterfactuals asserted in (2.3) are true, as I am suggesting, then, because it is clear that the events involved are distinct, the definition (IDC) would give us the undesirable result that e was a cause of c.

A natural response to this argument is to deny at least one of the counterfactuals asserted in (2.3), thereby avoiding the result. How might we argue that (2.3) is false while maintaining, as we must, that the counterfactuals asserted in (2.2) are all true? For purposes of argument, let us suppose that we wish to deny the counterfactual:

(2.3′) If the light had not gone on, then event b would not have occurred.

In order for (2.3′) to be true, the following would have to be true, given (DST):

(2.4) There is some world in which the light does not go on and in which event b does not occur which is closer to our actual world than is any world in which the light does not go on but in which event b does occur.

The question then becomes, is (2.4) true? At this point, it is necessary to consider what is to count when we are comparing worlds in terms of closeness. We must ask what would be a closest alternative world in which the light does not go on; and would such a world also be one in which event b does not occur?

One way to guarantee a negative answer to these questions is to allow among the possible worlds we are comparing those in which minor violations of actual world laws occur, for then we can suppose a world in which event b occurs (after the button is pushed) but in which the light simply fails to go on because of a minor violation of some law(s) of nature.[24] There does not appear to be any closer world in which the light fails to go on. If so, then (2.4) is false, and so is the counterfactual (2.3'), and hence the joint assertion (2.3). This would be sufficient to establish that there is *no* causal chain from e to c.

But is this line of argument sufficient to give us the asymmetry we are looking for? If we allow consideration of worlds in which minor violations of actual world laws can occur, then the argument is sufficient to show that there is no causal chain from e to c. Virtually the same argument can be used, however, to show that there is no causal chain from c to e. If there is such a causal chain, then the counterfactuals in (2.2) must be true. Again, let us concentrate on only one of these counterfactuals.

(2.2') If the button had not been pushed, then event b would not have occurred.

For this counterfactual to be true, the following must be true:

(2.5) There is some world in which the button is not pushed and in which event b does not occur which is closer to our actual world than is any world in which the button is not pushed but event b occurs anyway.

If we are going to allow consideration of worlds in which minor violations of law take place, one way to construct a world in which the button is not pushed but in which event b occurs anyway is to suppose that the occurrence of event b is a result of some minor violation of law. Moreover, I cannot think of any convincing reasons to suppose that a world in which the button is not pushed and event b does not occur would be any closer.

It might be argued in the following way that some such world would be closer than the one I am imagining. What would be the closest world we can imagine in which the button is not pushed? This would be a world just like the actual world right up to the time of the pushing of the button but then a minor violation of law takes place and the button is not pushed. In that world, it

24. This appears to be Lewis's suggestion in "Causation," pp. 565–567.

seems, event *b* would not then occur. To have it occur would require a *second* minor violation of law, one that gets things going again. So, we have two worlds to compare, one in which one violation of law takes place, and one in which two violations of law take place. It is clear that the former is closer to our actual world than the latter, so (2.5) is true after all. In response, I would question the suggestion that we need to suppose *two* violations of law in the world I am imagining. Let me introduce the somewhat fanciful notion of a pure deletion miracle. This is a violation of law the 'result' of which is to delete from actuality an event that would otherwise have occurred but that leaves the *rest* of the actual world entirely unchanged. We can get the world I want, which falsifies (2.5), simply by supposing that the button is not pushed because of some pure deletion miracle. Fanciful? Of course! But, is it any more fanciful than talk of any other kind of law violation? I submit that if we are warranted in saying that (2.4) is false, we are also warranted in saying that (2.5) is false. If so, then we fail to get causal chains either from *e* to *c* or from *c* to *e*; not only do we fail to guarantee asymmetry; we also lose the desired causal connection.

If these considerations are correct, they show that we must resist the temptation to allow for unbridled consideration of violation miracles when comparing worlds in respect of overall similarity. This does not mean that comparison of worlds in which violation miracles take place is *never* relevant when evaluating counterfactuals. (Consider: 'If a miracle were to occur, everyone would be amazed'.) But I would suggest that when we are considering counterfactuals that are involved in the analysis of causation among actual, occurrent, nonmiraculous events, we should consider irrelevant those worlds in which violation miracles take place.[25]

In the remainder of this section, I suggest another account of the asymmetry of our causal relation does not require consideration of miraculous worlds.[26] I assume, contrary to the argument above, that there *are* causal chains both from *c* to *e* and from *e* to

25. This is tantamount to holding that the possible worlds to be considered will be worlds in which the laws of this actual world hold (unviolated).

26. If my argument above against the miraculous worlds approach to dealing with asymmetry fails and that approach turns out to be acceptable, I would favor it, on grounds of simplicity, to what follows.

c in Case 1. It is nevertheless possible to imagine worlds in which event *e* occurs but event *c* does not, and to imagine worlds in which event *c* occurs but event *e* does not. The worlds that we imagine in each case are, however, not as close to the actual world as are the worlds we would consider in establishing the truth or falsity of the counterfactuals in (2.2) and (2.3). The idea I want to develop is that there is a relevant difference between the closest worlds we would need to imagine in order to imagine that *c* occurred but *e* did not occur and the closest worlds we would need to imagine in order to imagine that *e* occurred when *c* did not occur. This relevant difference (soon to be made explicit) is sufficient to establish the asymmetry we are looking for.

Consider first the sort of world in which event *c* occurs but event *e* does not, that is, a world in which the button is pushed but the light does not go on. There are many nonmiraculous ways in which this could have happened: there might have been a power failure or the filament in the bulb might have been broken. I do not know which of these worlds would be closest to the actual world, but it suffices to imagine a world in which some actual occurrent event other than *c* upon which the event *e* was causally dependent *failed* to occur.[27]

Now let us ask what we would need to imagine in order to have a world in which *e* occurred but *c* did not. This would be a world in which the light goes on but the button is not pushed: perhaps the person pushing the button dropped dead instead. Then, however, we would also have to imagine that something *else* caused the light to go on: perhaps another button was pushed instead. In the case at hand, to have *e* without *c*, requires *that something prevented c from occurring and that something else caused e,* but to get *c* without *e* requires only that *something prevented c from causing e*. This way of putting the matter neatly begs the question concerning the causal facts in Case 1, but the difference noted provides the key to capturing asymmetry. I suggest the following expanded version of (IDC) as a noncircular way of defining our causal relation to guarantee asymmetry.[28]

27. Throughout this discussion I use 'occurrent' and 'actually occurrent' to mean that the event in question actually occurs in this world of ours.

28. In clause (ii) I am assuming that world w_1, in which event *a* fails to occur, is also a world in which any event that is causally dependent upon *a* (including *e*) also fails to occur. 'Only' is somewhat misleading here.

(IDC') Where c and e are specific events that occurred, c is a cause of e iff:

    (i)   there is a causal chain of occurrent events from c to e; and

    (ii) where w_1 is a world in which c occurs and e does not occur, and w is the actual world, w_1 would have to have been different from w only in that some event a (other than c) that occurs in w and upon which e depends causally in w fails to occur in w_1; and

    (iii) where w_2 is a world in which e occurs and c does not occur, and w is the actual world, w_2 would have to be different from w in at least the following respects: (1) some event f (other than e) that occurs in w and upon which c depends causally in w fails to occur in w_2; and (2) some event g occurs in w_2 such that e is not causally dependent upon g in w but e is causally dependent upon g in w_2.

In Case 1, all three clauses are satisfied for c as a cause of e. For e as a cause of c, however, clause (i) is satisfied but (ii) and (iii) are not. This is sufficient to guarantee that c is a cause of e and that e is not a cause of c, and this is the asymmetry that we are seeking.

These conditions are also sufficient to deal with a problem that is often difficult for analyses of causation, namely, the common cause problem. We can illustrate this problem by a simple addition to Case 1. Suppose the button is also wired to a bell, so that when the button is pushed (c), the light goes on (e) and the bell rings (d). Here we have two effects of a common cause, but we must be careful to avoid the result that one of these effects turns out, by our definition, to be a cause of the other.[29] To adopt only the preliminary definition (IDC) would yield this unhappy result, for there is a causal chain from e to d and also one from d to e. We can see that there is such a chain from e to d as follows. Let 'b' again designate the complex event consisting of everything between c and e, and let 'h' designate everything between c and d. Given that the events involved are distinct, the existence of the

---

29. This kind of example is especially difficult for the regularity view of causation.

causal chain from e to d is established by the truth of the following joint assertion of counterfactuals:

(5)   If e had not occurred, then b would not have occurred, and if b had not occurred, then c would not have occurred, and if c had not occurred, then h would not have occurred, and if h had not occurred, then d would not have occurred.

Fortunately, the conditions (ii) and (iii) of the revised definition (IDC') are sufficient to guarantee that e is not a cause of d. Consider clause (ii), which is satisfied by e and d in this case. To have a world in which e occurs but d does not requires only that some event other than e upon which d causally depends fails to occur; for example, suppose the coil in the bell is broken. Clause (iii), however, is not satisfied for e and d in this example. To have a world in which d occurs but e does not, we need only suppose that something prevents e from occurring (perhaps a broken filament), but that c causes d anyway.

4. *Overdetermination*

A type of causal situation that has proved to be a source of difficulty for many approaches to the analysis of causation is that in which an event, $e,$ is causally overdetermined by two or more events.[30] Let us say that if e is overdetermined by exactly two events, then we have a case of dyadic overdetermination. If e is overdetermined by exactly three events, then this is a case of triadic overdetermination. In general, if e is overdetermined by exactly n events, then we have n-adic overdetermination. This discussion focuses on cases of dyadic overdetermination; however, the results will be stated in definitions that are fully general with respect to n-adic cases.

I want to distinguish between cases of *genuine* overdetermination and cases of *pseudo* overdetermination. In both types of cases we have an event, $e,$ and two events, c and $d,$ all of which occurred and are related such that, if either c or d alone had occurred, there would have been a causal chain from the event in

30. For a very useful discussion of this problem and for references to other discussions, see Louis E. Loeb, "Causal Theories and Causal Overdetermination," *Journal of Philosophy* 71 (1974): 525–544.

question to e. We have a case of genuine overdetermination if both c and d have equal claim to being called a cause of e, and a case of pseudo overdetermination if only one of the two can properly be called a cause of e.[31] I shall give examples of each kind of overdetermination and provide appropriate definitions. The motivation for this is twofold: first, examples involving genuine overdetermination are counterexamples to the definition (IDC′) of causation developed in preceding sections; second, in succeeding chapters of this book, examples involving both kinds of overdetermination will be of special importance for the epistemological theory that I am developing.

Let us first consider an example of genuine overdetermination.

Case 2. Suppose two switches, S1 and S2, are wired to a light bulb and to a live electrical source. Let us specify that the wires connecting S1 and S2 with the bulb are exactly the same length, that the switches are identical in construction, and so forth. Now suppose the two switches are pushed at precisely the same time. The light bulb goes on, which is event e. Let the pushing of switch S1 be event c and the pushing of S2 be event d.

In this case, it seems, each of the events c and d has equal claim to being a cause of e. If either had occurred alone, there would have been a causal chain from that event to the bulb's going on. What are the causal facts in this case? There are two primary alternatives: we can say that neither event c nor event d is a cause of e, or we could say they are both causes of e. Of the two alternatives, the second is intuitively stronger from my point of view, and hence it is the one I shall develop. I do not want to deny dogmatically that the first alternative represents a viable approach, but if we take that alternative, then we must say what event or events other than c and d are causes of e, and this is likely to involve us in unpalatable considerations concerning disjunctive and conjunctive events. Moreover, even though I shall develop the second alternative, I believe that the first alternative could also be developed within the framework of a counterfactual approach to causation.

If I say, in Case 2, that c was a cause of e and that d was also a cause of e, then the definition (IDC′) will not serve my purposes.

31. In "Causation," p. 567, Lewis discusses an example of what I call pseudo overdetermination but declines to discuss genuine overdetermination.

The conditions specified in (IDC′) require that there be a causal chain from cause to effect, and thus I would have to say there is a causal chain from c to e and from d to e. But even though there is a chain of actually occurring events linking c with e and a chain of actually occurring events linking d with e, neither of these is a *causal* chain. For simplicity, suppose the chain of events from c to e and the chain of events from d to e have only one member in common, namely e. (This is probably false, but that should not affect the point being made.) Let the predecessor of e in the chain from c to e be called 'c'', and let the predecessor of e in the chain from d to e be called 'd''. In order for the chain from c to e (for example) to be a causal chain, the counterfactual 'If c' had not occurred, then e would not have occurred' must be true. This counterfactual is false, however; if c' had not occurred, the chain of events from d to e would have been completed anyway and event e would have occurred. An analogous argument will show that the chain of events from d to e is not a causal chain. Consequently, cases of genuine overdetermination fail to satisfy my conditions, under the assumption that in such cases each of the overdetermining events is a cause.

To deal with this problem I shall provide a definition of the genuine overdetermination relation:

(DGO) Where c and e are occurrent events, c is a genuine over-determinant of e if and only if: There is some set of occurrent events $D = \{d_1, d_2, \ldots, d_n\}$ (possibly having only one member) such that

(1) if c had not occurred and if any member, d_i, of D had occurred, but no other members of D had occurred, and if e had occurred anyway, then there would have been a causal chain of distinct actually occurrent events from d_i to e, and d_i would have been causally prior to e; and

(2) if no member of D had occurred, and if c and e had occurred anyway, then there would have been a causal chain of distinct actually occurrent events from c to e, and c would have been causally prior to e.

In this definition, I have introduced the term 'causally prior to' merely as a simplifying device. To say that one event is causally prior to another is to say that the asymmetry relation discussed in the previous section holds between those events, and I shall take it that this relation holds between any two events that satisfy conditions (ii) and (iii) of the definition (IDC').

In Case 2 we will get the result that c and d are both genuine overdeterminants of e by (DGO). Consider event c. There is a set of events, D, in this case consisting of only event d, which is such that both (1) and (2) are satisfied. Similarly, event d is a genuine overdeterminant of e, for there is a set, D, consisting in this case of only event c, such that both conditions (1) and (2) are satisfied.

Given this definition of genuine overdetermination, I propose the following definition of causation:

(DC)   Where c and e are specific events that occurred, c is a cause of e if and only if:
        either (1)   (i), (ii), and (iii) as in (IDC');
        or   (2) c is a genuine overdeterminant of e.

The first disjunct of this definition guarantees the results arrived at in preceding sections. We have just seen that in Case 2, events c and d both qualify as genuine overdeterminants of event e by (DGO). Hence, the definition (DC) guarantees, by its second disjunct, that these events are also causes of event e.

Let us now consider an example of pseudo overdetermination:

Case 3. As in Case 2, suppose two switches are wired to a bulb, and let events c, d, and e be the two pushings of the switches and the lighting of the bulb, respectively. This time, however, imagine that switch S1 is equipped with an overriding device such that if S1 is pushed, then the circuit between the switch S2 and the bulb is broken. Switch S2 is not equipped with any sort of overriding device.

Case 3 is a clear case of pseudo overdetermination. Two events, c and d, occurred such that if either had occurred alone, there would have been a causal chain from that event to the occurrence of event e. But unlike Case 2, in this example only one of the two events, namely c (the pushing of switch S1), can properly be called a cause of event e. Even though the pushing of switch S2 would have been a cause of e, this event was not a cause of e because the pushing of switch S1 resulted in a breaking of the circuit between S2 and the bulb. We may say that the causal relation between S1's being pushed and the bulb's lighting *preempted* the potential causal relation between S2's being pushed and the bulb's lighting.

Superficially, such cases appear to present a problem for the counterfactual analysis of causation expressed in (DC). Considering only events *c, d,* and *e,* we may note that the counterfactual 'If *c* had not occurred, then *e* would not have occurred' is false, for even if *c* had not occurred, event *d* (the pushing of switch S2) would have been a cause of *e.* Similarly, the counterfactual 'If *d* had not occurred, then *e* would not have occurred' is false, but this fact is of no great importance. It is the falsity of the former counterfactual which might make us think we have a counterexample to (DC). It is clear that we want to say *c* was a cause of *e,* but it appears that the counterfactual relation required by clause (1) is not present, and moreover, *c* is not a genuine overdeterminant of *e.* Closer scrutiny will reveal, however, that this example is not a counterexample to our definition after all. Clause (1) requires that there be a causal *chain* of actually occurrent events connecting *c* and *e* if *c* is to be a cause of *e.* In Case 3 there is such a chain connecting *c* and *e,* and this chain contains events intermediate to *c* and *e.* For example, once *c* occurred, the electrical current passed through the first inch of the wire, then through the second, and so on up to the socket, then through the wires leading to the filament, and then *e* occurred. Each successive event in this chain was counterfactually dependent upon its predecessor; and this is so even though the counterfactual 'If *c* had not occurred, then *e* would not have occurred' is false. On the other hand, considering event *d,* it is obvious that there is no counterfactual chain of *actually occurrent* events linking it with *e;* although *d* occurred, it was prevented from inaugurating a causal chain. At best, we can say of event *d* that if event *c* had not occurred, there would have been a causal chain between *d* and *e.* But this causal chain would have contained events that did not actually occur.

Given these considerations, we can see that the definition (DC) establishes *c* as a cause of *e.* Condition (i) of clause (1) is satisfied, as we have just seen. Moreover, condition (ii) is satisfied. In order to have a world in which switch S1 is pushed without the light's going on, it would be sufficient to have a world that differs from ours only in that some occurrent event *a,* such as the current's going through the wire, upon which the light's going on was causally dependent, failed to occur. We might suppose, for example, a world in which there was a power failure. Finally, condition (iii) is satisfied. In order to have a world in which the bulb lighted without switch S1's being pushed, it would have been necessary to have a world in which some occurrent event, f—such as the person's deciding to push switch S1—upon which the pushing of S1 was causally dependent, failed to occur. But such a world would *also* have to be one in which the light's going on was causally dependent upon some event g such that in fact e was not dependent causally on g.

I conclude, then, that cases of pseudo overdetermination, such as Case 3, do not present a problem for the definition (DC).[32] Nevertheless, it is important to have a definition of the relation of pseudo overdetermination.

(DPO) Where c and e are occurrent events, c is a pseudo overdeterminant of e iff:
(1) c is not a cause of e (that is, there is no causal chain from c to e and c is not a genuine overdeterminant of e); and
(2)   there is some set of occurrent events, $D = \{d_1, d_2, \ldots, d_n\}$ (possibly having only one member), such that
(a)   each d_i in D is a cause of $e;$ and
(b)   if no member of D had occurred, but c and e had occurred anyway, then there would have been a causal chain from c to e, and c would have been causally prior to e.

In Case 3 we get the result that event d (the pushing of switch S2) is a pseudo overdeterminant of the bulb's going on and that event c (the pushing of switch S1) is a cause of the bulb's going on.

Let us note, finally, three considerations concerning over-determination. First, it should be clear that the relation is-a-pseudo-overdeterminant-of is not a 'real' causal connection. Pseudo overdeterminants do not contribute causally in any way

32. This solution to the problem of psuedo overdetermination is the same in essential detail as that proposed by Lewis in "Causation," p. 567; by Mackie in *The Cement of the Universe*, pp. 44–47; and by Loeb in "Causal Theories and Causal Overdetermination," p. 541.

CAUSATION

to those events of which they are overdeterminants. At best, we may say of pseudo-overdetermining events that they are potential causes. Nevertheless, throughout this book I shall treat pseudo overdetermination as a causal relation. Although this involves some stipulative stretching of the extension of the term 'causal relation', there are good reasons for doing so which will become clear as we proceed.

Second, the discussion so far has treated any given case of overdetermination as either a case of genuine overdetermination or a case of pseudo overdetermination. It is true that any given pair of events could be related by, at most, only one of these kinds of overdetermination. A given effect, e, however, can be overdetermined in both ways at a given time. For example, if our light bulb in Cases 2 and 3 were wired to three switches, S1, S2, and S3, and if S1 and S2 were both equipped with devices that override the circuit between S3 and the bulb, then if all three were pushed at the same time we would have a "mixed" case of genuine and pseudo overdetermination.[33] The pushing of S1 and the pushing of S2 would be genuine overdeterminants of the light's going on, whereas the pushing of S3 would be only a pseudo overdeterminant of that event.

Third, the examples have been designed to serve as particularly clear illustrations of the two kinds of overdetermination. Most examples, including many in later chapters, will not be nearly so clear with respect to the kind of overdetermination they exemplify. For example, if a person dies of a heart attack and is poisoned at the same time, is this a case of genuine or of pseudo overdetermination? The answer depends on precisely which events and chains of events actually occur. Any actual case could be settled only by empirical investigation and is not a matter to be determined by philosophical speculation. We can be sure, however, that any case of overdetermination will be an instance of one of the two types defined above; for my purposes this will often be enough.

33. See Loeb, "Causal Theories and Causal Overdetermination," p. 542. For considerations that cast doubt on Loeb's handling of this problem, see John O'Connor, "Causal Overdetermination and Counterfactuals," *Philosophical Studies* 29 (1976): 276–277. Loeb replies in "Causal Overdetermination and Counterfactuals Revisited," *Philosophical Studies* 31 (1977): 211–214.

5. *Summary and Concluding Remarks*

This chapter has suggested definitions of certain causal concepts that will figure prominently in the account of knowledge and justification to be developed in the remainder of this book, specifically, the notions of event causation, causal chain, and overdetermination. In the next chapter I return to epistemological matters, primarily to detailed discussion of the conditions under which a belief is based upon reasons. The basing relation is a central concept throughout this book, and its importance is evident from the definition (IDK) developed in Chapter One. My account of the basing relation is a causal one; beliefs are based upon reasons just in case there is an appropriate causal connection between those reasons and the belief in question. The appropriate kinds of causal connections are, or can be characterized in terms of, the causal concepts developed in this chapter. In later chapters (particularly Chapter Six) I extend the degree of involvement of causation beyond the basing relation and suggest a general causal account of knowledge, which holds that all our knowledge is ultimately dependent upon the causal ancestries of the reasons upon which our beliefs are based.

CHAPTER THREE

REASONS

Chapter One considered some traditional requirements for factual knowledge. According to the traditional definition (IDK) developed in that chapter, a person, S, has factual knowledge that h only if h, S believes that h, and S's belief that h is justified. From this point on, our primary concern will be the third of these requirements. As shown in Chapter One, the justification requirement involves several clauses:

(1.6)   A person, S, has factual knowledge that h at a time, t, only if there is some set of reasons, R, such that
    (1) S's belief that h is based upon R at t; and
    (2) S's believing that h on the basis of R is justified at t; and
    (3)   If, at t, S has any other reasons, R', that are relevant to whether S is justified in believing that h, then S would be justified in believing that h on the basis of $R \cup R'$ at t.

The necessary conditions for knowledge in (1.6) are expressed in familiar language. The philosophical literature on epistemology, however, contains a bewildering variety of viewpoints concerning the way in which these conditions (or appropriate substitutes) are to be understood. How are we to understand the requirement that S's belief that h must be *based* upon a set of reasons, R? What is meant by saying that a person *has* a set of reasons that are relevant to justifiably believing some proposition, h? Under what conditions is a belief that is based upon a set of reasons *justified*? To these and related questions there are virtually as many answers as there are philosophers who have

[73]

discussed them. In this chapter and the next I shall explicate the main concepts in my formulation of the justification requirement. This chapter is concerned with reasons and reason-based belief. Chapter Four deals with the troublesome concept of justified belief.

1. *Reason States*

Under what conditions is a person's belief that h based upon a set of reasons, R? The causal view that I want to defend may be expressed in the following way:

(DB) S's belief that h is based upon the set of reasons R at t = df.

    (1) S believes that h at t; and

    (2)   For every member, r_j, of R, there is some time, t_n (which may be identical with or earlier than t), such that

        (a) S has (or had) r_j at t_n; and

        (b)   there is an appropriate causal connection between S's having r_j at t_n and S's believing that h at t.

This definition requires further elucidation. First we must be clear about the kinds of things that are or can be members of a set of reasons, R. Second and most important, we must be clear about the kinds of causal connections that are appropriate for the basing relation, as required by clause (2b). This section considers the first question, the next section the second.

In Chapter One I indicated that I take all forms of belief states to be causally efficacious; that is, they are states of a person that can be caused and can be causes of other states. In constructing a causal account of the basing relation, I hold that the members of the set of reasons, R, upon which a belief is based are also causally efficacious. This means that the members of the set R must be events (or states).[1]

---

1. Most of the examples in Chapter Two concerned events; in this chapter most of the examples will involve states of affairs or states of a person. Hence, I shall often speak of various states as standing in causal relations to one another. Because I intend my account of causal relations to apply both to events and to states of affairs, for my purposes there is no need to distinghish between them.

When we think of the reasons for which a person believes something, it is natural to think of some set of propositions that the person believes (or perhaps knows). Propositions, however, are not entities that can be causally related to other entities. How, then, can the set of reasons upon which a belief is based consist of a set of events or states? To answer this we should distinguish between two kinds of reasons. First, there is the kind of reasons we refer to when we talk about a person's evidence, and it is here that talk of believed (or known) propositions is appropriate. Second, there are causal reasons for a belief. Causal reasons are, among other things, events or states of the person who has the belief, and they are events or states that enter into the (causal) explanation of the having of the belief in question. In (1.6) and (DB), the term 'reasons' is intended to designate causal reasons, not evidential reasons. But this does not mean that a person's evidential reasons are unimportant for the theory of justification that I am developing. A person's beliefs (which are states of that person) are often among the causal reasons upon which a belief that h is based. The proposition believed may very well be among the *evidential* reasons that this person has, and whether the belief is justified may depend upon the evidential connections between these propositions and h. Later I shall consider in greater detail the role evidential reasons play with respect to the justification of a belief. For now I restrict my discussion to causal reasons and drop the qualifier 'causal'. Whenever I am talking about evidential reasons, I shall be explicit.

We have noted that some of a person's belief states will often be among the reasons upon which a given belief that h is based. It is tempting to suppose that *only* belief states should be counted as reasons upon which another belief is based. But I want to use the term 'reasons' in a more inclusive way: I want to allow that the set of reasons upon which a belief is based can (and usually will) consist partly of certain kinds of *non*belief states that the person is in, and that this can be so even if the person has no beliefs about those nonbelief states. No doubt this extension of the scope of the term 'reasons' will be met with protest. If we think of reasons as believed propositions or as evidential reasons, then if we want to talk about states of a person as reasons, it would be only natural to restrict the scope of 'reasons' to beliefs that have the propositions in question as their objects. On that conception of reasons, it would indeed be peculiar to talk about nonbelief states as reasons. But I am talking about causal reasons, not evidential reasons, and so this motivation for restricting reasons to beliefs carries no force.

Simply saying that certain kinds of nonbelief states may serve as reasons does not provide any motivation for doing so. It is also necessary to say what kinds of nonbelief states are to be allowed as reasons. I shall consider the second of these problems first and then return to consider the question of motivation. Rather than attempt an exhaustive catalog of types of reason states, I shall give some examples and then provide a general characterization of this class of states.

First, there is a class of states that I shall call perceptual states, which I distinguish from perceiving. For example, suppose I perceive (see) a good friend of mine on a day when he is unhappy. I may come to believe that he is unhappy as a result of observing subtle bits of behavior, such as facial expressions, tone of voice, and bodily demeanor. The observed features of his behavior are causes of my having this belief. I would not, however, want to say that his behavior is among the reasons upon which my belief is based, for this is not a state of me. Rather, his behaving in the way that he does inaugurates a causal chain of events leading to my belief that he is unhappy, and among the links of this chain is a set of perceptual states of me.[2] Suppose my friend is behaving F-ly. Then, we might characterize my perceptual state as that of being appeared to F-ly, or perhaps as the state of sensing F-ly, or perhaps even as the state of having an F-ish sense datum. (I am not concerned in the present context about which philosophical theory concerning such states is correct.) Because this perceptual state is a link in a causal chain leading to my belief that my friend is unhappy, it is itself a cause of that belief. This perceptual state (or complex of perceptual states) is among the reasons for which I believe my friend to be unhappy. But this perceptual state is distinct from the event of my perceiving my friend's behavior, for I could have been in this perceptual state even if I were not perceiving my friend at all but were perhaps hallucinating instead. Al-

2. See definition (DCC) on page 55 of Chapter Two for the notion of a causal chain.

though the perceptual state and the event of my perceiving my friend's behavior are distinct, they are related by the compound/component event distinction utilized in definition (DD) of Chapter Two.

If it be granted that the perceptual state (or complex of perceptual states) involved in this example is causally related in some appropriate way to my belief that my friend is unhappy, then this state is a reason upon which that belief is based. Let us also note, however, that the observed features of my friend's behavior which are reflected in this perceptual state may be so subtle that I do not come to have any specific beliefs about those features. I may not even be able to describe these features if asked. Moreover, this perceptual state is not itself a belief state. Such states are, then, nonbelief states that can serve as reasons.

Perceptual states may be associated with any of the external senses. Moreover, if there is extrasensory perception, then some perceptual states may be associated with this kind of perception. I do not pretend, however, to understand extrasensory perception.

Perceptual states are one major class of nonbelief states that can function as reasons. I have called such states perceptual states because they are intimately associated with perception through the external senses. There is, perhaps, a somewhat blurred distinction between the class of perceptual states and the next major class of nonbelief reason states, namely, sensation states. This includes such states as being in pain, feeling overheated, and other states not associated in any clear fashion with the external senses. If I have a headache, I am in a state of pain, but my being in this state would not normally be associated with my perception of anything. This distinction is, however, not very clear. If I touch a very hot object, I will feel pain; is my being in pain in this instance a perceptual state? I cannot think of any *very* convincing reason for saying that it is not.[3] If it is, then some sensation states will also be perceptual states. In any event, it seems clear that sensation states can serve as reasons upon which a belief is based

3. It might be argued that each of the external senses has its proper objects: for sight, colors; for hearing, sounds; and so forth. Then, if painfulness is not among the proper objects of any of the external senses, we could say that the state of being in pain is not a perceptual state. In suggesting this argument, I do not intend to endorse it.

and that they can serve this function even under circumstances in which a person does not have any beliefs about being in the states in question. For example, if a person is becoming ill, some of the symptoms of the illness may take the form of very subtle sensation states. These sensation states may be too subtle to be precisely noticed and yet may be sufficient to serve as a cause of the belief that one is becoming ill.

Having introduced perceptual and sensation states as examples of nonbelief reason states, I shall now attempt to give a general characterization of reason states. Once that is done, I shall consider a few additional examples. Because I am concerned with a general characterization of reason states, I shall define the concept expressed by the locution 'r is a potential, or possible, reason state of S with respect to some actual or possible belief state of S'. Hence, if an actual state, r, of S qualifies as a potential reason state, it will not follow that it actually functions as a reason upon which any belief is based. I am concerned, in other words, to single out a class of states that *can* serve as reasons.

One characteristic of reason states may be elicited in the following way. I have intimated above that perceptual states can serve as reasons, but that perceivings cannot serve this function. The motivation for excluding perceivings from the class of reason states will be explored later in some detail. For now I shall note only that if a person, S, perceives some entity, or perceives *that* some entity has a given property, then the entity in question is thereby guaranteed to exist or to have the property in question. This feature of perceivings renders them undesirable as reason states within the framework of my theory of justification. I want to exclude from the class of possible reason states any state that guarantees the existence of some entity other than itself or the person, S, of whom it is a state. This can be effected by adopting the following necessary condition for possible reason states:

(3.1) r is a potential reason state of S at t with respect to some actual or possible belief state of S only if no entity, e, whose existence is entailed by 'S is in r at t' is such that, possibly, e exists at t and neither r nor S exists at t.

This necessary condition excludes perceivings but allows most perceptual states. Two comments are in order. First, I say it allows *most* perceptual states because some perceptual states may entail the existence of entities other than S and r. For example, suppose S is in a perceptual state that could be characterized thus: S is appeared to in the way in which object o appeared to her yesterday. It is plausible to hold that S's being in this perceptual state entails that object o existed yesterday; if so, then, assuming o could exist without S's existing, it is to be excluded from the class of potential reason states. Second, I intend this necessary condition to exclude self-perception as well as perception of entities other than the perceiver. For example, suppose S is perceiving his left foot. Then, his being in the state of perceiving his left foot entails that his left foot exists. His left foot, however, is an entity such that, possibly, it exists at t even though S does not exist at t.

Another characteristic of potential reason states may be described as follows. The states that I am calling perceptual and sensation states have often been characterized by philosophers in a way that implies a special status. Some philosophers will say that such states of a person are introspectively *given* in some sense, or that they are introspectively *immediate,* or *self-presenting.* Efforts to define this characteristic precisely have been many and varied, and there is no general agreement. But there *is* something special about these states, even if philosophers have been unable to get clear about the matter. I myself prefer to say that such states are at least possible objects of *direct awareness,* although I cannot justify this choice of terminology on grounds other than simple philosophical prejudice. If a person is in pain or is in the state of being appeared to redly, then, typically, the person will be aware of that state. As I understand it, being aware of such a state (or of anything) does not entail that one is consciously or purposefully attending to the occurrence of that state, nor does it entail that one has any beliefs or any knowledge about being in that state. Moreover, awareness is not restricted to the introspective realm; one can also be aware of tables, noises, and many other kinds of things. I have said, however, that perceptual and sensation states are possible objects of direct awareness. How are we to characterize *direct* awareness? And why say these states are *possible* objects?

We may characterize the notion of direct awareness intuitively by saying that one is directly aware of x just in case one is aware of x but that one's being aware of x is not dependent upon being aware of anything else. In so characterizing direct awareness I am taking the generic notion of awareness as undefined. Even so, this intuitive formulation requires greater precision. For example, suppose y is a proper part of x, and S is aware of x only because S is aware of y. Our rough formulation would exclude the possibility that S is directly aware of x, which is undesirable. Or suppose x is a state of S, perhaps a perceptual state. It is plausible to suppose that, necessarily, for any x, if S is aware of some state of x, then S is aware of x. If so, S's being aware of the state in question is dependent upon S's being aware of x. If x is identical with S, as we have supposed, our intuitive formulation will exclude the possibility of S's being directly aware of the state in question. Such problems can be avoided if we adopt the following definition of direct awareness; in this definition I take the generic notion of awareness as undefined and assume that the notion of essential dependence can be explicated with the aid of definition (DC_fDe) of Chapter Two:

(DDA) S is directly aware of x at t iff:
    (1) S is aware of x at t; and
    (2)   there is no other entity y such that all the following are true of x and y:
        (a) y is neither identical with nor a component of x;
        (b) x is not a component of y;
        (c) y is not identical with S; and
        (d) S's being aware of x at t is essentially dependent upon S's being aware of y at t.

We are, I submit, often directly aware of our perceptual and sensation states in just the way proscribed by the definition (DDA). If a person is directly aware of a perceptual or sensation state, then such a state is a possible object of direct awareness, by virtue of being an actual object of such awareness. It also seems possible, however, for a person to be in one of these states without being directly aware of that state. That is why I have said that such states are possible objects of direct awareness.

I have suggested that nonbelief reason states are possible objects of direct awareness. Are belief states, too, possible objects of direct awareness? As noted in Chapter One, there appear to be various kinds of beliefs. We may, for example, distinguish between occurrent beliefs and dispositional beliefs. Dispositional beliefs, at least, do not seem to be very likely objects of direct awareness. Therefore, I do not assume that all (or even any) belief states are possible objects of direct awareness; nevertheless, I do not want to assume that *none* of them are. If some belief states are not possible objects of direct awareness, and if all belief states are potential reason states, then belief states do not share the direct awareness characteristic with other potential reason states. I suggest the following definition of potential reason states:

(DPR) State r is a potential reason state of person S at time t with respect to some actual or possible belief state of S iff:
- (1) r is a state of S at t; and
- (2) either r is a belief state of S at t or r is such that, possibly, S is directly aware of r at t (or both); and
- (3) no entity, e, whose existence is entailed by 'S is in state r at t' is such that, possibly, e exists at t and neither r nor S exists at t.

In accordance with (DPR), beliefs, perceptual states, and sensation states qualify as potential reason states. Other kinds of states also qualify. For example, we often say of ourselves that we *seem* to remember a person, a place, an event, or having learned something. The state of seeming to remember is a potential reason state in accordance with (DPR). Other examples include hoping, wishing, feeling angry, and trying.

Thus, the class of states that can serve as reason states includes a wide variety of kinds of states other than (but including) belief states. There is a threefold motivation for including these non-belief states. First, some of these reason states traditionally have been viewed as intimately connected in some fashion with sources of knowledge. Belief states, perceptual states, sensation states, and seeming-to-remember states have often been discussed in this context. If we adopt the traditional metaphor of the internal versus the external world, such states have often been considered to fall approximately at the interface between these two realms: they have been looked upon as internal states that somehow provide us with our access to the external world. But the manner in which such states thus function as sources of knowledge has been unclear. By taking such states to be reason states I hope to provide them with a clear role in the acquisition of knowledge. Second, beliefs *about* the kinds of states that qualify as potential reason states by (DPR) have often been accorded a special epistemic status. According to some epistemologists, such beliefs are epistemically justified in such a way that they may be called evidentially basic, initially credible, noninferentially justified, or directly evident.[4] Such beliefs do, in my opinion, enjoy some such privileged position. By allowing the very states that are the objects of such beliefs to be among the reason states upon which those beliefs can be based, I hope ultimately to provide a way of explaining the privileged position they enjoy. Third, the theory of justification I defend requires that *every* epistemically justified belief be so justified only on the basis of reasons, including beliefs that are epistemically justified but are not based upon any other beliefs. Hence, my theory of justification requires that some beliefs be based upon nonbelief reason states.

Having explicated the notion of a potential reason state, let us note finally that the notion of *having* reasons, which is employed in condition (2a) of (DB) as well as in condition (3) of (1.6), receives a straightforward explication on my causal account of reasons. To say that S has or had reason r_j at a time t_n is to say that r_j is, or was, a potential reason state of S at t_n.

2. *Beliefs Based upon Reasons*

Let us now consider the conditions under which a person's belief is based upon a set of reasons. Let me note at the outset that I am concerned in this section to define the basing relation without regard to justificatory considerations. That is, I am not presently concerned to define reason-based *justification*; even a belief that is totally unjustified may be based upon a set of reasons in accordance with the concept of basing to be dealt with here.

The primary task is to specify the kinds of causal connections that are appropriate to the basing relation defined in definition (DB). Given the detailed discussion of causation in the preceding

4. For examples and references, see Roderick Chisholm, *Theory of Knowledge*, 2d ed. (Englewood Cliffs, N.J.: Prentice-Hall, 1977), chapter 2, and John L. Pollock, *Knowledge and Justification* (Princeton, Princeton University Press, 1974), pp. 25–33, 71–79.

chapter, this is a relatively easy task. It is clear that one kind of appropriate causal connection is the relation is-a-cause-of, defined in definition (DC) of Chapter Two. According to (DC), there are two kinds of situations in which one event may be designated as a cause of another: situations in which there is a causal chain of events from the one to the other, and situations in which one event is a genuine overdeterminant of another.[5] Let us consider epistemic examples of each.

Cases in which there is a causal chain from a reason state, *r*, to a belief are not difficult to find; the examples given above of the various kinds of reason states will serve. In the case in which I come to believe that my friend is unhappy by perceiving subtle bits of behavior, a number of reason states are involved in the formation of this belief, For example, there are the various perceptual states that I am in about which I do not have any specific beliefs. In addition to these perceptual states, it is reasonable to suppose that some belief states of mine are also causes (via causal chains) of the belief that my friend is unhappy. I may, for example, have a vague belief that there is something about my friend's behavior that tells me he is unhappy, and presumably I also believe that it is my friend whom I am perceiving. Each of these reason states is such that there is a causal chain of events from that state to the belief that my friend is unhappy.

Some of the belief states that thus serve as reasons may themselves be based upon reason states, and some of the nonbelief states involved presumably could be caused by other reason states via causal chains. This indicates that if we start from a given belief, such as the belief that my friend is unhappy, and trace its causes back along the various causal chains that lead to that belief, the result will be a complex of events that forms a treelike pattern.[6] Some of the events along the branches will be reason states, and others will be events or states that are not reason states. The branches of this causal tree will, I assume, extend indefinitely into the past. The branches of such a causal

5. I am assuming that the other requirements for causation are also satisfied; see definition (DC) on page 68 in Chapter Two.

6. Some might prefer the image of a pyramid. See, for example, Ernest Sosa, "How Do You Know?" *American Philosophical Quarterly* 11 (1974), 113–122, reprinted in George S. Pappas and Marshall Swain, eds., *Essays on Knowledge and Justification* (Ithaca: Cornell University Press, 1978).

tree represent one of the main kinds of causal connections that I want to specify as appropriate for basing. If it is possible to go from a specified reason state, r, to the belief that h along a branch that represents an unbroken causal chain, then r is a state upon which the belief that h is based. Let us also note that if there is a causal chain of distinct events from reason state r to the belief that h, then the belief that h is based upon r even if some of the events (or states) in that causal chain are not themselves reason states.

Suppose my belief that my friend is unhappy is based upon the various reason states suggested above. Now suppose this belief is in turn a cause of yet another belief of mine, namely, the belief that my friend will be unusually aggressive in our tennis game today. This new belief will be based upon all the reasons that form the basis of my belief that my friend is unhappy, and presumably on some additional reasons as well. For example, my new belief might also be based upon the belief that my friend tends to be aggressive when he is unhappy. In such a case, the causal tree leading to my belief that my friend will be unusually aggressive includes, but is more extensive than, the causal tree leading to my belief that my friend is unhappy. This is to be expected, given that the former belief is based upon the latter.

Other kinds of causal patterns are possible. Two are worthy of note. First, a given reason-based belief may be a common cause of two or more additional belief states that are not otherwise causally related. For example, suppose my belief that my friend is unhappy is a cause of my belief that he will be unusually aggressive in his tennis game, and also a cause of my belief that his wife has been nagging him this morning, although neither of these latter beliefs is a cause of the other. In such a case, the causal trees that lead to these two beliefs will have some branches in common (namely, those that lead to their common cause), but may not be such that the ancestry of one is otherwise included in the other. Second, two reason-based beliefs may be such that they have no reason states in common; if so, then the causal trees that lead to them may (but there is no guarantee that they will) be wholly distinct.

Genuine overdetermination, defined in (DGO) of Chapter Two, is the second kind of situation in which one event can be a cause of another. Suppose I am watching a news-service ticker tape on my cable television set and at the same time listening to a radio announcer reading the same ticker tape. The ticker tape and the announcer both tell me at precisely the same time that the Dow Jones average has just fallen below 700. I come to believe that the average has just fallen below 700. This belief is genuinely over-determined by various reason states that I am in. Suppose r_1 is the complex perceptual state involved in my seeing the ticker tape on the television set, and r_2 the complex perceptual state associated with my hearing the announcer read the tape over the radio. Each of these reason states, r_1 and r_2, is a genuine over-determinant of my belief that the Dow Jones average has just fallen below 700. We could expand this example in such a way that my belief is also genuinely overdetermined by two (or more) belief states. Thus, suppose b_1 is the belief that the ticker tape says the average has just fallen, and b_2 the belief that the an-nouncer has said this. Then, b_1 and b_2 may each be a genuine overdeterminant of my belief that the average has fallen below 700.

In considering causal chains, we imagined the causal history of a given belief as forming a treelike pattern extending indefinitely into the past, each branch representing a causal chain leading to that belief. We can expand this idea by adding branches that go back to genuine overdeterminants. Given our definition (DGO) of genuine overdetermination, such branches will not represent causal chains. Consider the example above. If we begin to trace the causes of my belief that the average has fallen, we im-mediately encounter the two beliefs, b_1 and b_2, that genuinely overdetermine this belief. These beliefs presumably will them-selves be based upon reason states, perhaps r_1 and r_2 above. Suppose belief b_1 is based, via a causal chain, on reason state r_1. Then the portion of the branch from r_1 to my belief about the average that consists of the series of events from r_1 to b_1 is a causal chain (assuming b_1 is not itself overdetermined), but the entire branch is not a causal chain. The segment from b_1 to my belief about the average is an instance of genuine overdetermina-tion. As before, the branches of these expanded causal trees rep-resent an appropriate type of causal connection. If it is possible to go from a given reason state r to the belief that h along a branch each segment of which is either a causal chain or an instance of genuine overdetermination, then the belief that h is based upon r.

Finally, let us consider another kind of causal connection that is appropriate to the basing relation, namely, the relation of pseudo overdetermination, defined in definition (DPO) of Chapter Two. As noted there, an event that is a pseudo overdeterminant of another does not have a 'real' causal connection to that event; it is not any part of the actual causal ancestry of that event. I shall argue later that it is necessary to include this relation, even though it is not a 'real' causal connection, if the account of justified reason-based belief is to be fully adequate. For now I note only that this relation is to be included among the appropriate causal connections.

As with genuine overdetermination, we can expand the causal tree leading to the formation of a given belief by adding branches that go back to pseudo-overdetermining reason states. Because the pseudo-overdetermination relation is not a 'real' causal connection, however, only those branches that contain only events that were causes of the belief will represent the actual causal ancestry of the belief.

We are now in a position to be more precise about the kinds of causal connections that are appropriate for the basing relation. If we consider a given belief that h, we may represent its causal ancestry by constructing a tree that traces out the proximate causes and pseudo overdeterminants of that belief. Such a tree will also trace out the more remote causes and pseudo overdeterminants of those proximate causes and pseudo overdeterminants. A reason state, then, is connected with the belief that h in an appropriate fashion just in case it lies along one of the branches of this tree. To capture this, I shall replace condition (2b) of definition (DB) with this condition, which is intended to be recursive:

(2b)   Either (1) S's having r_j at t_n is a cause (including genuine overdetermination) of S's believing that h at t or S's having r_j at t_n is a pseudo overdeterminant of S's believing that h at t;

or   (2)   for some r_i and t_i that satisfy condition (1), with 'r_i' substituted for 'r_j' and 't_i' for 't_n', S's having r_j at t_n is either a cause or a pseudo overdeterminant of S's having r_i at t_i;

or   (3)   for some r_k and t_k that satisfy condition (2), with 'r_k' substituted for 'r_i' and 't_k' for 't_i', S's having r_j at t_n is either a cause or a pseudo overdeterminant of S's having r_k at t_k;

or . . . , etc.

This condition completes my definition of the basing relation. In the next section I shall consider a variety of likely objections. I hope that this will serve both to clarify the proposal and to illustrate its application in specific examples.

3. *Objections*

In the justification requirement (1.6) formulated at the beginning of this chapter and in the definition (DB), I have included explicit reference to times. These temporal considerations may lead to some confusion concerning the basis of belief.

One potentially confusing consideration involving temporal matters concerns what I call the *problem of distant reasons*. A belief is a state that can persist through time even though the reason states that were originally causes of that belief no longer obtain. If there is a long interval between the time when a person was in the reason states that originated a belief and some later time when the belief is still held, it may seem odd to say the belief is, at this later time, still based upon the defunct set of reason states which originated the belief. For example, many adults believe things that their parents told them in childhood; in some such cases the belief has persisted via an unbroken causal chain from that much earlier time. Typically, many of the reason states that originated the belief will not also have persisted. Moreover, in such cases a person typically will have acquired over the years a new set of reasons for the belief in question. The originating reasons are distant reasons, and many may find it odd to call them reasons at all.

Why would it appear odd to include such a distant reason among the set of reasons upon which a current belief is based? One likely explanation involves an incorrect assumption about the basing relation. This assumption can be elicited by considering a possible argument against the result arrived at in the distant reasons situation. It might be argued that there is a close connection between

(3.2) S's belief that h is based upon reason state r at t

and some or all of the following:

(3.3) S takes r at t to be a reason for which S believes that h;

(3.4) S believes at t that S's belief that h is based upon r;

(3.5) S would at t cite or describe r if S were asked to provide the reasons upon which S's belief that h is based;

(3.6) S remembers at t that S was in r at some earlier time.

More precisely, it might be assumed that some or all of (3.3)–(3.6) are necessary conditions for (3.2). Then, it might be argued, if a person has held a belief for a very long time, the chances are that the distant reason states that originated the belief would not satisfy any of (3.3)–(3.6). Hence, S's belief that h could not be said to be based upon any such distant reason states. In response to this (imagined) argument, I would appeal to examples in which it is clear that a person's belief *is* based upon a set of reasons, but in which none of (3.3)–(3.6) is satisfied. I have already considered such situations in section 1 above. Although they are not examples of distant reasons, they show that (3.3)–(3.6) are not necessary for (3.2). Hence, I will let my case rest on the examples discussed there.

There is another possible explanation of the apparent oddity of allowing distant reasons to be included among the basis for a belief. This explanation involves the role that the concept of basing plays in our account of justified belief and knowledge. Whether a belief is justified or whether a person has knowledge is partly a function of the set of reasons upon which the belief is based; this manifests itself in the formulation of the justification requirement (1.6). Distant reasons do not seem very likely candidates for reasons upon which a belief might be justified or upon which a belief might count as an instance of knowledge. I agree with this, but let us note that there is much more to justification and knowledge than is found in the basing relation. If the *only* set of reasons upon which a person's belief that h is based is a set of very distant reasons, then my account of justification and knowledge almost certainly will *not* yield the result that the belief is an instance of knowledge. But in those cases in which the analysis does yield these results they will be found to be appropriate.

Yet another line of argument might be that the conditions in (DB) are not fully sensitive to the fact that a person's reasons can change over a period of time. For example, suppose I come to have a complex set of beliefs about Lefty, namely, that Lefty robbed the bank and murdered Jones. These beliefs are a cause of my belief that Lefty has a criminal personality. Suppose that my belief that Lefty has a criminal personality persists over a period and that there is an unbroken causal chain from my original reasons to the current belief. During this time, a friend of mine in the police department tells me that Lefty did not in fact do the things I once thought she had done; rather, Lefty stole a car and murdered Smith. At this later time my belief that Lefty has a criminal personality comes to be based upon this new set of beliefs, and the causal connection involved is a form of overdetermination. Because there is an unbroken causal chain from my original reasons to my current belief that Lefty has a criminal personality, however, we also have the result that my belief about Lefty is *still* based upon the old beliefs that Lefty robbed the bank and murdered Jones. Surely, it will be argued, this is a mistake, for I have now come to believe that my old beliefs about Lefty are false and I have relinquished those beliefs. Not only have I come to have new reasons for believing that Lefty has a criminal personality, but also this belief has ceased to be based upon the old reasons.

I deny, however, that my belief about Lefty has ceased to be based on my earlier beliefs. If, as the example requires, there is an unbroken causal chain from the earlier beliefs to my current belief about Lefty's criminal personality, then the latter is based upon the former. It is true that many things have changed: I have acquired some new beliefs about Lefty and I have given up some old beliefs, while my belief about her criminal personality has persisted. We may say that the set of reasons that I *have* has changed, but according to my conditions the total set of reasons upon which the belief is based still includes the earlier belief states.

The arguments considered so far are designed to show that the conditions suggested in (DB) are not sufficient for the basing relation. Keith Lehrer suggests a different kind of example that might appear to be a counterexample to the necessity of these conditions.[7] This is an example in which a lawyer, who is also a gypsy, comes to believe that his client is innocent of a murder on the basis of a reading of his cards. His belief that the cards say his client is innocent is a cause of his belief that his client is innocent. These beliefs in turn cause him to reconsider the evidence against his client, which up to this point has been interpreted by everyone as showing that his client is guilty. He finds that the evidence in fact conclusively establishes his client's innocence and he then claims to know that his client is innocent on the basis of this evidence. The case, however, is an emotionally charged one, and the gypsy lawyer

> agrees that it is extraordinarily difficult to be convinced by the evidence because of the emotional factors surrounding the crime. The evidence is quite conclusive, as shown by his complicated chain of reasoning, but even he would find himself unable to believe his client could be innocent of that murder were it not for the fact that the cards told him that his client is innocent of the . . . murder, and it is that which nurtures and supports his conviction. . . . On the other hand, were his faith in the cards to collapse, then emotional factors which influence others would sway him too.[8]

Lehrer argues that in this example the gypsy lawyer's belief is based upon a set of reasons that do not "explain why he believes as he does, his faith in the cards explains that, and the evidence in no way supports, reinforces, or conditionally or partially explains why he believes as he does."[9] Moreover, Lehrer offers this example in the context of a discussion of "causal accounts of what is involved when the justification of a belief is based upon evidence,"[10] and it constitutes his primary argument for the conclusion that "all such theories must be rejected."[11] I believe, however, that there is at least one such theory that need not be rejected, namely, the one suggested in (DB).

7. This example is developed in Keith Lehrer, *Knowledge* (Oxford, Oxford University Press, 1974), pp. 124–125.
8. Ibid.
9. Ibid.
10. Ibid.
11. Ibid.

The point of the example is that the gypsy lawyer's belief that his client is innocent is based upon his belief that the evidence conclusively establishes the innocence of his client. There is, however, no causal connection of any sort between these beliefs. Thus, it is not a necessary condition for the basing relation that there be a causal connection. I suggest that this example can be interpreted in such a way that there *is* a causal connection between the gypsy lawyer's justifying reason state and his belief in his client's innocence. The relation is one of pseudo overdetermination. Let '*h*' designate the proposition that the client is innocent; '*c*', the proposition that the cards say the client is innocent; '*q*', the proposition that the evidence conclusively establishes that *h* and '*S*', the gypsy lawyer. Then, *S*'s belief that *c* is a cause of *S*'s belief that *h* and *also* a cause of *S*'s belief that *q*. This, then, is an example in which one belief (reason state) is a common cause of two other beliefs. It is also an example in which there is no 'real' causal connection between the two beliefs that have the common cause. My suggestion is that *S*'s belief that *q* can plausibly be construed as a pseudo overdeterminant of *S*'s belief that *h*.

Someone might argue that *S*'s believing that *q* is not a pseudo overdeterminant of the belief that *h* because, as Lehrer has constructed the example, *S*'s believing that *q* is causally dependent upon *S*'s believing that *c*; hence, if *S* had not believed that the cards say his client is innocent, then *S* would not have believed to begin with that there is a conclusive argument from the evidence to his client's innocence. But these facts do not show that *S*'s believing that *q* is not a pseudo overdeterminant of the belief that *h*. Whether that is so depends upon whether *S*'s believing that *q* would be a cause of the belief that *h* if nothing else were *and* if *S* were still in the state of believing *q*. That counterfactual may very well be true even though, as a matter of fact, *S* would not have believed that *q* unless *S* had believed that the cards say his client is innocent. Moreover, it is plausible to say that *S* would be caused to believe that his client is innocent partly by his belief that the evidence is conclusive if he were to have this latter belief and did not have the belief about the cards. On the other hand, if the belief that the evidence is conclusive is *not* at least a pseudo overdeterminant of the belief in innocence, I see no ground for claiming that the gypsy lawyer has knowledge.

I conclude, then, that Lehrer's example does not provide a reason for rejecting the causal analysis of the basing relation. Moreover, this example illustrates the *need* for including the relation of pseudo overdetermination among those that are appropriate for the basing relation. We have agreed with Lehrer that the gypsy lawyer knows his client is innocent. This means that the gypsy lawyer's belief must be justifiably based upon some set of reasons. It is obvious that the set of reasons consisting of his belief that c is not a set of reasons upon which the belief that h is justifiably based. The only other set of reasons that the gypsy lawyer has is the set that includes his belief about the evidence. Because the relation between that belief and the belief that h is most plausibly constred as psuedo overdetermination, we must include this kind of causal connection in our account of basing.

4. *Summary and Concluding Remarks*

In this chapter I have developed a causal account of the basing relation, which has two main components. First, I have specified a class of states of a person that can serve as reasons upon which a belief may be based. This class of states includes, but is not limited to beliefs. Second, I have defined the basing relation in terms of causal relations among the members of a set of reason states and the belief that is based upon those reason states. In addition, I have endeavored to formulate and answer the most obvious and most difficult kinds of problems that my causal account faces. It may prove necessary to expand the list of appropriate causal connections, but any such revision would, I take it, be in the spirit of my account of basing.

This causal account of the basing relation is of central importance in my causal account of knowledge, but it is only one area in which causation enters the picture. Knowledge requires reason-based belief; because basing is causal, knowledge requires at least that much causation. But knowledge requires more causation than this, for reason states themselves are caused, and their causal ancestries are relevant to whether one knows. I shall discuss this feature of knowing in Chapter Six. For now, I turn to a consideration of *justified* reason-based belief.

CHAPTER FOUR

JUSTIFIED BELIEF

Supposing S believes that h on the basis of a set of reasons, R, the question remains whether this belief is justified in a way that might provide S with knowledge. A person's belief, even though based upon reasons, may be completely unjustified. I shall follow a fairly well-established usage and call the kind of justification that might provide a person with knowledge epistemic justification. My task in this chapter is to define a concept of epistemic justification adequate to the total analysis of knowledge to be developed in this book. That is, I shall define a notion of epistemic justification such that, if a person satisfies all other conditions for knowing specified in my final definition of knowledge, then satisfaction of the justification condition is all that would be needed for that person to have knowledge.

The problem of justification is, to my mind, the single most difficult and recalcitrant of all epistemological problems. I cannot pretend that the account of justification suggested here is adequate to every context in which epistemologists and others have used the term. Even so, I believe that the definition of justification that I give is faithful on the whole to the intuitions that underlie current discussions of knowledge and justification.

1. Some Examples

Before turning to the theory itself I shall suggest some examples of epistemically justified and unjustified belief. I believe these are examples about which there would not be any significant controversy among epistemologists (and others) concerning the justificatory status of the beliefs involved.

[93]

Example 1. Suppose Sally has an intense headache. Being in a state of pain causes her to believe that she is in pain. Let us suppose, moreover, that Sally is wide awake and attentive, that she understands the concept of being in pain, and that she has no problem in distinguishing sensations of pain from other bodily sensations. Because sensation states are among the states allowed as reasons by definition (DPR) of Chapter Two, we may say that Sally's belief that she is in pain is based upon her being in pain. I take it as uncontroversial that Sally's believing that she is in pain on the basis of her reasons is an instance of epistemically justified belief.

Example 2. Suppose Alfred is sitting in his study and is looking out the window. It is snowing outside. Alfred is wide awake, attentive, has normal vision, and is of at least normal intelligence and educational background. Moreover, it is daytime, the window through which Alfred is looking is clear, and there are no objects outside the window to block Alfred's view. Alfred is sober, undistracted, and has taken no hallucinatory drugs. Alfred comes to be in certain reason states, consisting in part of sensation states and perhaps also the belief that he sees snow falling outside. He also has beliefs about how things look when it is snowing, understands the relevant concepts, and in general has no trouble distinguishing snow from other sorts of weather conditions. Alfred's various reason states cause him to believe that it is snowing outside. As in Example 1, I take it as uncontroversial that Alfred's belief that it is snowing outside on the basis of his reasons R is epistemically justified.

Example 3. Throughout her childhood Roberta has believed that whales are fish, largely because she knows they live in water and swim like fish. While studying her high school biology book, however, she reads that whales are actually mammals and not fish. Somewhat amazed by this news, she asks her biology teacher if there isn't perhaps a mistake in the text. Her teacher assures her that the text is correct. Over the weekend she goes to the local sea aquarium and studies the whales there, noting certain mammalian characteristics for herself. On the basis of the various beliefs that she has thus acquired, she comes to believe that all whales are mammals. Her belief in this generalization on the basis of her reasons is, I take it, epistemically justified.

Example 4. Ralph is studying logic. One of his homework exercises instructs him to prove that the sentence '[A ⊃ (B ⊃ C)] ⊃ [(A · B) ⊃ C]' is true, where 'A', 'B', and 'C' represent sentences. Ralph is a good student, has mastered the fundamentals of elementary logic, and understands what is involved in proving that a sentence has a tautologous form. In this instance he abstracts the form of the sentence, proceeds to construct a truth table, fills in all the truth values correctly, checks it twice, and then notes that there are only 'T's' under the main connective. He (justifiably) believes that a schematic formula having such a truth table is tautologous. On the basis of these various reason states, he comes to believe that the schematic formula is a tautology and that the sentence in question is true. His belief that this formula is a tautology on the basis of his set of reasons *R* is, I take it, epistemically justified. Similarly, his belief that the sentence in question is true is epistemically justified. Finally, suppose Ralph also comes to believe that *h* on the basis of his reasons *R,* where the proposition that *h* is the proposition expressed by the sentence in whose truth Ralph has become a believer. This belief, like the others, is epistemically justified.

These four examples are all instances of epistemically justified reason-based belief. For each we can imagine similar examples in which the belief in question is *not* epistemically justified. Consider Example 1, in which Sally justifiably believes that she is in pain. Suppose Sally has great difficulty in discriminating between kinds of sensation states. Perhaps she has a propensity to confuse pain with tickling. If so, then it is considerably less clear that Sally's belief that she is in pain is epistemically justified on the occasion in question. Or, somewhat more fancifully, imagine that Sally has been wired to a highly sophisticated cerebroscope, and that the art of cerebroscope reading has become so advanced that mistakes about the subject's sensation states are negligibly rare. Sally knows all about the cerebroscope. On the occasion in question, her sensation state causes her to believe that she is in pain. But the cerebroscope indicates she is not in pain, and she is aware of the cerebroscope reading. It is questionable, I should think, whether Sally's belief that she is in pain is epistemically justified.

In each of the other examples given, it is easy to imagine variations in which the person is not justified. In Example 2 we might suppose that Alfred is not looking out the window, does not see the snow falling, but comes to believe that it is snowing outside simply because he would like it to be snowing outside. In Example 3 we might suppose that Roberta has some other source of information about whales, a source that would generally be regarded as unreliable and that she does not bother to follow through with questions and observations of her own. In Example 4 we could imagine that Ralph is not a good logic student and could not construct a respectable proof of tautologousness if his life depended upon it. Rather, he comes to believe that the sentence is true simply because he likes the way it looks; sentences that are aesthetically pleasing to him tend to strike him as true. In these variations it seems intuitively clear that the subject is not epistemically justified, even though the belief is based upon reasons. There are, of course, many other examples that we could consider. For now, however, this small sample will suffice.

2. *Justification and Reliability*

I shall first develop the intuitive idea behind the theory of epistemic justification I want to suggest, and then turn to a more precise formulation. The theory begins from the observation that people are, in some respects, rather like barometers and thermometers.[1] A barometer, for example, has a structure, or composition, that makes it sensitive to changes in atmospheric pressure in its region. Such changes in pressure cause changes in various states of the barometer, the result of which is the pointing of the

---

1. In *Belief, Truth, and Knowledge* (Cambridge: Cambridge University Press, 1973), David Armstrong suggests what he calls the "Thermometer Model" of noninferential knowledge. Consider this remark: "When a true belief unsupported by reasons stands to the situation truly believed to exist as a thermometer-reading in a good thermometer stands to the actual temperature, then we have noninferential knowledge" (p. 166). As I pointed out in Section 5 of Chapter One, the view I develop in this chapter is related, at least on an intuitive level, to this view suggested by Armstrong. My view differs from his, however, in at least two major respects. First, Armstrong is constructing a reliability view of *knowledge,* whereas I am suggesting an account of epistemic justification. Second, the account of reliability that Armstrong suggests is surely too strong, for it requires that the subject's being in the state of believing that p be nomically sufficient for the truth of p. My account is considerably weaker than this.

needle to a certain position on the face of the barometer. If the barometer is in good working order, then, on a given occasion, the fact that the barometer registers a certain atmospheric pressure, P, is related in an important way to the proposition that the atmospheric pressure *is* P. Let us call the set of characteristics that are sufficient for saying that the barometer is in good working order the set C. Then, we may say, given that the barometer has the set of characteristics C, the barometer's registering P is a reliable indicator of the way the world is with respect to barometric pressure. The barometer's registering P is a reliable indication that the barometric pressure is P.

People, like barometers, are causally sensitive to certain aspects of the world around them. A barometer registers changes in atmospheric pressure by coming to be in correlative states as a causal result of those changes. People register changes around them by coming to be in various perceptual states, sensation states, and belief states as a causal result of those changes. We would normally not say of a barometer that its registering a given pressure is justified; we do say, however, that its registering this pressure is reliable. We can also say of people that their being in certain states is reliable, and mean by this something very like what we mean when we say the same thing of a barometer.

Consider Example 2, the case of Alfred who is sitting in his study watching the snow fall outside. Alfred has come to be in certain reason states, R, as a causal result of the event of the snow's falling. Moreover, Alfred comes to believe that it is snowing, and this belief is based upon his set of reason states, R.[2] This belief is analogous to the state of the barometer that consists in the pointing of its needle to the mark P on its dial. Moreover, in constructing this case, we have supposed that Alfred is in good working order; he is wide awake, sober, has good vision, and so forth. There is, in other words, some set of relevant characteristics, C, that Alfred has, and by virtue of his having these characteristics it can be said that he is in good working order. Just as we

2. In discussing the barometer, I did not introduce any explicit analogue for the notion of a set of reasons, for normally we would not speak of barometers as having point readings based upon reasons. We could, however, speak of reasons in the case of a barometer if we wanted to, for there are various states of the barometer to which its needle-pointings bear appropriate causal relations.

say of the barometer, given its condition, that its being in the state of registering P is a reliable indicator of the atmospheric pressure, we can also say of Alfred that his believing that it is snowing outside on the basis of his reasons R is, given the condition C that he is in, a reliable indication that it is snowing outside.

In addition to reliability there is, of course, unreliability. If the barometer is not in good working order, then even if it should happen to indicate the correct atmospheric pressure on a given occasion, we would not say that its indication of that pressure is reliable. The same is true of people. The variation on the example involving Albert, in which Albert comes to believe that it is snowing outside simply because he would like it to be snowing, is not only an instance of unjustified belief but also an instance of unreliable belief. Alfred has certain relevant characteristics, including the characteristic of being prone to believe things he would like to be true, such that, given these characteristics, Alfred's belief that it is snowing is not a reliable indication of the way the world is. In each of the variations on the other examples considered, in which the subject's belief is unjustified, we also will find that the belief in question is not a reliable indicator of the way the world is.

Having noted the analogy between believers and other sorts of indicators, and having noted the correlation between facts about reliability and facts about the justificatory status of beliefs, we can proceed to an initial formulation of the theory of justification that I want to defend. Section 6 of Chapter One presented a version of the traditional analysis of knowledge in the incomplete definition (IDK). The third condition of (IDK) was the justification requirement, and we saw that some care must be taken in the formulation of this requirement. I shall take the conditions suggested in the justification requirement as definitive of epistemic justification; we thus obtain the following general definition:

(DEJ) S's belief that h is epistemically justified at t iff: There is some set of reasons, R, such that
    (1) S's belief that h is based upon R at t; and
    (2) S's believing that h on the basis of R is epistemically justified at t; and

(3)   if, at *t*, *S* has any other reasons, *R'*, that are rele-
      vant to whether *S* is justified in believing that *h*,
      then *S* would be epistemically justified in believing
      that *h* on the basis of $R \cup R'$ at *t*.

The relation employed in condition (2) of this general definition
needs to be defined. This is where reliability enters the picture. I
propose to define this notion in the following way:

(DEJR)   *S*'s believing that *h* on the basis of *R* is epistemically
         justified at *t* iff: *S*'s believing that *h* on the basis of *R*
         is a reliable indication that *h* at *t*.

The task of defining the concept of reliability will be the primary
concern in the remainder of this chapter. From this point on,
clauses such as '*S*'s belief is reliable', '*S* reliably believes that *h*',
and '*S*'s belief that *h* is epistemically reliable' should be understood as stylistic variations on the expression that is the definiens
of (DEJR).

3. *Reliability and Probability*

In the analogy between barometers and believers, ascriptions
of reliability and unreliability were based on two conditions: a set
of relevant characteristics, and a certain state of the entity (such
as a needle's pointing or a reason-based believing) that is said to
be a reliable or unreliable indication of the way the world is. In
the original example involving Alfred and his belief that it is snowing, "his belief that it is snowing outside on the basis of his
reasons *R* is, given the condition *C* that he is in, a reliable indication that it is snowing outside." What are we saying of Alfred, his
belief, and his characteristics when we say that these things provide a reliable indication that it is snowing? My answer is that
ascriptions of reliability are *evidential* claims, that is, claims that
these facts about the subject constitute good evidence for the
truth of the proposition believed. The information that Alfred has
the set of characteristics *C* (where these characteristics would be
specified) and that Alfred believes that it is snowing on the basis
of the set of reasons *R* (where the reasons would also be

[99]

specified) constitutes good evidence for the claim that it is snowing outside; that is, we would have better evidence for the claim that it is snowing outside than for the claim that it is not snowing (assuming that we did not also have negative evidence).

Claims to the effect that a certain body of information constitutes better evidence for h than for the denial of h can be represented using conditional inductive probability expressions. Of Alfred we might say, "The probability that it is snowing outside, given that Alfred believes that it is snowing outside on the basis of the set of reasons R and given that Alfred has the set of characteristics C, is greater than the probability that it is not snowing outside, given those same facts about Alfred." Using such expressions, I can formulate a first, approximate definition of the concept of reliable belief.

(4.1) S's believing that h on the basis of the set of reasons R is a reliable indication that h at t iff: there is some set of relevant characteristics, C, such that

(1) S has C at t (that is, each member of C is a characteristic of S at t); and

(2) the probability that h, given that S has C and that S believes that h on the basis of R, is greater than the probability that not-h, given those same facts about S.

Because the concept of reliable belief is to be defined in terms of probability and the concept of justified belief is defined in terms of reliable belief, I call my theory of justification the *probabilistic-reliability model of epistemic justification*; in shortened form the PR model of justification.

In each of the four examples of Section 1, the conditions suggested in (4.1) appear to be satisfied. Those examples were suggested as instances of justified belief, and justified belief has been defined in terms of reliable belief. Hence, we have some initial support for (4.1). There are, however, a number of problems with (4.1); by considering these problems we may progress to an adequate definition of reliable belief, and hence to an adequate theory of epistemic justification. Before turning to these matters, however, I want to consider some respects in which the PR model of justification might initially be misunderstood.

One likely source of misunderstanding is the use of conditional

JUSTIFIED BELIEF

inductive probability expressions in the definiens of (4.1). I have
said that such expressions can be taken to represent claims to the
effect that a body of propositions is good evidence for the truth of
some further proposition. Given that the concept defined in (4.1)
is used in turn to define the concept of justified belief, one might
think that this system of definitions is thereby rendered circular;
for, one might argue, there is no way to define the relations expressed by '*e* is good evidence for *h*' and '*e* is better evidence for
h than for the denial of *h*' except by reference to conditions under
which one would be justified in believing that *h* when *e* is one's
evidence. Because I am using the concept of evidential support in
defining justified belief, I agree that there is a close connection
between these notions. Moreover, I agree that the concept of
evidential support *could* be defined in terms of the concept of
justified (or reliable) belief. These various concepts are members
of a family of epistemic concepts many of whose members are
definable in terms of others. We are not, however, entitled to
conclude that a definition of one family member in terms of others
is circular. There are two ways in which the circularity may be
avoided: one is to take the concept employed in the definiens (in
this case, the concept of evidential support) to be undefined; the
other is to provide a definition of the concept used in the definiens
in terms of concepts outside the family (provided that these ex-
trafamilial concepts are not in turn defined by the original family).
Because I am not in a position to take the second course—I do not
know how to define the concept of evidential support—I take it as
undefined.

Another respect in which my strategy may be misunderstood
emerges from the earlier remark that "ascriptions of reliability
are *evidential* claims, claims to the effect that these facts about
the subject constitute good evidence for the truth of the proposition believed." One might ask, *for whom* do these facts constitute good evidence? For us? For God? For the subject in question? The answer is, perhaps these facts do not constitute good
evidence *for anyone.* In saying that Alfred's belief that it is snowing on the basis of his reasons is, given his relevant characteristics, a reliable indication that it is snowing, we do not imply that
these facts about Alfred are a reliable indication for anyone. It
may be that no one is aware of these facts, not even Alfred him-

[101]

self. To this degree, ascriptions of reliability are objective and independent of whether anyone knows or believes them to obtain. We may note that these things are also true of barometers. A deserted barometer's indications of barometric pressure may be every bit as reliable as those of a barometer in daily use.

In a related argument, a critic might say, "You have suggested a way of defining the concept of justified belief in terms of objective facts about the subject's reliability. In doing so, you have completely ignored the *subject's* own evidence for the proposition believed. It is clear, however, that questions of justification are often questions of the subject's evidence. Thus, your suggested approach must be inadequate." In response, I would point out that although I have not yet explicitly mentioned the subject's evidence, this does not mean that my theory ignores such evidence. On the contrary, the PR model of justification is fully sensitive to the role that the subject's evidence plays in questions of justification. To say that a person has evidence for some proposition is at least to say that this person has some *beliefs* such that the propositions believed (the evidence) bear some appropriate evidential relation to the proposition for which they are evidence. As we shall see later, the PR model of justification requires that evidential beliefs of this sort be among the set of reasons, *R,* upon which some further belief is based if those evidential beliefs are to contribute to the justification of that further belief. Moreover, the PR model requires that evidential beliefs of this sort be epistemically justified themselves if they are to contribute to the justification of other beliefs. I shall indicate later the manner in which the PR model imposes such requirements.

Many justification theorists have endeavored to account for epistemic justification solely by reference to the subject's evidence, relations of evidential support among believed propositions, and related concepts. A distinction is commonly made between beliefs that are, in some sense, evidentially basic, and those that are evidentially nonbasic. One way of drawing this distinction is to define a class of justification-making relations that can hold among propositions. Accordingly, a belief that h is evidentially basic if it qualifies as justified independently of the need for other justifiably believed (or known) propositions that bear some justification-making relation to the proposition that h.

A belief that *h* is evidentially nonbasic if it is justified only because the person justifiably believes (or knows) some evidence that bears an appropriate justification-making relation to the proposition that *h*. For those who have defended such theories, the main tasks have been to define clearly both a class of evidentially basic beliefs and a class of appropriate justification-making relations. Despite considerable philosophical effort expended on both tasks and despite all we have learned from these efforts, little agreement has been reached on either problem. One of the primary motivations for development of the PR model is to find an account of epistemic justification which does not require solutions to these problems. I cannot, however, claim complete success in this regard. For one thing, the PR model takes the relation of evidential support to be undefined, and this relation is one of the justification-making relations that epistemologists have been concerned about. For another, the PR model requires an account of evidentially basic beliefs; happily, it also provides for a satisfactory solution to this long-standing problem.

Another major motivation for development of the PR model is the fact that consideration of the subject's evidence does not alone seem sufficient to account for epistemic justification. Whether a person's belief is justified on a given occasion depends in part upon characteristics of that person which are relevant to the reliable gathering and processing of information. Such characteristics may have nothing to do with the subject's evidence. Consider Example 1 again, in which Sally believes that she is in pain. In one variation we imagined that Sally has a difficult time discriminating between kinds of sensation states and often confuses pain with other kinds of states (such as tickling). Now suppose Sally is unaware of this defect: on some occasions she correctly believes that she is in pain; on other occasions she incorrectly believes that she feels a ticklish sensation; and on still other occasions when she feels a ticklish sensation she incorrectly believes that she is in pain. On all these occasions she is unaware of when she is correct or incorrect, and so she has no *evidence* that she herself is an unreliable discriminator of sensation states. On any given occasion when Sally believes that she is in pain we would not say her belief is justified even if she happens to be correct. And, I believe, the explanation of this does not lie in

considerations of Sally's evidence. Rather, it is Sally's dispositional characteristic of being prone to confuse sensation states
with one another that motivates our judgment that her belief that
she is in pain is unjustified. The PR model attempts to account for
such factors by explicitly including reference to relevant characteristics of the believer.

Having noted these considerations, I now turn to the problems
that face our initial definition of reliable belief (4.1).

4. Relevant Characteristics

The first problem concerns the notion of relevant characteristics used in (4.1). It is time to provide precise indication of what
sorts of characteristics are to be considered relevant to determining whether a person's belief is epistemically reliable.

First, however, (4.1) requires an important modification. This
tentative definition of reliability has required only that there be
some set of relevant characteristics satisfying the conditions
given. This must be modified somewhat, for conditional probabilities are subject to variation depending upon the conditioning
evidence. For example, suppose that C is the total class of relevant characteristics of S for the determination of epistemic reliability in some situation. The conditional probability of h given
some subset of C (and holding other factors constant) may be
different from the conditional probability of h relative to the entire set C or some other subset of C. The current definition (4.1)
allows our determination of epistemic reliability to depend upon
some arbitrary selection of a subset of C. To prevent arbitrariness
we must impose a version of the total evidence requirement on
the set of characteristics C. This can be accomplished by requiring that the set C of relevant characteristics be a *maximal* set. A
set of relevant characteristics, C, is maximal just in case (1) every
member of set C is relevant and (2) for every other *relevant*
characteristic or set of relevant characteristics, C', of S, the
union of C with C' would not affect the conditional probabilities
referred to in the definiens of (4.1) if substituted for C, all else
being held constant. This characterization of maximality does not
require that *every* relevant characteristic of S be a member of C.
C need only be inclusive enough to guarantee that no other rele-

vant characteristics will affect the conditional probabilities involved. In what follows, I assume that the expression 'There is some set of relevant characteristics, C' in (4.1) is replaced by 'There is some *maximal* set of relevant characteristics, C'.

Which characteristics of a person are relevant? The answer would be easy if one could say, "All characteristics of the person are relevant." But it is not difficult to see that this liberal account generates counterexamples to the conditions suggested in (4.1). Consider again Example 2, in which Alfred believes reliably that it is snowing outside. Given the situation, Alfred has a number of characteristics that, taken by themselves, *guarantee* it is snowing outside. For instance, Alfred has the characteristic of being such that he correctly believes that it is snowing outside. He also has the characteristic of being such that he sees (perceives) snow outside his window. Either of these characteristics, if included in the set of characteristics C, would make it possible to say, "The probability that it is snowing outside, given that Alfred believes that it is snowing on the basis of his reasons R, and given that Alfred has C, is 1." Indeed, this probability statement would be true no matter what reasons Alfred's beliefs were based upon, just so long as Alfred has either of these snow-guaranteeing characteristics. In general, anyone who happens to have a correct belief that h, for whatever reasons, would have an epistemically reliable belief that h if we allow the characteristic of being such that the person correctly believes that h to be included among the set of relevant characteristics C. Our restrictions must exclude characteristics of this sort. Similar considerations apply to barometers. Suppose the barometer is broken, and hence unreliable, but that it happens coincidentally to register the correct barometric pressure. Then, the barometer would have the characteristic of being such that it correctly indicates the barometric pressure, and this characteristic alone would guarantee the probabilistic facts required for reliability. As with people, reliability of barometers must be measured relative to some restricted set of characteristics.

Similar considerations indicate the need for another restriction on the kinds of characteristics that are relevant for determining epistemic reliability. As we have seen, if a person correctly believes some proposition, then that person has a characteristic that alone guarantees that the proposition is true. Suppose, however, someone incorrectly believes some proposition; that is, suppose S believes that h when h is false. Then, S will have the characteristic of being such that S incorrectly believes that h, and this characteristic alone guarantees that h is false. Hence, the probability that h, given that S has this characteristic (and given whatever reasons and other characteristics S may have), is 0. (4.1) will then yield the result that S's belief that h is epistemically unreliable. In general, we would have the result that any false belief is unreliable, and thus unjustified. Some philosophers would welcome this conclusion.[3] As I shall argue in Chapter Five, however, we must allow for epistemically justified belief in false propositions. Consequently, our account of relevant characteristics must exclude those characteristics that alone guarantee the falsity of the proposition believed.

Perhaps we may say this: "A characteristic, c, of a person, S, is relevant to determining whether S's belief that h is epistemically reliable *only if S's* having c entails neither that h is true nor that h is false." While this is a step in the right direction, it must be modified. In Example 4, in which Ralph comes to justifiably believe that h, where h is tautologous, the proposition believed is such that it is entailed by every proposition. Hence, no characteristic of Ralph's would be relevant to whether he reliably believes the tautology in question, and that is, as we shall see, an undesirable result. Taking this into account, we may express one necessary condition for relevance in the following way:

(4.2)   A characteristic, c, of a person, S, is relevant to determining whether S's belief that h is epistemically reliable only if S's having c entails neither that h is true nor that h is false, unless h is such that the probability that h, given any evidence, e, is 0 or 1.

Although (4.2) places some needed restrictions on the class of relevant characteristics, even further restrictions are needed. Some of these may be elicited by considering characteristics that are similar in some respects to those that led to (4.2). Just as we

3. See, for example, Robert Almeder, "Truth and Evidence," *Philosophical Quarterly* 24 (1974): 364–368.

do not want to allow as relevant any characteristics that alone *guarantee* either that *h* or that not-*h*, we also do not want to allow characteristics that alone guarantee the probabilistic facts required for reliable belief. Suppose our subject, *S*, reliably believes that *h*. Then, *S* will have a characteristic, namely, the characteristic of reliably believing that *h*, such that the probability that *h*, given only this characteristic of *S*, will be greater than the probability that not-*h*. This characteristic must be excluded, at least on grounds of circularity, from the class of relevant characteristics. It will not be excluded by (4.2), however, for the characteristic in question is not such that *S*'s having it entails either that *h* or that not-*h*. There are other characteristics of this sort which *S* may have. For example, suppose *S*'s friend, Jones, reliably believes that *h*. Then, *S* will have the characteristic of having a friend who reliably believes that *h*, and this characteristic alone will guarantee the probabilistic facts required for reliability. If *S* also believes that *h*, *S*'s belief automatically will be a reliable one even if the reasons upon which *S*'s belief that *h* is based would not otherwise support that conclusion. To take yet another example, suppose *S* has a crystal ball that happens to be a reliable source of information about the world. *S*, however, is not aware that the crystal ball has this feature. When gazing into the ball, *S* comes to believe what it tells him, but only because he has been conditioned to do so by his gypsy upbringing. On any such occasion, *S* will have a characteristic that alone guarantees the probabilistic facts required for reliable belief, namely, the characteristic of being such that he is told that *h* by a reliable crystal ball. Even so, we would not say that *S*'s believing that *h* is a reliable indication of the way the world is, nor would we say that his belief is epistemically justified. Having access to a reliable source of information does not render one's beliefs justified nor even reliable unless one justifiably believes that the source is reliable.

These examples have in common some characteristic that has an illegitimate effect on the conditional probabilities required for reliable belief: a belief that may well be unreliable (or unjustified) turns out to be reliable simply because the subject happens to have a characteristic that alone guarantees that the probabilities work out. We can also imagine examples in which a person reliably (justifiably) believes that h but also happens to have some characteristic that illegitimately prevents the probabilities from working out. Consider this variation on the example involving Alfred and his belief that it is snowing outside. As in the original example, Alfred is looking out the window, is in good working order epistemically, and seems to see snow falling. He believes that it is snowing on the basis of the reasons specified in the original case. This time, however, suppose Alfred has been tricked: there is no snow falling outside his window; rather, there is a machine out there producing imitation snow. Now suppose Alfred's friend, Jones, reliably believes that such a machine is producing the stuff that Alfred sees. Then, Alfred will have a characteristic, namely, the characteristic of having a friend who has this reliable belief, such that, if this characteristic is allowed as relevant, the probabilities will not work out in the way required for reliable belief by (4.1).

In order to rule out characteristics that illegitimately affect the conditional probabilities, we must require that a characteristic be counted as relevant only if it is, when taken *alone,* probabilistically neutral with respect to h and not-h. We may characterize this notion of probabilistic neutrality in the following way: a characteristic, c, of a person, S, is probabilistically neutral with respect to whether h if and only if the probability that h, given tautologous evidence, T, is equal to the probability that h given T and given that S has c. In the example we have been considering, the unwanted characteristics do not satisfy the neutrality requirement. Those characteristics that do seem relevant, however, also seem to be characteristics that are neutral when taken alone. In the original example involving Alfred, one such characteristic might be that of having normal eyesight. Although it is clear that this characteristic is relevant to determining whether Alfred reliably believes that it is snowing, it is, when taken *alone,* probabilistically neutral to whether it is snowing. Whatever value we would assign to the probability that it is snowing, given *only* tautologous evidence T, we would assign precisely the same value to the probability that it is snowing, given T and given (only) the additional information that Alfred has normal eyesight.

Although the characteristic of having normal eyesight is probabilistically neutral when taken alone, Alfred's having this characteristic can have an effect on the conditional probabilities when taken in conjunction with the other conditioning evidence referred to in (4.1). Given that Alfred believes that it is snowing on the basis of reasons that include various perceptual states, the added information that Alfred has normal eyesight is positively relevant (probabilistically) to whether it is snowing. On the other hand, if Alfred's eyesight were poor and uncorrected, or if Alfred were a poor discriminator of snow from other forms of precipitation, these characteristics would be negatively relevant. All these characteristics, however, when taken alone, are probabilistically neutral to whether it is snowing. In general, the class of relevant characteristics includes those that are relevant to whether the subject is a reliable information-gathering and -processing entity. Good versus poor eyesight, good versus poor reasoning habits, ability or inability to discriminate among kinds of entities, and many other kinds of characteristics will turn out to be relvant, provided that they are probabilistically neutral when taken alone.

Following these considerations, I propose the following necessary condition for the relevance of a characteristic:

(4.3)   A characteristic, c, of a person, S, is relevant to determining whether S's belief that h is epistemically reliable only if S's having c is probabilistically neutral with respect to h when taken alone, unless h is such that the probability that h, given any evidence, e, is 0 or 1.

Three additional comments are in order. First, a characteristic that is relevant to determining the reliability of one belief may not be relevant to determining the reliability of another. In some cases it is quite important to be aware of this. Consider Alfred again. Suppose Alfred comes to believe that he has good eyesight. Then, the characteristic of having good eyesight will *not* be relevant to whether his belief is reliable, for it is not, when taken alone, probabilistically neutral to the proposition believed. Second, the exclusionary clause 'unless h is such that the probability that h, given any e is 0 or 1' in (4.3) is as important as it was in (4.2), for without it no characteristics of a person would be relevant to reliable belief in tautologies and other propositions that have the extreme probabilities relative to any evidence. Third, (4.3) entails (4.2): if S's having some characteristic c entails that h is true or that h is false, then S's having this characteristic will not be probabilistically neutral to h, when taken alone.

(4.2) and (4.3) constitute efforts to exclude characteristics that might illegitimately affect the conditional probabilities in the definition of reliable belief. Another type of characteristic also should be excluded from the class of relevant characteristics, though not because such characteristics would illegitimately affect the conditional probabilities involved. These are, rather, characteristics that do not affect the conditional probabilities *at all*. For instance, in Example 2 I assume that Alfred's height, weight, and hair color are not relevant characteristics vis-à-vis the question whether his belief that it is snowing is epistemically reliable. Such characteristics are technically harmless, but in the interest of accuracy they should be excluded as irrelevant. To do this, I adopt the following additional necessary condition, modeled after standard definitions of probabilistic relevance:

(4.4)   A characteristic, c, of a person, S, is relevant to determining whether S's belief that h is epistemically reliable only if c is a characteristic such that the probability that h, given (only) that S believes that h on the basis of R, is not equal to the probability that h, given (a) that S believes that h on the basis of R and (b) that S has characteristic c, unless the probability that h is either 0 or 1 given any evidence e.

In Example 2, suppose the probability that it is snowing outside, given only that Alfred believes that it is snowing on the basis of his set of reasons R, is p. Then, let c be the characteristic of having brown hair. It seems clear that conditional probability p will remain the same even if we add to our evidence the information that Alfred has characteristic c. In this manner we may exclude the probabilistically irrelevant characteristics.

(4.2), (4.3), and (4.4) have excluded those cases in which h has a probability of either 0 or 1 relative to any evidence, e, from the requirements imposed. But how are we to distinguish relevant from irrelevant characteristics in those cases in which the proposition believed has one of the extreme probabilities relative to any evidence? The problem is broader than the question would indicate, for such cases also provide counterexamples to the tentative definition of epistemic reliability suggested in (4.1). We must give special treatment to such cases by introducing considerations that will allow us to distinguish relevant from irrelevant characteristics in this special class.

Let us begin treatment of these special cases by considering the tentative definition (4.1) of epistemic reliability and Example 4, in which Ralph comes to believe that a tautology is true on the basis of reasons that include his belief that he has correctly proved that the sentence is a tautology. This example was suggested as a clear instance of reliable belief, and the conditions of the tentative definition (4.1) seem to be satisfied. In a variation on that example, however, Ralph's belief is not epistemically reliable: "We could imagine that Ralph is not a good logic student, and indeed could not construct a respectable proof of tautologousness if his life depended upon it. Rather, he comes to believe that the sentence is true simply because he likes the way it looks; sentences that are aesthetically pleasing to him tend to strike him as true." This variation provides a counterexample to (4.1). For the moment, let us pretend we have already decided how to tell which characteristics of a person are relevant to determining whether a belief is epistemically reliable; then, conditions (1) and (2) of (4.1) are satisfied. The crucial consideration has to do with condition (2). Because the sentence believed to be true is a tautology, the probability that it is true, given any evidence e whatever, is 1, and thus is greater than the probability that it is not true, given that same evidence e. Hence, condition (2) is trivially satisfied. Assuming condition (1) is also satisfied, we get the undesirable result that Ralph's belief is epistemically reliable in this variation on Example 4. How can we avoid this result?

To answer this question we must consider what in the example inclines us to say that Ralph's belief is *not* epistemically reliable. Ralph's belief is in some sense arbitrary even though it is based upon reasons. Whereas it is no accident that the proposition he believes is true, it is accidental that he believes a true proposition. If, instead of the sentence '$[(A \supset (B \supset C)] \supset [(A \cdot B) \supset C]$', Ralph had been confronted with the very similar-looking sentence '$[A \supset (B \supset C)] \supset [A \supset (B \cdot C)]$', and if he had found it pleasing, he also would have come to believe that the second sentence is true. But this second sentence is not a tautology, and is in fact false. Ralph, in other words, has the characteristic of being prone to believe to be true any sentence that looks nice to him, regardless of the truth value and logical status of that sentence. In this respect Ralph is an unreliable indicator of the way the world is. I suggest that this is the feature of the situation that disinclines us from saying that Ralph's belief is epistemically reliable. Can this feature be made any more precise?

Suppose that you do not yourself know whether the sentence that Ralph believes to be a tautology is a tautology or not. Suppose, moreover, that you know Ralph believes that this sentence is a tautology on the basis of reasons R, and that you know what his relevant characteristics are, including the characteristic of being prone to believe to be true sentences that are aesthetically pleasing to him. Presumably you would not take this as good evidence that Ralph has a true belief, and thus would not take the fact of his having this belief as good evidence for the truth of the proposition believed. Whereas any evidence whatever is good evidence for a tautology, the same cannot be said concerning evidence that a person's belief that some sentence is a tautology is a correct belief. In the case at hand, let 'h^*' designate the following: 'Ralph believes some *true* proposition or other on the basis of reasons R'. And let 'q^*' designate this: 'Ralph believes some proposition or other on the basis of R'. Then we may say that q^*, conjoined with the evidence that Ralph has the (relevant) characteristics C, is not good evidence for h^*. In other words, the probability that h^*, given q^*, and given that Ralph has C, is no greater than the probability that not-h^*. These probabilistic facts hold even though the proposition that Ralph in fact believes has a probability of 1 relative to any evidence whatsoever. By reference to these probabilistic facts we may explain our inclination to say that Ralph's belief is not a reliable one. A person with Ralph's characteristics is no more likely to have a true belief than a false one in circumstances of the sort we are imagining; therein lies the unreliability.

It is possible to treat these special cases by generalizing on this analysis of the example involving Ralph. Any given instance of reason-based belief will be either a case in which the proposition believed has an extreme probability relative to any evidence, or a case in which the proposition believed has a nonextreme probability relative to some evidence. For convenience in formulating various conditions, I refer to propositions of the former sort with the term 'noncontingent' and to propositions of the latter sort with the term 'contingent'.[4] Our special cases, then, are those in which the subject has a belief in a noncontingent proposition. To deal with such cases, I propose the following tentative definition of epistemic reliability, which is intended to supersede (4.1):

(4.5) S's believing that h on the basis of the set of reasons R is a reliable indication that h at t iff: There is some maximal set of relevant characteristics, C, such that

    (1) S has C at t; and

    (2) (a)   For those cases in which h is contingent: the probability that h, given that S has C and given that S believes that h on the basis of R, is greater than the probability that not-h, given those same facts about S;

         (b)   For those cases in which h is noncontingent: the probability that h^*, given that S has C and given q^*, is greater than the probability that not-h^*, given that S has C and given q^* (where 'h^*' designates 'S believes some true proposition or other on the basis of R' and where 'q^*' designates 'S believes some proposition or other on the basis of R').

In the variation on Example 4, clause (2b) is the operative one, and it is not satisfied for Ralph and his belief that h. In cases of this sort, (2b) will yield the correct result concerning reliable belief in noncontingent true propositions.

Condition (2b) is formulated in a way that allows for reliable belief in noncontingent *false* propositions. Suppose Ralph of our example is involved in yet another kind of circumstance. This time a famous logician has told him that a certain very complicated logical formula is logically true. The logician claims to have proved that this formula is a theorem of logic, and Ralph knows that the logician's past record about such matters is impeccable. Nevertheless, the logician is mistaken this time: the formula in

4. I do not mean to suggest, however, that this usage coincides in any precise fashion with the various other usages to which these terms have been put by philosophers. I would gladly use some other pair of terms if I could think of one less misleading.

question is false (and logically so). Ralph's belief, on the basis of the reasons available to him, is epistemically reliable, assuming that Ralph is the sort of person who is cautious about believing things on the basis of testimony. Moreover, this is the result we get on condition (2b). Given Ralph's characteristics and his reasons R, the probability that he correctly believes some true proposition is greater than the probability that he does not, even though the proposition that he believes is in fact logically false.

Having considered the problems presented by noncontingent propositions for our earlier tentative definition (4.1), we are still left with the question: "In these special cases, which characteristics of the person S are relevant and which irrelevant with respect to determining epistemic reliability?" Although the conditions imposed in (4.2), (4.3), and (4.4) do not apply, there are analogous conditions that do. Consider again the variation on Example 4, in which Ralph believes that a sentence is tautologous because it looks nice to him. Now consider clause (2b) of the tentative definition (4.5) of epistemic reliability. This clause involves h^*, which says (in this instance) that Ralph believes some true proposition or other on the basis of R. Unlike h itself, h^* is not a logical truth. Given that Ralph believes that h, however, there is a characteristic of Ralph such that Ralph's having this characteristic entails that h^* is true. This characteristic is that of being such that he correctly believes some true proposition or other on the basis of R. As with the considerations that led to the requirement expressed in (4.2), this consideration prompts an analogous requirement centering on h^* in these special cases, namely, the requirement that characteristic c not be the one that alone entails either the truth or the falsity of h^*.

Similarly, our subject may have characteristics that are not probabilistically neutral to h^*, when taken alone. Such characteristics may illegitimately affect the probabilities required for reliability. This suggests a requirement analogous to that imposed by (4.3) centering on h^*.

Finally, considerations analogous to those that led to the formulation of (4.4) prompt a requirement that centers on h^*. This requirement would exclude as irrelevant those characteristics probabilistically irrelevant to h^* (rather than to h) relative to the given fact that q^* is true, where q^* is as stated in condition (2b) of (4.5).

[114]

Combining these considerations, I propose the following definition of relevant characteristics:

(DRC) A characteristic, c, of a person, S, is relevant to determining whether S's belief that h on the basis of R is epistemically reliable iff:

    (1)   For those cases in which h is contingent:
        (a) S's having c is probabilistically relevant to h, given that S believes that h on the basis of R; and
        (b) S's having c is probabilistically neutral to h, when c is taken alone;

    (2)   For those cases in which h is noncontingent: let 'h^*' designate 'S believes some true proposition or other on the basis of R' and let 'q^*' designate 'S believes some proposition or other on the basis of R',
        (a) S's having c is probablistically relevant to h^*, given q^*; and
        (b) S's having c is probabilistically neutral to h^*, when c is taken alone.

Assuming this definition of relevant characteristics, have we then achieved a satisfactory account of epistemically reliable belief in (4.5)? Unfortunately, a number of difficult problems remain.

5. *Reason States and Conditional Probabilities*

One of the remaining problems has to do with probabilistic considerations that are in some respects similar to those that led to restrictions on the class of relevant characteristics. In the tentative definition (4.5), the conditional probabilities in question are conditioned upon two distinct kinds of facts about the person S: facts concerning S's relevant characteristics (the aspect that we have been concentrating on), and facts concerning the basis of S's belief that h—that is, facts concerning S's set of reason states, R. Consider clause (2a) of (4.5):

(2a)   For those cases in which h is contingent: The probability that h, given that S has C and given that S believes that h on the basis of R, is greater than the probability that not-h, given those same facts about S.

In Chapter Three I defined the expression 'S believes that h on the basis of the set of reasons R'. If we replace this expression with its definiens in (2a) the resulting expression is very complex. It is instructive, however, to consider what happens if we thus rewrite (2a). I shall use the simple definition expressed in the first formulation of (DB) on page 74 of Chapter Three.

(2a′)   For those cases in which h is contingent: The probability that h, given that
   (a) S has C; and
   (b) S believes that h at t; and
   (c)   for every member, r_j, of R there is some time, t_n, (which may be identical with or earlier than t) such that
      (i) S has (or had) r_j at t_n; and
      (ii)   there is an appropriate causal connection between S's having r_j at t_n and S's believing that h at t,
   is greater than the probability that not-h, given those same facts—namely, (a), (b), and (c)—about S.

In considering characteristics that should be excluded from the class of relevant characteristics, we noted that some (such as the characteristic of correctly believing that h) must be excluded because they illegitimately affect the conditional probabilities involved. A class of cases involving clauses (b) and (c) of (2a′) leads to similar restrictions. Consider again Example 1, in which Sally believes that she is in pain. In that example, one of the reason states upon which Sally's belief is based is the state of being in pain. Hence, if condition (c) of (2a′) were instantiated to a conjunction of statements of the forms (i) and (ii), each dealing with one of Sally's reason states, one of these statements would assert that Sally is in pain. The proposition that Sally is in pain is, in other words, entailed by clause (c) in this example. But this will give us the result that the probability that Sally is in pain, given the facts expressed in (a), (b), and (c), is 1. This does not yield an undesirable result in Example 1, for that is an example of epistemically reliable belief. In some possible variations on Example 1, however, Sally's belief that she is in pain is not epistemically reliable because of certain characteristics that she has. In these variations, Sally's belief that she is in pain may still be based upon the state of her being in pain. In such a case, the conditional probability that she is in pain, given the relevant characteristics *and* a description of all of her reasons, will again be 1. Consequently, Sally's belief that she is in pain would turn out to be epistemically reliable, and that would be an undesirable result.

Generally, there are a number of propositions entailed by conditions (b) and (c) of (2a$'$), and if one of these happens to be the very proposition h that S believes, then S's belief will turn out trivially to be reliable even in cases in which it is clear that the belief is not reliable. Other examples include cases in which h is the proposition that S believes that q, or in which h is the proposition that there is an appropriate causal connection between S's having r_j at t_n and S's believing that h at t. We must grant that a person can reliably believe such propositions, but we must be careful not to guarantee that this result follows trivially.

This problem can be dealt with by placing restrictions on the evidence class to be considered when determining the conditional probabilities in these cases. In Example 1, we are not interested in the trivial claim that the conditional probability that Sally is in pain, given that she believes she is in pain on the basis of being in pain, is greater than the probability that she is not in pain, given those same facts. Rather, in such cases we are interested in the conditional probability that Sally is in pain given *only* that she believes that she is in pain (along with a listing of relevant characteristics of Sally). The needed restriction can be effected by adding a clause to the definition (4.5) of epistemic reliability which specifically restricts the facts upon which the conditional probabilities are to be assessed in these cases. Rather than rewrite the entire definition (4.5) at this point, I shall for now merely suggest the needed condition:

(4.6)   If h fails under clause (2a) and is entailed by 'S believes that h on the basis of R', then the probability that h, given (only) that S believes that h and given that S has C, is greater than the probability that not-h, given (only) those same facts about S.

In Example 1 we will still get the result that Sally's belief that she is in pain is epistemically reliable, for the probability that she is in pain, given (only) that she believes that she is *and* given that she has the relevant characteristics C, is greater than the probability that she is not in pain, given only those same facts. In those variations in which Sally's belief is not epistemically reliable, however, we will also get the correct result even though her belief is based upon the state of her being in pain; for, given her relevant characteristics C (including the tendency to confuse pain with other states), the mere fact that she believes that she is in pain makes it no more probable that she is in pain than that she is not.

Someone might raise the objection that if we adopt the restriction suggested in (4.6), we will rule out some legitimate examples of epistemically reliable belief. Consider Sally again. Suppose, as in the variation on Example 1, that Sally is easily confused between pain and other sensation states. On this occasion, however, she is wired to the sophisticated brain machine described in another earlier variation, and the machine tells her that she is in pain. Her belief that she is in pain is based in part upon the belief that the machine says she is in pain. Then, it would seem, Sally's belief that she is in pain is epistemically reliable, even though the conditional probability of her being in pain, given *only* that she believes that she is in pain (and has the characteristics C), is not sufficient to warrant this conclusion: she has an *independent* set of reasons which renders her belief reliable. In response to this kind of objection, I would note that the definition (4.5) is not a definition of epistemic reliability *simpliciter,* but rather a definition of 'S's belief that *h on the basis of R* is epistemically reliable'. In the example under consideration, Sally has a set of reasons, R^*, such that her believing that she is in pain on the basis of R^* is epistemically reliable in accordance with (4.5). But this set of reasons is not such that Sally's believing that h on the basis of these reasons entails that h. The restriction suggested in (4.6) is aimed at cases in which such an entailment holds. When a person has several sets of reasons, the belief in question may be reliable on the basis of one set but not on the basis of the others. Each set must be judged independently of the others by separate applications of the definition (4.5).

Another kind of example that illustrates the restriction suggested in (4.6) deserves brief mention, not because it raises any fundamentally new points but because it is likely to occur to seasoned epistemologists. Suppose S has some belief or other, the belief that q (where q may be any proposition whatever). Moreover, S's believing that q is a cause of S's believing that S believes that q. In such a case, as in the case of Sally and her pain, one of S's reason states (namely, the belief that q) is both a cause and the object of another of S's beliefs. Hence, where 'h' stands for 'S believes that q', S's belief that h on the basis of the set of reasons R entails that h. The restriction suggested in (4.6) must therefore be applied. To determine whether S's belief that h is epistemically reliable, we must ask whether the conditional probabilities satisfy the consequent of (4.6). This requires asking whether the probability that S believes that q, given (only) that S believes that S believes that q and given S's relevant characteristics C, is greater than the probability that S does not believe that q, given those same facts about S. Many epistemologists would argue that one's own belief states are introspectively available in such a way that the probabilities will *always* be favorable to epistemic reliability in such an instance of nested belief. Thus, they will say, in normal cases nested beliefs are epistemically reliable. But there is no reason to suppose that this is always so. Surely a person may, for example, have the tendency to confuse beliefs with other sorts of intentional attitudes (such as hoping, desiring, or suspecting), and such a characteristic may affect the conditional probabilities in a way adverse to the claim that a given nested belief is epistemically reliable. There is no essential difference between such situations and the example in which Sally is imagined to be prone to confusion about pain states. Except that such cases must be dealt with in accordance with the restriction (4.6), beliefs about one's own beliefs do not form a significantly special class of beliefs.

There is yet another kind of problem for the tentative definition (4.5) of epistemically reliable belief. It has been implicit in the discussion thus far that the set of reasons, R, upon which a given belief is based will often contain other belief states of the person in question. A generally accepted principle stipulates that a belief that is based upon other beliefs can be epistemically justified on the basis of those other beliefs only if those other beliefs are themselves epistemically justified. On the PR model, this translates into the principle that a belief that is based upon other beliefs can be epistemically reliable only if those other beliefs are reliable as well. This principle is one I adopt. Because our tentative definition (4.5) of epistemic reliability does not guarantee that this principle is satisfied, the definition must be revised. There are, however, two important exceptions to our general principle that show we must be careful about the manner in which we make these revisions.

The first exception to this principle may be illustrated by the example of nested belief discussed above. In cases in which S believes that h, where 'h' is 'S believes that q' and where S's belief that q is among the reasons upon which the belief that h is based, we should not require the belief that q itself to be a reliable one, for the belief that q is serving as a reason solely by virtue of the fact that it is a state of the person, and the question whether S's belief that S believes q is reliable refers only to the reliability of S as an indicator of *what* S believes. The object belief (the belief that q) needs only to be a belief state in such a case; it need not also be a reliable indicator that q. An accurate formulation of the principle should excuse such cases from the requirement imposed. Thus, any revisions to our definition (4.5) that are designed to guarantee satisfaction of this principle should also excuse these cases.

The second exception may be elicited by considering examples in which S's belief that h is based upon a set of reasons, R, which contains epistemically reliable beliefs along with, say, one unreliable belief. Let us say that a reason state, r, is an essential member of a set of reasons, R, with respect to S's reliably believing that h on the basis of R, if S's belief that h would still be reliable even if r were deleted from R. In the cases we are considering, if the unreliable belief is also an inessential member of R, then S's belief that h may well be reliable even though our principle is violated. We want our principle to apply only to beliefs that are essential members of the set of reasons upon which some further belief is based.

Having noted these two exceptions, I now suggest a formulation of that principle.

(4.7) S's believing that h on the basis of R is epistemically reliable only if: for every belief state, b, of S such that (1) b is an essential member of R and (2) S's being in belief state b does not entail that h, there is some set of reasons, R^*, such that S's having b on the basis of R^* is epistemically reliable.

Clause (1) is designed to account for the second of the exceptions noted above; (2) is designed to account for the first. The principle (4.7) points to a straightforward revision of the definition (4.5). This revision will be introduced in the final definition of epistemic reliability at the end of the next section.

6. *Competition and the Lottery Paradox*

One final but significant group of problems must be addressed before presentation of the definition of epistemic reliability These problems arise from the fact that conditional probabilities are used in defining this concept. According to the tentative definition (4.5), once we are given a person's relevant characteristics and reasons, epistemic reliability of a belief is largely a function of the comparative conditional probability of h and the denial of h (or, in the cases covered by (2b), of h^* and its denial). In the examples we have considered, these comparative conditional probabilities have been sufficient to illustrate the points being made. Other examples, however, show that we must compare the conditional probability of h with the conditional probabilities of a much broader class of propositions if we are to have an adequate account of epistemic reliability. Perhaps the clearest example is the one that has become known as the lottery paradox.[5]

Suppose a lottery has been organized in the following fashion. There are 1,000 tickets numbered 1 through 1,000, all of which have been sold. The stubs from these tickets have been placed in the standard sort of barrel, which will be rotated, and a stub will be selected by a blindfolded person. The person who has the ticket matching this stub is the one and only winner of the lottery. The ticket stubs are alike in size, shape, texture, and every other way that might be relevant to the lottery's being fair; each stub has the same chance of being selected. Suppose Connie has purchased one of the tickets, which happens to be numbered 1. She knows all the conditions of the lottery—that it is a fair lottery, that exactly one ticket will be drawn, and so forth. Hence, she has each of the following reliable beliefs (I am simply assuming, as part of the problem, that these beliefs are reliable):

5. The lottery paradox was discovered by Henry E. Kyburg, Jr., and its formulation can be found in his book *Probability and the Logic of Rational Belief* (Middletown, Conn.: Wesleyan University Press, 1961), p. 197.

b_1: the belief that there are exactly 1,000 tickets in the lottery;

b_2: the belief that the lottery is totally fair;

b_3: the belief that q, where q is the proposition that exactly one ticket from the tickets numbered 1 through 1,000 will be the winning ticket.

In addition to these beliefs, suppose Connie has various reliable background beliefs about lotteries in general, about probability theory, and whatever other beliefs a normal person would bring to such a situation. Moreover, Connie is well educated, alert, sober, and unencumbered by mental handicaps. She considers the likelihood that her ticket will win the lottery and realizes that the probabilities are significantly against her winning. Hence, on the basis of her reasons, which include belief states b_1, b_2, b_3, she comes to have the additional belief

b_4: the belief that her ticket (number 1) will *not* win.

Can we say that this belief is epistemically reliable?

On the basis of our tentative definition (4.5) of epistemic relia-bility, Connie's belief that her ticket will not win appears to be epistemically reliable. The probability that ticket number 1 will not win, given that she has the relevant characteristics C and given that she believes that it will not win on the basis of her reasons R, is greater than the probability that ticket 1 will win, given those same facts about Connie. At first, the conclusion that her belief is reliable may seem correct; after all, the probabilities are overwhelming in favor of the truth of her belief b_4. There are, however, powerful reasons for rejecting this result.

The argument for rejecting the result that Connie's belief is reliable rests upon the adoption of certain principles that form part of the logic of justified belief. In many discussions of the lottery paradox, three such principles are considered which may be given a very rough formulation.[6] The *consistency principle* says that inconsistent beliefs cannot be simultaneously justified. The *deductive closure principle* says that if S justifiably believes

6. The rough formulations that follow are inadequate. I shall suggest more refined versions below. For a very useful discussion of these principles, see Henry E. Kyburg, Jr., "Conjunctivitis," in Marshall Swain, ed., *Induction, Acceptance, and Rational Belief* (Dordrecht: Reidel, 1970), pp. 55–82.

that h, and if h entails h', then the belief that h' is also justified. The *conjunction principle* says that if a person justifiably believes that h and also justifiably believes that h', then the belief that ($h \cdot h'$) is also justified. None of these principles is particularly convincing when formulated in this rough fashion, and many epistemologists have attempted to provide more accurate versions. Moreover, many arguments and examples have been given to show that one or another of these principles is mistaken. Rather than review the many versions that have been suggested or evaluate the arguments against them, I shall introduce my own (reliability) versions of the consistency principle and the deductive closure principle. I shall not use any version of the conjunction principle, for I do not believe that any interesting version of it is correct, and it is not needed to generate the lottery paradox.[7]

To formulate my version of the consistency and deductive closure principles requires a notion that has not been explicitly considered up to this point. I have been considering the definition of the locution 'S's believing that h on the basis of R is epistemically reliable', which implies that S believes that h on the basis of R. I now introduce the expression 'S's believing that h on the basis of R *would be* epistemically reliable', as an abbreviation of the following more complex expression:

(4.8) There is some maximal set of relevant characteristics C such that:
   (1) S has C; and
   (2) S has the set of reasons R; and
   (3) if S had believed that h on the basis of R, and if S (still) had the characteristics C, then it would have been the case that S's believing that h on the basis of R is epistemically reliable.

With this expression, we may now speak not only of actual beliefs that are epistemically reliable, but also of possible beliefs that would be reliable if the agent had them.

Let us consider the consistency principle. This principle (or, rather, various versions of it) is often formulated in a way that

---

7. Kyburg provides excellent reasons for rejecting the conjunction principle in "Conjunctivitis."

conflicts directly with one of our earlier examples, in which our subject reliably believes a proposition that is logically false on the basis of testimony from an expert mathematician. In that example, the proposition believed is self-contradictory. If we formulate the consistency principle in such a way that no inconsistent beliefs can be simultaneously reliable, then, if the belief in question is reliable, no *other* belief of the agent's could be reliable. That result must be avoided. Some restriction on the principle of consistency is needed which will allow for inconsistent beliefs in some cases and not in others. Which beliefs should be thus allowed for and which should be disallowed?

The required restriction can be motivated in the following straightforward way. A person can reliably hold an inconsistent belief (or set of beliefs) only if that person is not in a position reliably to believe that the belief (or set of beliefs) is inconsistent. To say that a person is in such a position does not require us to say that this person actually believes that the belief (or set of beliefs) is inconsistent. Rather, we need say only that such a belief *would be* reliable in the sense indicated in (4.8); that is, the person S must have some set of reasons, $R,$ and some set of relevant characteristics, $C,$ such that if S had believed that the belief (or set of beliefs) in question is inconsistent, then that belief would be epistemically reliable on the basis of R. In our example of a person who reliably believes an inconsistent mathematical proposition on the basis of believed testimony, it is reasonable to suppose that this person does not *also* have reasons such that believing that the proposition is inconsistent on the basis of those reasons would be epistemically reliable; for if the person *did* have such reasons, then, if he had believed that the proposition is inconsistent, and if this belief would be epistemically reliable, and if he had believed the proposition anyway, then he would have been in the epistemically unenviable position of believing a proposition that is not only inconsistent but which he reliably believes to be inconsistent. It would be intolerable to allow for such a possibility. Hence, we must restrict cases of epistemically reliable belief in inconsistent propositions to those in which the person is not in a position to reliably believe that the beliefs are inconsistent.

I suggest the following principle of consistency for epistemically reliable belief:

(PEC) If, for each h_i in the set of propositions $\{h_1, h_2, \ldots, h_n\}$, S's believing that h_i on the basis of R would be epistemically reliable, and if '$h_1 \cdot h_2 \cdot \ldots \cdot h_n \cdot q$' is inconsistent, and if S has some set of reasons, R^*, such that S's believing that '$h_1 \cdot h_2 \cdot \ldots \cdot h_n \cdot q$' is inconsistent on the basis of R^* would be epistemically reliable, then it is not the case that S's believing that q on the basis of R would be epistemically reliable.

In this formulation the antecedent provides three conditions that are jointly sufficient for a belief *not* to be epistemically reliable. The third of these conditions is designed to capture the intuition that inconsistent beliefs cannot be simultaneously reliable if the person is in a position to reliably believe that they are inconsistent. If this clause of the antecedent is not satisfied, then the principle does not yield a conclusion concerning reliable belief; in this sense, the principle allows for the possibility of epistemically reliable belief in inconsistent propositions.

The principle of deductive closure is not needed to get the results that constitute the lottery paradox. The principle is important in its own right, however, and will be referred to in later chapters. As with the consistency principle, some care must be taken in its formulation. The rough formulation suggested above will not do, for it yields results that are in conflict with some of our earlier examples. In one we supposed that Ralph has an unreliable belief in a logically true proposition. If, as is reasonable, we suppose Ralph has at least one reliable belief in *some* proposition h, then, because a logically true proposition is entailed by any proposition, our rough version of the deductive closure principle would yield the result that Ralph's belief in the logically true proposition is epistemically reliable after all. Other examples also indicate the need for a more precise rendition of the closure principle. Suppose S reliably believes some conjunction of axioms of a theory; let this conjunction of axioms be h. Then, suppose h' is an incredibly complicated theorem of this theory, a theorem that no one has ever been able to prove but which nevertheless is entailed by h. There is no reason to think that S's belief that h' would be epistemically reliable. In such examples, an intuitively straightforward restriction similar to the one imposed in the consistency principle (PEC) above will yield the correct results. I suggest the following version of a deductive closure principle for epistemically reliable belief, which incorporates such a restriction.

(PDC): If S reliably believes that h on the basis of R, and if h entails h', and if S has some set of reasons, R^*, such that S's believing that h entails h' on the basis of R^* would be epistemically reliable, then S has some set of resons, R^{**}, such that S's believing that h' on the basis of R^{**} would be epistemically reliable.

In this formulation the antecedent provides three conditions that are jointly sufficient for a person's believing some logical consequence of something justifiably believed to be epistemically reliable. The third condition is intended to express the idea that the person, S, is in a position to reliably believe that the one proposition is a logical consequence of the other. Note that the antecedent expresses only one set of sufficient conditions for such a belief to be epistemically reliable. Other conditions may also be sufficient. For example, suppose S reliably believes that h, and suppose h entails h'. Because S is not in a position to reliably believe that h entails h', the antecedent of (PDC) is not satisfied. S might still reliably believe that h', however, if, for example, S has independent testimony from a reliable expert to the effect that h' is true.

Given these two principles, let us now return to the lottery example. Connie has come to have the belief, b_4, that her ticket (number 1) will not win the lottery. Given the tentative definition (4.5) of epistemic reliability, this belief appears to be epistemically reliable. Now let us consider a set of *possible* beliefs (we need not suppose Connie actually has these beliefs) generated in the following fashion. Let 'h_1' designate the proposition that ticket number 1 will not win the lottery; 'h_2', the proposition that ticket number 2 will not win the lottery; and so forth to '$h_{1,000}$', which designates the proposition that ticket number 1,000 will not win the lottery. Then, 'b_4' (which is an actual belief of Connie's) designates the belief that h_1, 'b_5' designates the belief that h_2, and so forth. Consider b_5, the belief that ticket number 2 will not win the lottery. Would Connie's having this belief on the basis of her reasons R be epistemically reliable? Nothing distinguishes this belief from belief b_4; Connie's reasons are the same, her characteristics are the same, and the conditional probabilities are the same. Hence, by the tentative definition (4.5) we should conclude that b_5 would be epistemically reliable on the basis of R. But then, by parity of reasoning, there is no ground for distinguishing b_5 from b_6, b_7, and so forth. Each of these beliefs would be epistemically reliable by (4.5). Hence, we may assert

(4.9)   For each h_i in the set of propositions $\{h_1, h_2, \ldots h_{1,000}\}$, Connie's believing that h_i on the basis of R would be epistemically reliable.

One of the conditions of our example is the supposition that Connie reliably believes that q, where q is the proposition that exactly one ticket from the ticket's numbered 1 through 1,000 will be the winning ticket in the lottery. Now let us note that

(4.10) '$h_1 \cdot h_2 \cdot \ldots \cdot h_{1,000} \cdot q$' is logically inconsistent.

The conjunction of h_1 through $h_{1,000}$ tells us that *no* ticket from those numbered 1 through 1,000 will win the lottery, whereas q tells us that exactly one of them will win.

Another of the suppositions of this example is that "Connie knows all about the conditions of the lottery." I assume that this includes her having reasons such that, if she were to believe that '$h_1 \cdot h_2 \cdot \ldots \cdot h_{1,000} \cdot q$' is inconsistent on the basis of these reasons, then this belief would be epistemically reliable. In other words,

(4.11) Connie has some set of reasons, R^*, such that Connie's believing that '$h_1 \cdot h_2 \cdot \ldots \cdot h_{1,000} \cdot q$' is inconsistent on the basis of R^* would be epistemically reliable.

Now (4.9), (4.10), and (4.11) together with the consistency principle (PEC) entail

(4.12) It is not the case that Connie's believing that q on the basis of R would be epistemically reliable.

(4.12), however, contradicts one of the assumptions of our example, and thus we have arrived at inconsistent results.

What is the source of the problem in the lottery example? Some would argue that the consistency principle (PEC) should be rejected. I have attempted, however, to formulate the principle so that it is free from the sorts of problems typically raised for consistency principles. Have we perhaps made some illicit assumptions about our subject? We have supposed only that Connie reliably holds beliefs b_1, b_2, b_3, and that she has some set of reasons, R^*, by virtue of which we may assert (4.11). Surely these suppositions are not farfetched; indeed, they seem to characterize precisely the sort of position that many people are in with respect to lotteries and other similar games of chance. The only remaining assumption of the example is the tentative definition (4.5) of epistemic reliability. This definition yields the result that Connie's belief that h_1, as well as (possible) beliefs in the propositions h_2 through $h_{1,000}$, is or would be epistemically reliable on the basis of her reasons R. This leads to the contradiction. Hence, I conclude that these (actual and possible) beliefs are not or would not be epistemically reliable. The tentative definition (4.5) must be revised to avoid this result.

Revision is required because (4.5) is not sensitive enough to the element of *competition* inherent in questions of epistemic reliability.[8] If we are asking whether a person's believing that h on the basis of a set of reasons, R, is a reliable guide to the way the world is, we must consider other (possible) beliefs that the person might have had and compare the reliability of those beliefs with the reliability of the belief that h. According to the P-R model of justification, reliability is explicated in terms of certain conditional probabilistic facts. In the tentative definition (4.5), the conditional probability of h is compared only with the conditional probability of the denial of h in cases covered by clause (2a). This is tantamount to taking the denial of a proposition to be its only competitor vis-à-vis epistemically reliable belief. In many situations such as the lottery example, however, a believed proposition competes also with propositions other than its denial. In such cases, the belief that h is epistemically reliable only if it is more reliable than belief in any of the propositions that compete with h,

8. I suggested the notion of competition in my doctoral dissertation, "The Logic of Epistemic Consistency," University of Rochester, 1963. Keith Lehrer uses this concept in dealing with the lottery paradox in *Knowledge* (Oxford: Oxford University Press, 1974), pp. 192–198.

where the class of competitors is broader than the one that includes only the denial of h. We can easily revise definition (4.5) to reflect this if we can determine what the competition class is for a given believed proposition.

If a believed proposition has a probability of 0 or 1 on any evidence, then in one sense it has no competitors. If the proposition is thus guaranteed to be true, it wins all competitions, whereas if it is guaranteed to be false, it loses all competitions. But as we have seen in our discussion of such propositions in connection with clause (2b) of (4.5), belief in such a proposition may be reliable or unreliable independently of its extreme probability. This is why I have introduced the special clause (2b) in the tentative definition (4.5). As far as I can determine, this clause is adequate to handle such cases, and so no special considerations need to be introduced concerning competition in the cases covered by clause (2b). Thus, I assume that such propositions compete only with their denials.[9]

My primary concern is with competition among propositions in the cases covered by clause (2a) of (4.5). As we have noted, if h' is equivalent to the denial of h, then h' is an epistemic competitor of h.[10] Moreover, if h' entails, but is not equivalent to, the denial of h, then h' should be countenanced as a competitor of h. Generally, any proposition that is a contrary of h competes with h, for contrary propositions cannot both be true. These logical relations (contrariety and contradictoriness) are sufficient for competition if they hold between h and h'. The lottery example shows us, however, that another sort of relation must also be countenanced as sufficient for competition.

In the lottery example Connie holds belief b_4, which is the belief that h_1 (where 'h_1' designages 'ticket number one will not win'). What propositions can be said to compete with h_1? Let us grant that any proposition equivalent to the denial of h_1 is a competitor and that any contraries of h_1 are competitors. In addition to these, the propositions $h_2, h_3, \ldots h_{1,000}$ must be countenanced

9. Another possibility is to take h^*, as in (4.5), and define a competition class for it.
10. I have added "equivalent to" for obvious reasons. Strictly speaking, the denial of h is not-h, but we would want any proposition that is equivalent to not-h to stand in the competition relation to h.

as competitors of h_1. Given that Connie justifiably believes that q ('exactly one ticket from the tickets numbered 1 through 1,000 will be the winner'), the members of the set of propositions $\{h_1, h_2, \ldots h_{1,000}\}$ cannot all be true relative to her reasons R. If we take these propositions in pairs, however, no member of any given pair is either the contradictory or a contrary of its mate. Hence, if we are to say that they are pair-wise competitors, we must find some other relation that holds between the members of this set of propositions, by virtue of which they may be said to compete.

Competition among propositions, like the notion of epistemic reliability itself, must be made to be relative to the person, S, and to S's reasons R and relevant characteristics C. In the lottery example, the propositions h_1 through $h_{1,000}$ have a relation that holds in pairs relative to Connie's reasons and characteristics, namely, the relation of negative relevance.[11] Consider h_1 and h_2, which tell us respectively that the tickes numbered 1 and 2 will not win. The probability that h_1 is true, given that Connie believes that it is true on the basis of her reasons R (including the reliable belief that q) and given that Connie has the relevant characteristics C, is 999/1,000. Suppose we add to the conditioning evidence the proposition that ticket number 2 will not win (h_2). Then, the conditional probability that h_1 is true, given this expanded conditioning evidence, is slightly lower than it was before, namely 998/999. The condition that one of the tickets does not win reduces the number of tickets that could win, and hence reduces the probability that each remaining ticket will *not* win. Thus, each of the propositions h_1, h_2, $\ldots h_{1,000}$ is negatively relevant to each of the others, relative to the conditioning evidence in our example.

If a proposition, h, and another proposition, h', are either contradictories or contraries, then they are also negatively relevant to each other; but the converse of this does not hold. We might thus be led to suppose that competition could be defined in the following way:[12]

11. This approach to characterizing competition was initiated by Lehrer in *Knowledge*, pp. 192–198, and in earlier writings.

12. In the following definition and the discussion afterward, I occasionally use the expression 'the usual facts about S' to abbreviate 'S has C and S believes that h on the basis of R'.

(4.13) h' is an epistemic competitor of h relative to person S, reasons R, and relevant characteristics C iff:

either (1) h and h' are such that the probability of each, given the usual facts about S, is greater than 0 and less than 1, and h' is negatively relevant to h given (i) S believes h on the basis of R and (ii) S has C;

or (2) h is covered by (2b) of (4.5) and h' is equivalent to the denial of h.

This definition is very close to what we need, but it must be revised because of a technical problem. The problem was discovered by Keith Lehrer in connection with a very similar definition of competition.[13]

To appreciate the problem, we must remind ourselves that the purpose of defining competition is to revise our definition of epistemic reliability. Roughly, this revision will result in the requirement that belief in a proposition, h, is epistemically reliable only if the conditional probability of h (given the usual facts about S) is greater than the conditional probability of any competitor of h (given those same facts about S). With this in mind, we can see that (4.13) is too weak: it allows some propositions as competitors which should not be allowed. Consider propositions h_1 and h_2 of the lottery example. Given the definition (4.13), h_2 is a competitor of h_1, and this is as things should be. For Connie's belief that h_1 on the basis of R to be epistemically reliable, the conditional probability of h_1 should be greater than that of h_2, given the usual facts about the subject. Now, suppose r is some proposition with the following characteristics: r is irrelevant to h_1 given the usual facts about Connie, but the probability of r, given those facts, is greater than the probability of h_1. Because r is irrelevant to h_1, r alone will not qualify as a competitor of h_1 by (4.13). The problem is that we can construct a proposition that may compete with h_1, given (4.13), such that its conditional probability is at least as great as that of r. The proposition is the disjunction of r with h_2 ($r \lor h_2$). Because h_2 is negatively relevant to h_1 and because r is irrelevant to h_1 (given the usual facts), this disjunction may itself be negatively relevant to h_1. If so, this disjunction

13. See Lehrer, *Knowledge*, p. 193.

will qualify as a competitor of h_1, given (4.13). Moreover, because r entails the disjunction $r \lor h_2$, the conditional probability of this disjunction is at least as great as that of r alone. Hence, for Connie's belief that h_1 to be epistemically reliable, given our projected revision of (4.5), the conditional probability of h_1, given the usual facts about the subject, would have to be greater than the conditional probability of r. This is an unhappy result, for r is no competitor of h_1 and there is no reason why its conditional probability should enter the picture at all.

In considering various ways of avoiding this problem, Lehrer argues against one obvious sort of restriction that might be added to (4.13), namely, the restriction that h' not be equivalent to a disjunction of propositions one of whose disjuncts is irrelevant to h. This restriction would rule out the illegitimate disjunction $r \lor h_2$ above. As Lehrer quite correctly notes, however, this restriction would also rule out all competitors of h except those that are either contradictories or contraries of h.[14] There is, however, a similar but less powerful restriction that Lehrer does not consider, namely, the restriction that h' not be equivalent to a disjunction of propositions one of whose disjuncts r has the following *two* characteristics: (a) r is irrelevant to h, given the usual facts about the subject; and (b) r is such that the conditional probability of r, given those facts about the subject, is greater than or equal to the probability of h, given those facts. This restriction will rule out the unwanted disjunction $r \lor h_2$ but not legitimate competitors. It is true, however, that every h' that is negatively relevant to a given proposition h (relative to the usual facts) but is neither a contrary nor a contradictory of h will be equivalent to *some* disjunction that contains a disjunct irrelevant to h. Such disjunctions are countenanced as competitors by this proposed restriction. No harm results, however, because the probability of any such disjunction must (by the probability calculus) be equal to the probability of h'. There is therefore no danger that h will compete with the irrelevant disjunct, for the probability of that disjunct must, by the above restriction, be less than the probability of h itself.

I suggest, therefore, that we define competition in the following way:

14. Ibid., p. 194.

(DComp) h' is an epistemic competitor of h relative to person S, reasons R, and relevant characteristics C iff:
    either   (1)   (a) h and h' are contingent; and
                     (b) h' is negatively relevant to h given the usual facts about S; and
                     (c) h' is not equivalent to a disjunction of propositions one of whose disjuncts, q, is both (i) irrelevant to h given the usual facts about S and (ii) such that the probability of q, given those facts about S, is greater than or equal to the probability of h, given those facts:
    or   (2) h is noncontingent and h' is the denial of h.

It should be noted that the expression 'the usual facts about S' is intended to cover situations in which h is entailed by 'S believes that h on the basis of R' as well as those in which h is not thus entailed.

In the lottery example, each of the propositions h_2 through $h_{1,000}$ is a competitor of h_1, relative to Connie, her reasons, and her relevant characteristics. If we assume the tentative definition (4.5) of epistemic reliability to have seen revised to require that a believed proposition must probabilistically outstrip all its competitors, then Connie's belief that her ticket will not win *fails* to be epistemically reliable, and the lottery paradox is solved. Generally, whether we are dealing with situations of the sort involved in the lottery example or with any other epistemic situation, a belief can be judged epistemically reliable only relative to those beliefs (actual or possible) with which it competes.

7. A Definition of Epistemic Justification

All the considerations of the preceding pages can now be brought together in a final definition of epistemically reliable belief. As might be expected, given the many problems that have been discussed, the final definition is rather complicated.

(DER) S's believing that h on the basis of R is a reliable indication that h at t iff: there is some maximal set of relevant characteristics, C, such that

(1) S has C at t; and

(2)   Whichever of (A), (B), or (C) is appropriate to the situation:

   (A)   (i) h is contingent and is not entailed by 'S believes that h on the basis of R' and (ii) the probability that h, given that S believes that h on the basis of R and that S has C, is greater than the probability that q, given those same facts about S, for every q that is a competitor of h relative to S, C, and R;

   (B)   (i) h is contingent and is entailed by 'S believes that h on the basis of R' and (ii) the probability that h, given (only) that S believes that h and that S has C, is greater than the probability that q, given those same facts about S, for every q that is a competitor of h relative to S, C, and R;

   (C)   (i) h is noncontingent and (ii) where 'h^*' designates 'S believes some true proposition or other on the basis of R', and where 'q^*' designates 'S believes some proposition or other on the basis of R', the probability that h^*, given q^* and given that S and C, is greater than the probability that not-h^*, given q^* and given that S has C; and

(3)   for every belief state, b, of S such that (i) b is an essential member of S's set of reasons R and (ii) S's being in belief state b does not entail that h there is some set of reasons, R_b, and some maximal set of relevant characteristics, C_b, such that b is based upon R_b, S has C_b, and condition (2) above is satisfied for b, *mutatis mutandis*.

Despite its length and complexity, this definition is not as fearsome as it appears. Clause (A) of condition (2) applies in most of the examples with which epistemologists concern themselves. This clause covers what might loosely be called justified belief in propositions about the external world, including contingent generalizations. The other two clauses, (B) and (C), cover the two major kinds of special cases. Clause (B) applies in those special situations in which the object of the subject's belief is a proposition that ascribes one of the reason states in R to the subject (and, more generally, when this proposition is entailed by S's believing that h on the basis of R). Clause (C) applies to special situations in which the subject believes some noncontingent proposition, such as a logical truth. Finally, condition (3) guarantees that the generally agreed-upon principle (4.7), introduced at the end of Section 5 above, is satisfied in any case of reliable belief.

8. *The Regress Problem*

On page 103 of Section 3 above, there occurred a discussion of a distinction that is often made by justification theorists, the distinction between beliefs that are evidentially basic and those that are evidentially nonbasic. At that point I remarked that "the PR model requires an account of evidentially basic beliefs; happily, it also provides for a satisfactory solution to this long-standing problem." I close this chapter with an attempt to provide that account.

Consider clause (3) of our definition (DER) and also the principle (4.7), which this clause is intended to guarantee. Someone might argue in the following fashion: "You have said that beliefs that are essential members of some set of reasons, R, upon which some further belief is reliably based must themselves be reliably based upon some set of reasons, R_b. What about beliefs that are essential members of R_b? Presumably they too must be reliably based upon yet another set of reasons. What about this new set of reasons? Suppose it contains essentially some beliefs of S? We will need still another set of reasons upon which these beliefs must be reliably based. Unless you can suggest some way in which this regress of reasons comes to an end, we will be faced either with an endless set of reasons involved in the reliability of any given belief or with sets of reasons which eventually are circular." This argument presents what is known as the *regress problem,* and it must be faced by any account of justification that embraces the principle (4.7).

In order to deal with this problem, I suggest a distinction that is similar to the distinction between evidentially basic and evidentially nonbasic beliefs mentioned above. We have noted that the account of reasons and reason-based belief which is part of the PR model allows for a set of reasons to include nonbelief states, such as sensation and perceptual states. It is my contention that many of our reason-based beliefs are reliable on the basis of sets of reasons which do not include any belief states at all. Consider again the original Example 1, in which Sally believes that she is in pain. The set of reasons, R, upon which this belief is based includes the very state of being in pain. We may allow, however, that this set of reasons also includes some belief states, perhaps Sally's belief that she has a headache. If we consider that subset of R, call it R', which consists of all those members of R which are *not* beliefs of Sally's, we can see that Sally's believing that she is in pain on the basis of R' is reliable. This case is one of those covered by clause (2B) of the definition (DER). For Sally's belief to be reliable, the conditional probability that she is in pain, given only that she believes that she is in pain and given that she has relevant characteristics C, must outstrip the probabilities of the competitors. And the probabilities are in order in this example. In effect, for cases covered by clause (2B), the actual membership of the subject's set of reasons is irrelevant to reliability. In this sense, such beliefs can be reliable on the basis of a set of reasons (such as R') which does not include any belief states at all. In general, when a belief qualifies as reliable by clause (2B) of (DER), there will be some belief-empty set of reasons upon which that belief is reliably based. For such beliefs, clause (3) of (DER), the clause that leads to the regress problem, is rendered inoperative because its antecedent is not satisfied.

Examples of this sort provide us with the beginning of what we need to counter the regress argument, for they are examples in which no further set of belief-laden reasons need be considered. Moreover, the class of beliefs which is rendered reliable by clause (2B) of (DER) is virtually coextensive with the class of beliefs which many justification theorists have wanted to call evidentially basic. Typically, the suggestion is that every justified belief is either evidentially basic or is justified on the basis of a chain of reasons which ultimately comes to an end in beliefs that are evidentially basic. The problem with this suggestion is that the class of beliefs which qualifies as reliable (justified) in accordance with condition (2B) of (DER) is not clearly a class that is extensive enough to serve as the ultimate basis for all other justified beliefs. I do not need to take a stand on this issue, however, for I believe the class of beliefs that are reliable on the basis of belief-empty reason sets is considerably broader than the class of beliefs that qualify as reliable by clause (2B) of (DER). This broader class of beliefs provides a proper stopping place for the regress of belief-laden reasons and is, I submit, broad enough to serve as the basis for all justified belief.

Consider again the original Example 2, in which Alfred believes justifiably that it is snowing outside. Upon which reasons is Alfred's belief based? Some members of this set of reasons are perceptual states, such as the state of seeming to see snow, the state of seeming to see a window, and so forth. Presumably Alfred's reasons will also include some belief states, such as the belief that snow looks like what he now seems to see. It may even be (although this is controversial) that the ascription to Alfred (or to anyone) of the perceptual states in question requires ascription of certain belief states; even so, we may distinguish the perceptual states from the belief states involved. Where R is the total set of reasons upon which Alfred's belief is based, let R' be that subset of R which contains no belief states. Then R' is one set of reasons upon which Alfred's belief is based. I submit that, given Alfred's relevant characteristics C (such as being able to distinguish snow from other forms of precipitation), Alfred's belief that it is snowing on the basis of R' is epistemically reliable. It is quite plausible, I believe, to say that the probability that it is snowing, given that Alfred seems to see snow, etc., and given that Alfred has the characteristics C, is greater than the probability of any competitors, given those same facts about Alfred. If so, then because R' is a belief-empty set of reasons, we have another example of a belief that is reliable on the basis of one set of reasons which does not include any belief states. Let me emphasize that I am not suggesting that Alfred's belief is not based on any beliefs; we have already supposed that R contains some beliefs. Rather, I am suggesting that Alfred's belief is reliable relative to at least one set of reasons (R') which does not contain any belief states.

The example involving Alfred is covered by clause (2A) of

(DER). Many examples of this sort are subject to a similar analysis, but do not fall within the category of beliefs that are evidentially basic, at least as that category is usually characterized. I said earlier that I want to introduce a distinction that is similar to the distinction between evidentially basic and evidentially non-basic beliefs. The distinction that I shall suggest does not make quite the same division among beliefs as does the more traditional distinction. Rather, I distinquish between those beliefs that are *belief-independently* reliable and those that are *belief-dependently* reliable. The former notion is defined as follows:

(BIR) S's believing that h on the basis of R is belief-independently reliable iff: S's believing that h on the basis of R is a reliable indication that h and would remain so even if R were restricted to the subset of its members that are not beliefs.

The latter is then defined in this way:

(BDR) S's believing that h on the basis of R is belief-dependently reliable iff: S's believing that h on the basis of R is a reliable, but not a belief-independently, reliable indication that h.

We have considered two examples of beliefs that are belief-independently reliable. Let us now consider the original Example 3, in which Roberta comes to believe justifiably that all whales are mammals, for this is an example of belief-dependently reliable belief.

In Example 3 we have supposed Roberta has come to believe that her textbook says that whales are mammals. She has also come to believe that her teacher has asserted that what the textbook says is correct. Roberta has also taken the trouble to observe a few whales for herself, and thus has come to believe that these whales have mammalian characteristics. Presumably she also has background beliefs concerning the manner in which textbooks are produced, the manner in which teachers are educated, and a belief to the effect that if some members of a species display mammalian characteristics, then they all do. Her belief that all whales are mammals is based on these beliefs. It is also based upon whatever reasons these beliefs are themselves based upon (see condition (2B) of the definition of the basing relation on page 86 of Chapter Three). It is plausible to say, then, that the total set of reasons, R, upon which Roberta's belief is based includes many beliefs and also some nonbelief states (such as the state of seeming to see a whale). Her believing that all whales are mammals on the basis of R is reliable. The probability that all whales are mammals, given that Roberta believes that they are on the basis of her reasons R and given her relevant characteristics C, is greater than the probability of any competitor. If, however, her set of reasons R were restricted to that subset of R which contains no beliefs, these probabilistic facts would not obtain. Hence, Roberta's belief is belief-dependently reliable.

There are many other examples of the distinction between belief-independently and belief-dependently reliable belief, but this small sample should suffice to make the intended distinction clear. Given this distinction, I propose to block the regress argument with the suggestion that every justified belief is either belief-independently reliable or is based upon a tree of reasons (see Chapter Three, pages 83–87) whose branches end in a set of reasons whose belief members are belief-independently reliable. According to this suggestion, the body of reliable reason-based beliefs which is attributable to a person at a time has a structure reminiscent of the kind of structure associated with foundationalistic theories of justification.[15] On the PR model, the foundation of justified belief includes beliefs other than beliefs about one's introspectively available mental states, and also includes reason states that are not beliefs at all. This broad foundation should be sufficient to ground all justified belief. I confess, however, that I do not know how to prove that this is so.

In Chapter Six, returning to a consideration of foundational themes, I shall suggest that knowledge, like justified belief, has a structure and a foundation. As might be expected, these facts are not unrelated.

15. For a sophisticated discussion of foundationalism, see James W. Cornman, "Foundational versus Nonfoundational Theories of Empirical Justification," *American Philosophical Quarterly* 14 (1977): 287–297, reprinted in George S. Pappas and Marshall Swain, eds., *Essays on Knowledge and Justification* (Ithaca: Cornell University Press, 1978).

9. *Summary and Concluding Remarks*

In this chapter I have developed the leading ideas of the probabilistic-reliability model of epistemic justification. According to the PR model, to say that a belief is epistemically justified is to say that the belief is a reliable indicator of the way the world is. Reliability is a function both of the reasons upon which the belief is based and of the relevant characteristics of the believer. Believers are viewed as complicated barometers of the world around them, with belief states themselves serving as analogues of barometer readings. Underlying this view are the assumptions that human beings are very much a part of the natural course of events and that the natural course of events is largely a complicated interplay of causal forces. We are belief-forming entities, and the mechanism of belief formation is causal. It is unlikely, I think, that we would have survived if it were not for the fact that most of the beliefs we form as a result of causal forces are correct or approximately correct. It cannot be denied that many of our beliefs are false; nor can it be denied that many of our beliefs are formed as a result of bias and faulty belief-forming equipment. But my theory of justification assumes that, despite our doxastic defects, we are in general reliable processors of the information we receive. If we reject this assumption and hold that human beings are not generally reliable barometers of the way the world is, then my theory of justification leads to skepticism. I believe, however, that if this assumption is rejected, then every theory of epistemic justification will lead to skepticism. My theory fares neither better nor worse than any other as a hedge against the persistent skeptic.

I assume, then, that many of our reason-based beliefs are epistemically justified in accordance with the PR model and that many of these justified beliefs are true. For many purposes this is sufficient. I am concerned, however, with our *knowledge* of the world around us. As we shall see in the next chapter, knowing is an even stronger epistemic position than epistemically justified, reason-based belief.

CHAPTER FIVE

DEFECTIVE JUSTIFICATION

At the end of Chapter One I noted that the traditional analysis of knowledge represented in the incomplete definition (IDK) is inadequate. Let us turn now to a detailed consideration of its inadequacies. Although the traditional requirements are necessary conditions for factual knowledge, a variety of examples show that the conditions are not jointly sufficient. Perhaps the best-known type of example is the one suggested by Bertrand Russell[1] and later made precise by Edmund Gettier.[2] I shall follow established usage and refer to such examples as 'Gettier examples'. It should be noted, however, that this name has come to have a considerably broader extension than the examples that Gettier actually suggested: a Gettier example is any example that shows the traditional requirements for knowledge to be insufficient. I shall begin by describing the kind of example that Gettier actually proposed; at later stages other kinds of Gettier examples will be considered. In my description of these examples and throughout this chapter, I shall use the terminology developed in this book unless doing so would seriously misrepresent the ideas.

We are asked to imagine a person, S, who has a justified belief that q on the basis of some reasons. Moreover, q entails h; S reasons correctly from q to h, thereby coming to believe justifiably that q entails h; and S believes that h on the basis of these

---

1. Bertrand Russell, *The Problems of Philosophy* (1912; reprint New York: Galaxy Books, 1959), pp. 131–132; and *Human Knowledge* (New York: Simon and Schuster, 1948), pp. 154–155.
   2. Edmund Gettier, "Is Justified True Belief Knowledge?", *Analysis* 23 (1963): 121–123, reprinted in Michael Roth and Leon Galis, eds., *Knowing: Essays in the Analysis of Knowledge* (New York: Random House, 1970).

beliefs. Because *q* entails *h* and because *S* has an epistemically justified belief that *q* and a justified belief that *q* entails *h*, *S*'s belief that *h* is also epistemically justified. (In the presentation of his examples, Gettier appeals to a deduction principle similar to (PDC) of the previous chapter in support of this claim.) We are to imagine, however, that *q* is false, whereas *h* is true. *S*, then, does not have factual knowledge that *h*, even though all the requirements for knowledge that we have elicited thus far are satisfied. Let us consider some examples that have this structure. Here are two situations suggested by Bertrand Russell:

> There is the man who looks at a clock which is not going, though he thinks it is, and who happens to look at it at the moment when it is right; this man acquires a true belief as to the time of day, but cannot be said to have knowledge. There is the man who believes truly, that the last name of the Prime Minister in 1906 began with a B, but who believes this because he thinks that Balfour was Prime Minister then, whereas in fact it was Campbell Bannerman.[3]

If we add, in the first case, that the man is epistemically justified in believing that the clock is working properly, and in the second that he is justified in believing that Balfour was the prime minister in 1906, then the examples can be made to fit the schema above, provided that the man has, in each case, reasoned correctly from a false proposition to a true one. In the first example, the man justifiably believes the false proposition that the clock is working and indicates the right time, which entails that the time is what the clock indicates it is. Similarly, in the second example he justifiably believes the false proposition that Balfour was the prime minister in 1906, which entails that the name of the prime minister in 1906 begins with a B.

In his paper Gettier also suggests two examples. Because his formulation is so admirably clear, I quote his presentation of the first example in its entirety.

> Suppose that Smith and Jones have applied for a certain job. And suppose that Smith has strong evidence for the following conjunctive proposition:

3. Russell, *Human Knowledge*, pp. 131–132.

(d)   Jones is the man who will get the job, and Jones has ten
        coins in his pocket.

Smith's evidence for (d) might be that the president of the company assured him that Jones would in the end be elected, and that he, Smith, had counted ten coins in Jones's pocket ten minutes ago. Proposition (d) entails

(e)   The man who will get the job has ten coins in his pocket.

Let us suppose that Smith sees the entailment from (d) to (e), and accepts (e) on the grounds of (d), for which he has strong evidence. In this case, Smith is clearly justified in believing that (e) is true.

But imagine, further, that unknown to Smith, he himself, not Jones, will get the job. And also, unknown to Smith, he himself has ten coins in his pocket. Proposition (e) is then true, though proposition (d), from which Smith inferred (e), is false. In our example, then, ... it is ... clear that Smith does not *know* that (e) is true.[4]

The second example provided by Gettier is similar in structure. In the second example, however, the inferred true proposition h is a disjunction ($q \lor r$) of two propositions, one of which (r) is true and the other (q) false. S infers the disjunction from the false proposition q, for q is a proposition that he justifiably believes to be true. S does not believe that r, nor does S have any reasons such that S would be epistemically justified in believing that r on the basis of those reasons.

In these examples the traditional requirements for knowledge are satisfied, but the subject lacks knowledge. Hence, these examples show that the traditional requirements are not sufficient for factual knowledge. A number of philosophers have objected to Gettier's examples, and have attempted to defend some version of the traditional analysis on the grounds that the justification requirement is falsely assumed to be satisfied.[5] Let us therefore elaborate on the first of Russell's examples, in order to satisfy ourselves that the three requirements for knowledge suggested in (IDK) are really satisfied. Suppose the clock that S is looking at is

4. Gettier, "Is Justified True Belief Knowledge?", p. 122.

5. See, for example, Irving Thalberg, "In Defense of Justified True Belief," *Journal of Philosophy* 66 (1969): 794–803; Charles Pailthorp, "Knowledge as Justified True Belief," *Review of Metaphysics* 23 (1969): 25–47; a follow-up exchange between Pailthorp and Keith Lehrer in the 1970 issues of *Review of Metaphysics* 24: 122–133, and Robert Meyers and Kenneth Stern, "Knowledge without Paradox," *Journal of Philosophy* 70 (1973): 147–160.

a clock that has been in his living room for years; he has looked at it every day, and it has always indicated the correct time, for up to this point it has worked perfectly. Suppose it is twelve noon, and at midnight on the previous night the clock developed a defect and stopped working. S is not aware of that fact. On this particular day, S is concerned to know exactly what time it is, for he is to meet a friend at twelve-thirty. He looks at his clock and reasons that because the clock has always worked perfectly in the past, it is working properly now. His belief that the clock is now working properly is thus based upon a set of reasons, R, which includes his belief about the clock's past performance. S also reasons that because it now indicates that the time is twelve o'clock and is working perfectly, it *is* twelve o'clock. Hence, there is a false proposition, q, that the clock is working properly and indicates it is twelve o'clock, such that S has an epistemically justified belief that q, and such that q entails h, that it is twelve o'clock.

It might be objected that it is improper to say of S that his belief that q is epistemically justified, for one cannot be epistemically justified in believing what is not the case. If, however, we require that it be the case that q if a person is to be epistemically justified in believing that q, then it is difficult to see what we shall say about the following. Suppose S's neighbor also has a clock in his living room and this clock also has worked properly every day in the past. Moreover, suppose S's neighbor is looking at his clock, which is working properly and indicates it is twelve o'clock. It seems we would say of S's neighbor that he *knows* his clock is working. If he knows it is working, then his belief that it is working is epistemically justified. What is the difference between the neighbor's reasons and those upon which S's belief is based? They have the same reasons for believing that their respective clocks are working and we may suppose their relevant characteristics to be the same. The fact that S's clock is not working whereas his neighbor's is, does not seem to make a difference with respect to whether S is epistemically justified in his belief. If we take epistemic justification to be defined as in (DEJ) of Chapter Four and assume S and his neighbor to be relevently similar in their reasons and characteristics, then the competition class and the conditional probabilities ought to be the same for each case.

Of course, the difference between the cases makes a great difference to whether S *knows* that his clock is working; the truth of the proposition believed is relevant to knowledge, but not to justification.

I shall continue to assume, therefore, that S is fully justified in his belief that (*q*) his clock is working properly and indicates it is twelve o'clock. The examples are not to be rejected on the grounds that only beliefs in true propositions can be epistemically justified. There is still room for objection to the examples, however, because we have also supposed that S reasons correctly from *q* to the conclusion that (*h*) it is twelve o'clock, and that S's belief that *h* is based partly upon the justified belief that *q* entails *h*. We have in effect assumed that the justificatory status of *q* transfers to *h* via the entailment relation. The previous chapter introduced the principle of deductive closure for epistemic justification (PDC), and it is obvious that acceptance of this principle is tantamount to the assumption just noted. Indeed Gettier suggests a principle similar to (PDC) in presenting his examples. Some philosophers have objected to principles of deductive closure for epistemic justification and have rejected the Gettier examples on those grounds. Those who have argued in this way have typically also been concerned to defend some version of the traditional analysis of knowing, represented in the tentative definition (IDK). There are two general responses to such arguments. The first is that even if (PDC) is rejected, there are Gettier examples that show the traditional analysis (IDK) to be defective without reliance upon (PDC). In the next section we shall consider some examples of this type. The second response involves an argument to the effect that if one accepts the traditional analysis of knowing (IDK), then one ought also to accept the principle of deduction (PDC).[6] If this argument is correct, then it seems misguided to attempt a defense of the traditional analysis of knowing, which involves rejection of the principle of deductive closure.

Our principle of deductive closure was formulated as follows (I shall here replace 'reliably' with 'justifiably' in the formulation given in Chapter Four, page 126):

6. This argument is based upon a similar argument suggested by David Coder in "Thalberg's Defense of Justified True Belief," *Journal of Philosophy* 67 (1970): 424–425.

(PDC) If S justifiably believes that q on the basis of R, and if q entails h, and if S has some set of reasons, R^*, such that S would be justified in believing that q entails h on the basis of R^*, then S has some set of reasons, R^{**}, such that S would be epistemically justified in believing that h on the basis of R^{**}.

Let us assume, with those who argue against (PDC), that the traditional analysis of knowing expressed in (IDK) is correct; that is, we assume that knowledge is justified true belief. The argument I have in mind requires one more assumption, the assumption that the following principle is unobjectionable.

(PDKJ) If S knows that q, and if S knows that q entails h, then S has some set of reasons, R^{**}, such that S would be epistemically justified in believing that h on the basis of R^{**}.

This principle is similar to the principle (PDC), except that the two antecedent conditions of (PDC) have been replaced by much stronger conditions to the effect that S *knows* the propositions in question to be true. I take this principle to be unobjectionable: surely if I know that q is the case and if I also know that q's being the case logically guarantees that h is the case, then I am in a position to believe justifiably that h. I cannot think of a single interesting objection to (PDKJ). I admit, however, that the argument that follows is only as good as this assumed principle.

Given (PDKJ) and the traditional analysis (IDK), let us now suppose q and h are any two propositions such that

(a) q is true and q entails h.

Let us suppose that some person, S, is such that

(b) S justifiably believes that q on the basis of (some set of) reasons, R; and

(c) S justifiably believes that q entails h on the basis of (some set of) reasons R^*.

Then (IDK), (a), and (b) entail[7]

7. I am assuming that clause (3c) of the justification requirement in the traditional definition (IDK) is satisfied in claiming that this entailment goes through, but this seems uncontroversial. See page 44 of Chapter One for a formulation of (IDK).

(i) S knows that q.

Moreover, (IDK), (a), and (c) entail

(ii) S knows that q entails h.

Finally, the assumed principle (PDKJ) along with (i) and (ii) entail

(iii) S has some set of reasons, R^{**}, such that S would be epistemically justified in believing that h on the basis of R^{**}.

Thus, we can see that (iii) follows from (b) and (c) if we assume the traditional analysis (IDK), the principle (PDKJ), and assume as in (a) that q and h are any two *true* propositions such that q entails h. But the conditional "if (b) and (c), then (iii)" is simply our principle of deduction (PDC). I take this argument to show that if knowledge is justified true belief, then for cases in which q and h are both true, (PDC) is satisfied. This argument will not hold in cases (such as the Gettier examples) in which q is false, for in those cases (a) would be false. All I have shown is that those who want to defend the view that knowledge is justified true belief are committed, on logical grounds, to (PDC) in cases where q and h are both true, provided they are also willing to grant the unobjectionable principle (PDKJ).

But if those who defend the justified true belief analysis are committed to (PDC) in cases in which q and h are both *true,* what grounds could they have for denying that this principle holds in cases in which q is false? If we allow that justification can transfer from belief that q to belief that h under the assumptions of (PDC) when q is true, what difference would it make if q were false? The truth or falsity of the propositions involved does not seem relevant to the question of justification, although it obviously is relevant to whether one has knowledge. Because I do not know of any persuasive arguments on this point, I shall continue to assume that the principle (PDC) holds and that the examples we are considering are genuine counterexamples to the view that knowledge is justified true belief.[8]

---

8. There are, however, some interesting arguments in Meyers and Stern, "Knowledge without Paradox."

1. *True Reasons*

In the Gettier examples we can say that even though the subject, *S,* has an epistemically justified belief, this belief is defectively justified from the point of view of knowing. In order to make the analysis of knowing impervious to such problems we must come to some understanding of the notion of defective justification and then require, in addition to the traditional requirements, that a person's belief be nondefectively justified if that person is to have knowledge.

Perhaps the most obvious feature of the Gettier examples is that *S* has reasoned through a false proposition in arriving at his belief that *h.* For those who take the examples to be genuine counterexamples, a natural response is to single out this fact as the source of *defectiveness* of the justification, with respect to knowing that *h.* In other words, we might say that *S*'s belief that *h* is defectively justified if and only if the set of reasons upon which *S* justifiably believes that *h* includes a false belief.[9] In the example, the set of reasons for which *S* believes that it is twelve o'clock includes the false belief that his clock is working properly, and so his belief is defectively justified in accordance with this suggested notion of defectiveness. Unfortunately, if we were to add to our basic requirements the requirement that *S*'s belief be nondefectively justified and interpret nondefectiveness in accordance with this suggestion, the resulting requirements would be neither necessary nor sufficient for factual knowledge.

Let us first imagine a situation in which *S*'s belief is defectively justified from the point of view of knowing, but wherein his reasons do not involve any false beliefs. Suppose Smith has wired a detonator box to a charge of TNT and is about to flip the switch. He has checked the wiring carefully and knows that the TNT is brand X and that the batteries are brand Y. He remembers that he has used those products many times and that in the past they have always worked. On the basis of these reasons he comes to believe that the TNT will explode when he flips the switch. He flips the switch and the TNT does explode. It explodes, however, because

9. See, for example, Michael Clark, "Knowledge and Grounds: A Comment on Mr. Gettier's Paper," *Analysis* 24 (1964): 46–48; and J. T. Saunders and Narayan Champawat, "Mr. Clark's Definition of knowledge," *Analysis* 25 (1964): 8–9. See also the discussion of Gilbert Harman's proposals in Section 3 below.

a hunter coincidentally fires a high-powered shell into the charge at the moment the switch is flipped. Had the hunter not done so, the charge would not have exploded, for in fact the battery in the detonator did not have enough power to cause the explosion. Hence, Smith's belief is defectively justified and he does not know the explosion will occur. We may suppose, however, that his reasons did not involve any false beliefs. Smith might have reasoned that the battery was powerful enough and hence the TNT would explode, and his belief might have been based upon such reasons; but he did not reason in that way, and his reasons are still sufficiently good to render his belief fully justified. Even so, from the point of view of knowledge, his belief is defectively justified.

We can also see that a person's belief might be based upon some false beliefs even though that person has knowledge; in such a case, the belief is not defectively justified from the point of view of knowing. There are two sorts of cases to be considered in this regard. The first involves a person's having *two* (or more) sets of reasons, each of which is sufficient to render the belief justified.[10]

We might imagine a variation on one of Russell's examples. *S* looks at a clock that is not working but happens to indicate the correct time. We may suppose, as above, that *S* justifiably believes that the clock is working properly. He also looks at his wristwatch, which is working properly and indicates the correct time. He justifiably believes that both the clock and his wristwatch are working properly and comes to believe that both indicate the correct time. We may imagine that his belief about the time is based on both sources of evidence via overdetermination. He knows, I should think, what time it is, and yet this belief is based upon a false belief.

We can also imagine a situation in which *S* has only one set of reasons for believing that *h* and in which, even though *S*'s reasons include a false proposition, *S*'s belief is not defectively justified with respect to knowing. For example, suppose *S* attends a wedding ceremony. Being knowledgeable about such matters, he knows that the ceremony has been performed without a single

10. This kind of example was suggested by Lehrer in "Knowledge, Truth, and Evidence," *Analysis* 25 (1965): 168–175, reprinted in Roth and Galis, *Knowing.*

error, that the person performing it is authorized to marry people, and so forth. On the basis of these reasons he comes to believe that the two persons involved were married in the ceremony and on the basis of that belief concludes that they are married. Unknown to him, however, the participants were married previously in a civil ceremony, and hence were not married in the ceremony he witnessed. He still knows they are married, but his belief is based partly on the false belief that they were married in the ceremony he witnessed. Even though his reasons include a false belief, his belief is not defectively justified from the point of view of knowing.

These examples suffice to refute the view, suggested by some, that a person's believing that h is nondefectively justified with respect to knowing just in case the set of reasons for which that person believes that h does not include any false beliefs. The examples show that this is neither necessary nor sufficient for nondefectively justified belief. How, then, shall we define this notion?

2. *Conclusive Reasons*

One thing the Gettier examples show is that it is possible for a person to have an epistemically justified belief that h when h is true, but that if h had been false the person would still have had the same reasons for believing that h. In the clock example, S looks at the clock at the moment when it happens to register the correct time. Suppose he had looked at the clock one hour later; the time registered by the clock would have been incorrect, but all S's reasons for believing that the time was what the clock indicated would have been the same. It is, in some sense, merely *coincidental* that S's epistemically justified belief is also a true belief. As long as we allow that the reasons upon which a correct belief is based could have been the same even if the proposition believed had been false, there is room for this element of coincidence. Consequently, some authors have suggested that in order for a person's epistemically justified belief to be an instance of knowledge, the conditions for knowing must be strong enough to rule out the possibility of coincidence. This suggestion is often expressed thus: A person can know that h only if the person has conclusive reasons for believing that h. On my account of reasons, this terminology is inappropriate, for reason states are states of a person and as such cannot be conclusive or inconclusive. It would be better to say that a person can know that h only if the person's belief is conclusively justified on the basis of the set of reasons R. I shall, however, speak of conclusive reasons in order to avoid unnecessary confusion.

How shall we formulate the conclusive reasons requirement? Peter Unger has suggested an analysis of knowledge which might be adapted to this purpose.[11] Unger notes that in Gettier examples it seems accidental that the subject has a true belief, and supports this with considerations similar to those in the previous paragraph. Unger suggests that such cases can be dealt with if we define knowledge this way: A person, S, has knowledge that h if and only if it is not at all accidental that S is right about its being the case that h. Although I do not subscribe to this analysis of knowing, Unger's suggestion may be promising if converted into an analysis of conclusive reasons.

(5.1)   A person, S, has conclusive reasons, R, for believing that h iff: it is not at all accidental that S correctly believes that h on the basis of R.

Given this we would add a condition to the traditional definition of knowledge expressed in (IDK) to the effect that the reasons, R, upon which S's belief that h is based must be conclusive reasons. In the clock example this restriction appears to yield the desired result, for it is accidental that S is right about what time it is.

The notion of accidentality, however, is too vague. When is it correct to say that it is not at all accidental that S correctly believes that h on the basis of a set of reasons, R? Unger says he does not intend the notion of accidentality to include such things as automobile accidents, but he does not say precisely what he does intend.[12] Let us consider the clock example again. As we have described the example, it does seem accidental in some sense that S correctly believes that it is twelve o'clock. We can now imagine a variation on that example. Suppose someone has cleverly arranged for S to be looking at the clock at just the moment when it indicates the right time. Then, in whatever sense

11. Peter Unger, "An Analysis of Factual Knowledge," *Journal of Philosophy* 65 (1968): 157–170, reprinted in Roth and Galis, *Knowing*.
12. Unger, "An Analysis of Factual Knowledge," section II.

it *is* accidental that *S* is right about what time it is in the original example, it is in that same sense not at all accidental that *S* is right in the revised example. Yet *S* does not have knowledge in either case. Similarly, in the Gettier example quoted above, suppose someone has cleverly staged the entire set of circumstances described by Gettier. The employer has been bribed to mislead *S*, ten coins have been placed in *S*'s pocket, and so forth. It is then not accidental that *S* correctly believes that the man who will get the job has ten coins in his pocket. Such examples indicate that the notion of accidentality is not the key to understanding conclusive reasons; something stronger is needed.

We could define a very strong notion of conclusive reasons in a straightforward way by saying that a person's reasons are conclusive just in case it is logically impossible that *S* have these reasons when *h* is false. But if we add to our traditional requirements for factual knowledge the requirement that one's reasons must be conclusive in this sense, the resulting analysis would rule out many things that we agree are known. Indeed, these requirements would rule out any instance of knowledge in which the belief is based on beliefs that provide only inductive evidence, such as knowledge that the sun will rise tomorrow. This notion of conclusive reasons is too strong.

A similar but weaker formulation of this requirement is the following: A set of reasons upon which *S* justifiably believes that *h* are conclusive reasons for believing that *h* if and only if it is physically impossible that *S* have these reasons when *h* is false.[13] Like its predecessor, however, this version of the conclusive reasons requirement will rule out too many things that are known. For example, suppose Alfred is looking at a vase on a table. The lighting is good, there is nothing wrong with Alfred's eyesight, and he knows a vase when he sees one. Surely we would say that Alfred knows there is a vase on the table. His belief is based upon reasons, namely, the way in which he is appeared to by the vase and the table, and his background knowledge about vases. Moreover, his belief is epistemically justified, and we may suppose he has no other reasons that violate clause (3c) of (IDK). Are his

13. By 'physically impossible' I mean simply that a description of the state of affairs in question conjoined with (true) laws of nature would yield a contradiction.

reasons conclusive? According to our current version of the conclusive reasons requirement, it seems not, for surely it is physically *possible* for Alfred to have the reasons he does even though there is no vase on the table. He might have been hallucinating without being aware that he is doing so, or he might have been looking at a cleverly concealed hologram image of a vase which is so realistic that he is deceived. Thus, if we were to add a conclusive reasons requirement to (IDK) in accordance with this suggestion, we should have to say that Alfred does not know there is a vase on the table. Unless we wish to adopt an insidious form of skepticism, this result must be judged unacceptable.

In arguing that Alfred's having the reasons that he does is physically compatible with there being no vase on the table, we had to imagine a possible situation different from the real situation. In this alternative situation the causal role of the vase with respect to Alfred's having the reasons that he does is superseded by something else, such as a hologram image of a vase or a hallucinatory drug. This suggests that we might further weaken the analysis of conclusive reasons by ruling out at least some alternative situations from consideration. We do not want the mere possibility of hallucination or the mere possibility of there being a hologram image to prevent knowledge. Consider Alfred's actual situation: he is seeing a vase on a table in normal light. Now suppose this situation is different in *only* the following way: the vase is not in fact on the table, but everything else about the situation remains the same, except what is required logically or causally by the supposition that the vase is missing. Then, it seems, Alfred would no longer have the reasons that he does for believing that there is a vase on the table. These considerations suggest the following revision of the analysis of conclusive reasons: A set of reasons for which S justifiably believes that h is conclusive if and only if, given S's actual situation, S would not have had these reasons if h had been false and if the situation had been different only in any other ways required causally or logically by the supposition that h is false.[14]

14. This proposal is essentially the same as one made by Fred Dretske in "Conclusive Reasons," *Australasian Journal of Philosophy* 49 (1971): 1–22, reprinted in George S. Pappas and Marshall Swain, eds., *Essays on Knowledge and Justification* (Ithaca: Cornell University Press, 1978). In his book, *Belief, Truth*

This conclusive reasons requirement is promising. For one thing, the analysis of factual knowledge incorporating this requirement is not susceptible to the vase counterexample suggested above. Moreover, this analysis avoids the Gettier cases we have considered. In the case in which a man is looking at a broken clock, h is the proposition that it is twelve o'clock, and the set of reasons upon which the man bases his belief includes his justified beliefs that the clock is registering the correct time and has always worked in the past. Now let us suppose, as at the beginning of this section, that this situation is changed only in that it is not twelve, but one o'clock. Even so, S would still have exactly the same reasons, for the clock would still register twelve o'clock even if it were one o'clock. Thus, an analysis of factual knowledge incorporating our current conclusive reasons requirement gives us the right result in this example; because the conclusive reasons requirement is not satisfied, the person does not know that it is twelve o'clock. Similarly, it seems that in any case like this one, in which it is only a coincidence that a person's epistemically justified belief is correct, this analysis of factual knowledge would give the correct result.

Unfortunately, there are examples that show that this way of formulating the conclusive reasons requirement is too weak. If added to our requirement for knowledge, the resulting definition would allow some cases to qualify which should be disallowed as instances of knowledge. Returning to the example of Alfred's looking at a vase on a table, let us imagine this time that someone has cleverly rigged a concealed network of mirrors such that anyone standing in front of the table would see a reflected image of the vase, and this reflected image would appear to be exactly where the vase really is.[15] Alfred is not aware of these mirrors. He comes to believe that there is a vase on the table. Alfred's reasons, however, are just what they would be if there were no mirrors and he were looking directly at the vase rather

---

and Knowledge (Cambridge: Cambridge University Press, 1973), David Armstrong defends a version of the conclusive reasons requirement (see, for example, p. 159). I believe that the following discussion raises problems for Armstrong's view as well as Dretske's.

15. This example is similar to one used by Gilbert Harman in *Thought* (Princeton: Princeton University Press, 1973), p. 174. Harman uses the example for different purposes, however.

than seeing an image of it. His reasons are just what they were in the original case; therefore, Alfred has an epistemically justified belief that there is a vase on the table, and his belief is correct. But this time he does not know that there is a vase on the table, for he is not aware of the network of mirrors. Sadly, our latest version of the conclusive reasons requirement is satisfied. Had the vase not been on the table, and had the situation otherwise been the same except for what is causally or logically required by that supposition, Alfred would not have had the reasons that he does, for he would then not have seemed to see any vase at all on the table.

I do not know of any obvious ways in which any of these proposals concerning conclusive reasons might be improved upon. Indeed, I am inclined to think this approach to the problem of defectively justified belief is doomed to failure. To be sure, we must do something to guarantee that instances of accidentally correct belief do not qualify as knowledge. On the conclusive reasons approach, this is guaranteed by requiring, in effect, that a person can know that h only if the person could not be mistaken in believing that h on the basis of the reasons that person has.[16] Some of our examples indicate, however, that a person can have knowledge even though that person might have been mistaken. To require the kind of immunity to error which is implicit in the conclusive reasons approach is, I conclude, a mistake. We must look elsewhere for the solution to our problem.

3. *Evidence One Does Not Possess*

In his book *Thought* and in a number of articles that preceded the publication of this book, Gilbert Harman has developed a comprehensive theory of warranted inference (justification) and knowledge.[17] In the course of his discussion Harman provides detailed consideration of the problems raised by the Gettier examples. Harman's suggestions point toward a solution of our problem.

16. Dretske, for example, in "Conclusive Reasons," p. 1, says: "Any subject, S, who believes that P and who has conclusive reasons for believing that P . . . *could not be wrong* about P [given these reasons]. . . ."

17. To avoid misrepresenting Harman's views, I shall use his terminology throughout this section.

According to Harman, the troublesome Gettier examples arise only in contexts in which a person's belief is the result of warranted inference. Harman argues that there is a class of beliefs that are not based on inference but that there are no Gettier problems associated with this class of beliefs.[18] Although there are a number of perplexities involved in what Harman says about noninferential beliefs and inference, I shall not consider these, for they do not have any serious bearing on what I want to discuss here.

Let us recall the situation in which S looks at his clock, which is broken but happens to indicate the correct time, and also looks at his wristwatch, which is not broken and indicates the correct time. On the basis of both sets of reasons S comes to believe correctly and justifiably that the time is what the two timepieces indicate. In such cases we can, according to Harman, ascribe several different inferences to S.[19] We can ascribe to S an inference from what the broken clock indicates to a conclusion about what time it is; we can also ascribe to S an inference from what his wristwatch indicates to a conclusion about what time it is, and we can ascribe to S an inference from what both timepieces say to the conclusion about what time it is. In saying we can ascribe all three of these inferences to S we are not committed to saying that there are three distinct mental processes involved. Rather, there are three distinct abstract structures of inference, each of which is instantiated in what might be a single mental process by which S comes to have a belief about the time.[20] In the terminology that I have adopted we can say that the set of reasons upon which S's belief about the time is based includes all these inferences. The example would be an instance of overdetermination.

This example was used earlier to show that we cannot provide an adequate analysis of factual knowledge simply by requiring that one's belief not be based upon any false beliefs. If, however, there are several inferences that can be ascribed to S, perhaps we can provide a more subtle requirement to the effect that S knows by inference only if at least one of S's inferences is sufficient to

18. See Harman, *Thought*, pp. 186–188.
19. Ibid., pp. 168–169.
20. Ibid., p. 48.

provide justification and does not involve any false beliefs. In the example, we can see that even though two of S's inferences involve false beliefs, there is one that does not, namely, the inference based on the belief about what time his wristwatch indicates. Because these reasons are such that S's believing it is twelve o'clock on the basis of them is epistemically justified and they involve no false beliefs, we are willing to ascribe knowledge to S. This is essentially the approach that Harman takes to the problem of analyzing knowledge. He puts the matter in the following way: "We know by inference only if one of our inferences remains warranted and leads to the acceptance only of truths when restricted in premises to the set of things we know ahead of time to be true."[21] Because the only thing the person in our example *knows* ahead of time to be true is that his wristwatch is working properly (along with background knowledge), and because his reasons (beliefs) concerning the wristwatch are alone sufficient for S to have an epistemically justified (warranted) belief, this proposal is satisfied and we get the right result in that example.

There are, however, examples that might make one think Harman's proposal is inadequate.[22] Suppose a friend of yours comes into the room and you recognize him. Normally there would be no doubt that you know your friend has come into the room. Suppose there is, however, unknown to you, someone else out in the hall who looks exactly like your friend; if this other person had walked into the room, you would have mistaken him for your friend. Therefore, you cannot in fact be said to know that your friend has walked into the room. The account of knowledge proposed by Harman appears to be satisfied, because your inference is warranted and would remain so even if restricted in premises to things that you know beforehand. In light of this kind of problem, Harman raises some considerations that are of fundamental importance for the analysis of knowledge.[23]

In the example just given, as well as in the Gettier cases, there is always some evidence that the subject does not in fact possess (believe), but such that if he *did* possess it he would no longer be

21. Ibid., p. 172. A more precise definition is given by Harman on p. 171.
22. This example is similar to one used by Harman on page 175.
23. Ibid., Chapter 9.

epistemically justified in believing what he does. If you knew there was someone in the area who looks exactly like your friend, then you would no longer be justified in believing that it is your friend, rather than this other person, who has come into the room. In the original clock example, in which S is not also looking at a wristwatch, if S knew that the clock was broken, then he would no longer be epistemically justified in believing that it is twelve o'clock. In these examples, the fact that there is such evidence available undermines the person's reasons and prevents that person from having knowledge. This is why we can say that the subject's belief is defectively justified with respect to knowledge. The defect lies not in the reasons themselves nor in the belief, but rather in the presence of this unpossessed evidence.

We have noted that in the Gettier examples there is evidence available such that if the subject came to have (believe) this evidence, then he would no longer be epistemically justified in his belief. In these cases, this evidence undermines his reasons. We must be careful not to suppose, however, that one's reasons are undermined *whenever* there is unpossessed evidence of this sort. To say that unpossessed evidence is undermining is not equivalent to saying that it would nullify your justification if you came into possession of it. Let us return to the example involving a friend who walks into the room. This time, instead of supposing there is someone around who looks just like your friend, suppose your friend's mother has gone insane and is telling someone that her son is dead. *If* you came to know (or justifiably believe) that your friend's mother had said this but did not also come to know that she had gone insane, then the epistemic justification of your belief that it is your friend who has just come into the room would be nullified. But surely we do not want to say that this unpossessed evidence undermines your reasons.[24] You know that your friend has just come into the room even if his mother has insanely stated that he is dead. Unpossessed evidence that would nullify your justification if you came to have it must be partitioned into two categories: that which also undermines your reasons and that which does not. We may then say that a person's belief is defectively justified, from the point of view of knowing, just in case

24. Ibid.

there is undermining evidence that the person does not possess. This is Harman's proposal.

Harman admits that he cannot find any formal way of distinguishing between cases in which unpossessed evidence is undermining and cases in which it is not. Consequently, he leaves the distinction unanalyzed and argues for the following principle concerning unwarranted inference:

(Q)   One may infer a conclusion only if one also infers that there is no undermining evidence one does not possess.[25]

Harman notes that if one is to accept principle (Q), then one must hold that the conclusions of inferences involve self-reference; otherwise, one could not make a single inference without first inferring that there is no undermining evidence to the conclusion that there is no undermining evidence, and so on to an infinite regress. Thus, a warranted inference, for Harman, is always an inference to a *conjunctive* conclusion of the form "*h* and there is no undermining evidence to this whole conjunction."[26]

If one accepts principle (Q), the Gettier problems are easily accounted for within Harman's general position that one knows only if there are no false premises or conclusions involved in at least one of your warranted inferences. In all such cases there is undermining evidence, and the required conjunctive conclusion is false even though the first conjunct is true.

There are two difficulties with the solution proposed by Harman. First, the principle (Q) seems too strong a requirement for warranted inference. If, for one's inference to be warranted, one must in fact infer that there is no undermining evidence, then in all probability hardly anyone ever makes a warranted inference. When one considers Harman's views about reasoning and inference, however, (Q) is not as counterintuitive as it first appears. The position that Harman defends is a functionalist one, according to which "the only way to discover *when* a person makes inferences is to discover what assumptions about inferences are needed to account for his knowledge."[27] In addition, Harman

25. Ibid., p. 151.
26. Ibid., pp. 153–154.
27. Ibid., p. 20.

holds that inference is often unconscious, where that includes the belief that is the result of the inference. Putting these things together, we might argue, as Harman does, that the introduction of principle (Q) provides the simplest account of the troublesome cases that we are concerned with, and because this account requires us to ascribe at least the unconscious inference to the conjunctive conclusion in question, we are thus justified in accepting both (Q) and the presence of these inferences. Even though this line of argument is worthy of respect, there is something unpalatable about the requirement that one must, in *any* sense of inference and belief, infer a conclusion as sophisticated as '*h* and there is no undermining evidence to this whole conclusion' if one's inference is to be warranted. An alternative account of knowledge which does not require this and does not introduce anything equally unpalatable would be preferable.

Second, Harman's account is incomplete because of the undefined distinction between undermining unpossessed evidence and unpossessed evidence that is not undermining. This is (as Harman would admit) the very distinction that needs to be clarified if any real understanding of the notion of defectively justified belief is to be gained. This is why I remarked earlier that Harman's results point toward a solution of our problem. It would not be accurate to say that a solution has been provided. In the succeeding sections, therefore, we shall continue our search for an account of defectively justified belief. From this point on, however, we may think of our task in the light of Harman's distinction between undermining and nonundermining evidence.

4. *Defeasibility and Ideally Situated Observers*

In each of the examples of defectively justified belief considered in the preceding sections, we can partially characterize the defect by noting that the subject, *S*, is less than ideally situated with respect to the reasons that form the basis of his belief. There is always some additional evidence that has in some way escaped his notice. These situations are similar in many ways to problematic situations that arise in ethical theory and have led to the distinction between prima facie and absolute obligation.[28] It is not an

28. A classic use of this distinction occurs in W. D. Ross, *The Right and the Good* (Oxford: Oxford University Press, 1930).

uncommon feature of our experience that we feel obligated, relative to what we know, to perform some action and discover later that we simply are not in a position to perform that action. In such cases, we say that our prima facie obligation to perform the action has been overridden, or defeated, by circumstances that we did not initially know about. Similarly, in the cases of defectively justified belief in the preceding sections, the subject S has a justified belief, given the reasons upon which that belief is based. Because he is less than ideally situated, however, his reasons may be overridden, or defeated, by evidence that he does not have. In any of those cases, if we imagine S coming to have some of the additional evidence, we can see that his belief would no longer be justified. For example, in the situation in which a man looks at a clock that has stopped working but happens to register the correct time, we can see that if he were to come to know, or justifiably believe, that the clock is not working, then the set of reasons consisting of this information combined with his old reasons would no longer form the basis for a justified belief that the time is what the clock indicates. The defeasibility approach to explicating knowledge is based upon the intuitively appealing idea that if a person's belief is justified in such a way that the person has knowledge, then if that person were to approach an ideal epistemic position by coming to have additional reasons, the belief would not cease to be justified as a result. The belief would be indefeasibly justified. According to this approach, to say that a person's belief is defectively justified, from the point of view of knowing, is to say that the belief in question is defeasibly justified.

The notion of an ideal epistemic position is, of course, only an epistemologist's pipe dream. In any full sense, anyone who falls short of omniscience is less than ideally situated epistemically. We can nonetheless make sense of the idea that we are better off at some times than at others with respect to the reasons we have for believing something. In contexts of inquiry and investigation it is natural to speak of the investigator as improving his epistemic position; indeed, we would not consider his investigation a success unless such an improvement occurred. There are, however, many different ways in which a person's epistemic position might improve. Given this variety, to characterize indefeasible justification in the simplistic manner suggested above is too vague to be useful. If we are to utilize the notion of indefeasible justification, we must find a precise characterization of the manner in which possible improvement of one's epistemic position is relevant to the question whether one's belief is indefeasibly justified.

5. Overriding

Let us begin by considering a proposal made some time ago by Roderick Chisholm in "The Ethics of Requirement."[29] In this essay Chisholm provides an explication of the ethical concept of defeasibility and suggests that an analogous explication can be given for the epistemic notion of defeasible justification. Taking the expression 'p requires q' as primitive and letting 'p', 'q', and 's' stand for events or states of affairs, Chisholm first defines the notion of overriding.

(5.2) There is a requirement for the state of affairs q which has been overridden = df. There are states of affairs, p and s, such that (i) p occurs and p requires q and (ii) s occurs and the joint occurrence of p and s does not require q.[30]

Chisholm then provides the following definition of defeasibility:

(5.3) A requirement for the state of affairs q is defeasible = df. There is a state of affairs, p, such that p requires q and this requirement may be overridden.[31]

To obtain the epistemic analogue of these definitions, we can take as primitive the expression 'e justifies h', where 'e' and 'h' stand for propositions.[32] We can then say:

(5.4) There is a justification for h which has been overridden = df. There is a body of evidence, e, and a body of evidence,

29. Roderick Chisholm, "The Ethics of Requirement," *American Philosophical Quarterly* 1 (1964): 147–153. In later writings Chisholm develops a highly sophisticated epistemology that goes far beyond the proposal made in this early paper.
30. Ibid., p. 148.
31. Ibid., p. 149.
32. In doing so, I switch from the reasons terminology employed in this book to the evidential terminology favored by Chisholm. I shall do this in a number of places in succeeding sections in order to avoid misrepresenting the views of the authors discussed. The following definition could, however, be reformulated in my own terminology.

e', such that (i) e is true and e justifies h and (ii) e' is true and the conjunction of e and e' does not justify h.

We can then say that a justification for h is defeasible in the following way:

(5.5a) A justification for h is defeasible = df. There is a body of evidence, e, such that e is true and e justifies h and this justification may be overridden.

In opposition to justifications that are defeasible are justifications that are indefeasible. It seems appropriate, given the above definition, to define this concept as follows:

(5.5b) A justification for h is indefeasible = df. There is a body of evidence, e, such that e is true and e justifies h and this justification cannot be overriden.

But the notorious word 'cannot' presents us (as usual) with a problem. Presumably, to say that a justification for h cannot be overridden is to say that there cannot be any body of evidence, e', such that e' in conjunction with the justifying body of evidence e fails to justify h. But how are we to understand the requirement that there cannot be any such body of evidence, e'? We might take this to mean that it is not logically possible that there is such a body of evidence. This conception of indefeasibility, however, is not satisfactory if we are concerned to analyze defective justification in terms of indefeasibility. We want to say that a person, S, knows that h only if S's belief that h is indefeasibly justified. On the suggestion under consideration this would amount to saying that S knows that h only if it is logically impossible that there should be some additional evidence, e', such that the set consisting of belief in this additional evidence, combined with S's reasons for believing that h, would no longer constitute a set of reasons upon which belief that h would be epistemically justified. This requirement is obviously too strong. If h is some contingently true proposition, then it is logically possible that h is false. But if it is logically possible that h is false, then it is logically possible that there is some body of evidence, e', such that the combination of the belief that e' with S's reasons would no longer be a set of reasons upon which belief that h would be epistemically justified. The denial of h would constitute such possible evidence, and it is clear that the combination of S's reasons with the belief that not-h would fail to be a set of reasons upon which the belief that h would be justified. This proposal, then, will yield the result that we can have knowledge only of noncontingent propositions. This is not a happy result.

Another way to interpret 'cannot' is to say that it is not *physically* possible that there should be a defeating body of counterevidence, e'. The resulting requirement for knowing, however, suffers from defects similar to the one just considered. Suppose h is the proposition that there is a red ball in front of me. It is not physically impossible that h is false: the conjunction of the denial of h with the laws of nature would not yield a contradiction. Hence, any belief that h would be defeasibly justified, and I could never know of any red ball (or of anything else) that it is in front of me. The skeptic would enjoy this conclusion, but I do not.

Yet another way to interpret 'cannot' is to say that there is in fact no true body of defeating counterevidence e'; that is, a person's belief that h is indefeasibly justified just in case there is in fact nothing about the world that overrides that person's reasons. This is compatible both with saying it is physically possible that there should be such counterevidence and with saying it is logically possible that there should be. Under this interpretation of defeasibility, we get the following requirement for factual knowledge: A person, S, knows that h only if there is no true body of evidence, e', such that the set consisting of the combination of belief that e' with S's reasons would fail to constitute a set of reasons upon which belief that h would be epistemically justified. The resulting analysis of knowledge has a great deal to recommend it. For one thing, it is immune to the problems raised by Gettier. It is readily established that in each of those examples there is some true body of evidence, e', such that the set consisting of the combination of a belief that e' with S's reasons fails to be a set of reasons upon which belief that h would be justified.

Despite this meritorious feature, an analysis of knowing incorporating this requirement will not suffice, for it is too strong. The following example will make this clear. Suppose S attends a wedding ceremony in which two of his friends become married. The ceremony is performed by the bishop without any errors, and S knows these things. It seems that S knows, after having witnessed the ceremony, that his friends are married. But we can easily imagine the world being such that S's belief is defeasibly justified in accordance with the interpretation under consideration. Imagine, for example, that at the time the ceremony is performed, but unknown to anyone involved in the ceremony (including S), the cardinal goes insane. He has long harbored a suppressed hatred of the bishop, and in his insanity falsely denounces the bishop as a fraud who is not authorized to marry anyone. There will then be a true body of counterevidence, e' (namely, the proposition that the cardinal says the bishop is a fraud), such that belief that e' combined with S's reasons would fail to be a set of reasons upon which the belief that the people are married would be epistemically justified. Thus, an analysis of knowing incorporating this requirement is too strong. Because I cannot think of any other obvious way of interpreting Chisholm's suggestion, I conclude that we must look elsewhere for an analysis of indefeasible justification.

6. *Evidence That One Could Be Expected to Know About*

In the wedding example just considered, the presence of the defeating counterevidence concerning the cardinal's remark is an entirely unexpected fact. There is no way in which S could reasonably be expected to know that the cardinal is saying the things that he is about the bishop. The problem with the last requirement considered in the previous section is that it allows *any* true proposition to serve as a defeating bit of counterevidence. We need somehow to restrict the range of admissible defeating counterevidence in order to avoid the kind of result reached in the wedding example. Perhaps we can take our clue from the fact that in this example the defeating counterevidence is not something that S could be expected to know about.

In an early paper on the analysis of knowing, Ernest Sosa suggests an explication of knowledge along these lines.[33] In order to illustrate the motivation behind this approach, Sosa provides an example in which we would deny knowledge to a person be-

33. Ernest Sosa, "The Analysis of Knowledge That *p*," *Analysis* 25 (1964): 1–8. In later writings Sosa pursues a somewhat different line but suggests that his later views are derivative from this first paper. See "Propositional Knowledge," *Philosophical Studies* 20 (1969): 33–43; "Two Conceptions of Knowledge," *Journal of Philosophy* 67 (1970): 59–68, and especially "How Do You Know?", *American Philosophical Quarterly* 11 (1974): 113–122, reprinted in Pappas and Swain, *Essays on Knowledge and Justification*.

cause there is available some evidence that the person has failed to take into account. We are asked to imagine that there are seven persons who are in a room, R. They emerge from the room and are interviewed by two other people, A and B. A interviews four people and B interviews the remaining three. They ask only one question: "Is there a chair in room R?" Those interviewed by A answer in the affirmative; those interviewed by B answer that there is no chair in room R. B then interviews the four people interviewed by A, but A decides that he does not need to interview anyone else. B concludes that he does not know whether there is a chair in room R, whereas A concludes that there is a chair in the room. As Sosa correctly points out, we would not say that A's belief is an instance of knowledge even if there is in fact a chair in the room. Even if we grant that A has a justified belief that there is a chair in the room, A's reasons are overridden by the countertestimony provided by the people not interviewed by A. The only difference between A and B is that B has this countertestimony in addition to the positive testimony possessed by A. Sosa's point is that the counterevidence in this example is evidence that A could reasonably have been expected to gather. Generalizing on this type of example, Sosa produces a set of conditions that can be construed as conditions for indefeasible justification, although Sosa does not himself use that terminology. The important part of his proposal may be stated in this way:

(5.6)   S's justified belief that h is indefeasibly justified if and only if there is no true proposition, e', such that (i) the combination of belief that e' with the set of S's reasons for believing that h fails to constitute a set of reasons upon which a belief that h would be epistemically justified, and (ii) S could reasonably have been expected to find out that e' is true and that condition (i) is satisfied.[34]

In the example provided by Sosa, it is clear that A's belief is defeasibly justified in accordance with this proposal, for there is testimonial counterevidence available such that A can reasonably have been expected to find out about that evidence. Moreover, in the wedding example described at the end of Section 5 above, it

34. Sosa, "The Analysis of Knowledge That p," p. 7.

seems that S cannot reasonably have been expected to find out that the cardinal is denouncing the bishop as a fraud; hence, his justification is not defeasible in accordance with this proposal. It would appear that Sosa's suggestion works in both examples. Moreover, in the cases provided by Gettier and in a number of the examples considered in the preceding sections, Sosa's conditions yield the appropriate result: in those cases there is some defeating counterevidence that S could reasonably have been expected to find out about.

Unfortunately, it is not always clear when we can say that a person could *reasonably* have been expected to find out about something. Presumably, what Sosa had in mind is something like the following. If a person can reasonably be expected to have found out about something, then if that person fails to find out about it or neglects to do so we would be warranted in criticizing that person for lack of thoroughness. We could point out that some obvious source of relevant evidence had been overlooked. But when would such criticism not be warranted? Let us suppose an investigator has undertaken to sample a large population, such as the population of the United States, in order to find out the approximate percentage of people who support a particular political candidate. The investigator makes every effort to ensure that the sample is large enough for that population, takes every precaution possible to ensure that the sample is random and well stratified, and keeps a very close check on the manner of polling used. The results indicate that 40 percent of the population is in favor of the candidate, 50 percent is not, and the remaining 10 percent is undecided. It is concluded that these percentages are approximately correct. Let us suppose that the sample selected was, despite the investigator's best efforts, grossly misrepresentative of the population as a whole. Would we then be warranted in criticizing the investigator for failing to take into account some additional relevant evidence? It seems that we would not, for the investigator had done the best that one could under the circumstances: to expect more would be unreasonable. There are, indeed, many sorts of situations in which a person's evidence is true but seriously misleading, and yet that person could not be expected to know that it is misleading. If, in such a situation, S's reasons are such that S's belief that h is justified, and if h should happen to be true, then given (5.6) we would have to say S knows that h, contrary to fact. In the situation just considered we would not say the investigator knows the percentages in any event, because the investigation has led to a justified *false* belief. Let us see if there are any similar cases in which the evidence leads to a justified true belief.

As a somewhat bizarre example, suppose a physician administers a dose of what he believes to be a very powerful drug, D, to a patient in order to relieve the patient of some symptoms of a disease. The drug has been thoroughly tested and its effects on patients suffering from this disease are well known. After administering the drug the physician watches closely for the appropriate reaction, which occurs exactly as expected. Suppose, in addition, that it is standard procedure before administering this drug to subject it to a battery of precise tests to guarantee quality, for it is a very unstable substance. The substance administered to the patient has passed all these tests. Moreover, this substance has been processed by the manufacturer in exactly the way that all other quantities of the drug have been processed in the past. In short, the physician and everyone else are fully justified in believing that drug D is being administered to the patient. Moreover, it *is* drug D, but in the manufacturing process a foreign substance was mixed in with the materials. This foreign substance rendered the product (drug D) impotent to affect patients with the disease in question. The foreign substance is, moreover, undetectable through any testing procedure known to science. When the substance was administered to the patient, it had no effect whatever. Through a remarkable coincidence, the patient's reaction was caused by something he had eaten for lunch. Thus, the result was the same, but the causes were not what the physician was epistemically justified in believing them to be.

It seems obvious in this example that the physician could not be said to *know* that the patient will display the predicted reactions, even though the physician justifiably believes this, and the belief is true. There is some defeating counterevidence in this situation. We cannot say, however, that the physician could *reasonably* have been expected to find out about this defeating counterevidence. All the usual tests were performed, and the manufacture of the substance was, to all appearances, correctly conducted. If any additional tests had been made at any time prior to the administration of the substance to the patient, the results would have supported the view that the substance was drug D. In accordance with (5.6) and our projected revision of the traditional analysis (IDK), we would conclude that the physician knew the reaction would occur, a result that seems to contradict the facts in our example.

Although (5.6) is plausible, we can see by example that it is too weak. In cases such as the one Sosa considers, there is defeating counterevidence that the subject could reasonably be expected to know about. In the example of the wedding, there is counterevidence that the subject could not reasonably be expected to know about, but we would not consider it defeating counterevidence. Such cases support (5.6), but, as our example shows, they do not illustrate all the possibilities.

7. *Evidence That One Would Be Justified in Believing to Be False*

In the example discussed in the previous section, we saw that the physician's belief that the patient would react in a certain way is defeasibly justified. The physician's reasons are overrridden by available counterevidence, but this evidence is not something the physician could reasonably be expected to know about. Although we could not reasonably expect the physician to know about this counterevidence, the reasons upon which the belief that the patient will react in the manner predicted is based are *also* reasons upon which a belief that the substance being administered to the patient is unadulterated drug D would be epistemically justified. This false proposition, which our subject would be justified in believing, is the defeating counterevidence. Proposal (5.6) was initially attractive because it provided a way of restricting the range of admissible defeating counterevidence, thereby avoiding some of the problems with the proposals considered in Section 5. Given what we have just noted about the example used against (5.6), perhaps it will be profitable to restrict the range of admissible counterevidence to true propositions that S would be epistemically justified in believing to be false. If we revise our definition of indefeasibility by incorporating this restriction, the resulting analysis is essentially the same as one considered by Keith Lehrer and Thomas Paxson.[35] This proposal may be stated as follows:

(5.7) S's belief that h is indefeasibly justified if and only if there is no true body of evidence, e', such that (i) the combination of belief that e' with S's reasons for believing that h fails to constitute a set of reasons upon which a belief that h would be epistemically justified and (ii) S would be epistimically justified in believing the denial of e'.

In the example involving the physician, there is a body of true evidence, e', which overrides the physician's reasons in accordance with this proposal. In the example involving the man who witnesses a wedding while the cardinal is insanely denouncing the bishop, however, it appears that the subject's belief is indefeasibly justified in accordance with this proposal. Even though the proposition that the cardinal is denouncing the bishop is counterevidence, it does not seem to be counterevidence that the subject would be epistemically justified in believing to be false. Hence, this potentially defeating counterevidence is ruled out by clause (ii) of (5.7) and is not eligible to serve as defeating counterevidence.

Let us grant for the moment that the counterevidence e' in the marriage example is not something that the subject would be epistemically justified in believing to be false. Even so, as Lehrer and Paxson show, this counterevidence can be used to construct a proposition that will override S's reasons in accordance with (5.7).[36] We need only to consider some proposition, r, such that S would be justified in believing it to be false but such that it is irrelevant to whether or not the two people are married. Suppose, for example, that r is the true proposition that Atlanta is west of Columbus and that the S of our example would be epistemically justified in believing r to be false. Then consider the conjunction of r and the counterevidence e' about what the cardinal is saying. This conjunction is also counterevidence, given that r is irrelevant to whether the two people are married. But because S would

35. Keith Lehrer and Thomas Paxson, "Knowledge: Undefeated Justified True Belief," *Journal of Philosophy* 66 (1969): 225–237.
36. Ibid., p. 230.

be justified in believing *r* to be false, *S* would be justified in believing the conjunction of *r* and *e'* to be false. Hence, there is a true proposition, namely, the conjunction of *r* and *e'*, such that in accordance with (5.7) it overrides our subject's reasons for believing that the two people are married. Because this gives us the wrong result concerning what *S* knows in this example, we must reject this proposal.

Noting this kind of difficulty, Lehrer and Paxson suggest an account of indefeasible justification which is designed to rule out artifically constructed defeating propositions such as the conjunction of *r* and *e'* above. They note that the defeating effect of the conjunction of *r* and *e'* stems solely from *e'*, whereas the reason why *S* would be justified in believing this conjunction to be false has to do solely with *S*'s reasons for believing the irrelevant proposition *r*. We need a closer connection in the satisfaction of clauses (i) and (ii) of the proposal. In order to guarantee a closer connection, Lehrer and Paxson suggest an analysis that may be expressed in this way:[37]

(5.8) *S*'s belief that *h* is indefeasibly justified if and only if there is no true body of evidence, *e'*, such that (i) the combination of belief that *e'* with *S*'s reasons for believing that *h* fails to constitute a set of reasons upon which a belief that *h* would be epistemically justified; and (ii) *S* would be epistemically justified in believing the denial of *e'*; and (iii) for any logical consequence, *q*, of *e'*, if the combination of belief that *q* with *S*'s reasons for believing that *h* fails to constitute a set of reasons upon which a belief that *h* would be justified, then *S* would be epistemically justified in believing that *q* is false.

With the addition of clause (iii), the conjunction of *r* and *e'* above is ruled out as defeating counterevidence, for *e'* [= *q* in (5.8)] alone is a logical consequence of this conjunction such that condition (iii) is not satisfied for *e'*. By hypothesis, however, *S* would not be justified in believing *e'* false.

This revised proposal handles not only the original Gettier cases, but also the other examples considered so far in this chap-

37. Ibid.

ter. Unfortunately, there are problems with the projected analysis of knowledge that would result from the adoption of this proposal. It can be shown that the resulting analysis of knowing is too weak.

The following example structure shows that the analysis of knowing incorporating (5.8) is too weak. Suppose S justifiably believes that h. But suppose that even though h is true and S justifiably believes that h, S does not know that h because there is some true counterevidence, e', such that S would be justified in believing e' to be false and e' overrides his reasons for believing that h. Then suppose there is a second body of true counterevidence, e'', available such that e'' also overrides S's reasons for believing that h but S would not be justified in believing e'' to be false. Consider, then, the disjunction of e' and e'' ($e' \lor e''$). This is a logical consequence of e', and because each disjunct is defeating counterevidence, the disjunction as a whole is defeating counterevidence. So, in accordance with clause (iii) of (5.8), S will have to be such that he would be justified in believing the disjunction ($e' \lor e''$) false. For any disjunction, however, S would be justified in believing it false if and only if S would be justified in believing, of each disjunct, that it is false; and we have already assumed that S would not be justified in believing e'' to be false. Because examples exhibiting this structure are not difficult to find, we may conclude that the projected analysis of knowing incorporating (5.8) is too weak. This analysis would allow some cases to be instances of knowledge which should be disallowed.

We began this section with the observation that in some of our troublesome examples of defective justification there is available some defeating counterevidence that the subject would be justified in believing to be false. As it turns out, none of our efforts to forumulate an analysis of defeasibly justified belief in accordance with this consideration have proved successful. Because I do not know of any other satisfactory proposals along these lines, I conclude that we must look elsewhere for an account of defeasibility.

8. *Evidence That One Might Come to Know About*

At the beginning of the discussion of defeasible justification in Section 4, the notion of defeasibility was characterized in terms of epistemic positions that are less than ideal. We also spoke of possible improvement of one's epistemic position, and in the proposals considered thus far it has been assumed that whether a person's belief is defeasibly justified is a function of the way the world is over and above what is represented in that person's reasons. Implicit in these notions is the idea that if some true body of defeating counterevidence is available, then this additional evidence is something one might come to know. To say that one might come to know this additional evidence is compatible both with saying that one could not reasonably have been expected to know it and with saying that one would not (given one's actual reasons and characteristics) be epistemically justified in believing it to be false. This idea is explicitly represented in a proposal put forth by Risto Hilpinen.[38] Hilpinen characterizes indefeasibility in terms of possible increases in knowledge; of the proposals considered thus far, this suggestion is perhaps the clearest representative of the notion of movement toward an ideally situated epistemic position. An increase in knowledge is surely one way of moving toward such an ideal state.

In constructing his characterization of indefeasible justification, Hilpinen refers to a principle put forth by Jaakko Hintikka. Hilpinen calls this the "extendability thesis."[39] The principle states that if a person genuinely knows some proposition h, then no matter what else he might come to know, he will not lose the knowledge that h as a result. Hintikka puts the matter in the following way:

> If somebody says "I know that p" in this strong sense of knowledge, he implicitly denies that any further information would have led him to alter his view. He commits himself to the view that he would still persist in saying that he knows p is true—or at at the very least persist in saying that p is in fact true—even if he knew more than he now knows.[40]

38. Risto Hilpinen, "Knowledge and Justification," *Ajatus* 33 (1971): 7–39. Virtually the same proposal was made independently by Peter Klein in "A Proposed Definition of Propositional Knowledge," *Journal of Philosophy* 68 (1971): 471–482.

39. Hilpinen, "Knowledge and Justification," p. 25.

40. Jaakko Hintikka, *Knowledge and Belief: An Introduction to the Logic of the Two Notions* (Ithaca: Cornell University Press, 1962), pp. 20–21.

Leaving aside the dubious parts about what people would persist in saying, we may express the extendability thesis as follows:

(ET)   If S knows that h, then for any true proposition, q, S would know that h even if S knew more than S now knows by knowing that q.

According to (ET), the corpus of propositions of which a person has genuine knowledge is always extendable to new instances of knowledge without detriment to any previous members of the corpus. Hilpinen suggests that the extendability thesis be adopted as "a condition of adequacy for the definition of defeasibility."[41] That is, our characterization of defeasibility must be such that any instance of knowledge in accordance with our defeasibility analysis of knowledge must satisfy the extendability thesis.

Let us consider whether (ET) is a principle we wish to accept. To begin, (ET) is vaguely formulated. A subjunctive clause is used, but we are not told what else is permitted to happen to S in the event that he should know *more* than he now knows by coming to know that q. What does the expression 'more than' in (ET) allow for? Let us look at some of the possibilities.

On one reading of 'more than', the extendability thesis (ET) turns out to be trivially true. We can express this sense of 'more than' as follows:

(5.9)   At $t2$, S knows more than S knew at $t1$ iff at $t2$, S knows everything that he knew at $t1$ and knows at least one thing that he did not know at $t1$.

We can interpret the extendability thesis in accordance with this sense of 'knowing more than' as follows:

(ET1) If S knows that h, then for any true proposition, q, S would know h even if S knew everything that S now knows and also knew that q.

(ET1), however, is a trivial truth, for it says that if S knows that h, then S would still know that h even if S continued to know that h and knew something else as well. This is not a very interesting principle. A more interesting interpretation of 'knowing more than' is the following:

41. Hilpinen, "Knowledge and Justification," p. 30.

(5.10) At $t2$, S knows more than S knew at $t1$ iff at $t2$, the sum of S's information about the world is greater than it was at $t1$.

The phrase 'sum of S's information' is not intended to express any very technical sense of information. If we assume that some rough measure of the cognitive content of sentences in natural languages is available, then the sum of S's information would simply be the measure assigned to the conjunction of everything that S knows. It is clear that the sum of S's information could increase over a period even if the items of information that S has were to change; that is, it is compatible with (5.10) that S should come to know more than S now knows even though S loses some present knowledge. Hence, we get the following nontrivial interpretation of the extendability thesis:

(ET2) If S knows that h, then for any true proposition, q, S would know that h even if the sum of S's information about the world were to increase as a result of S's coming to know that q.

There are a number of problems with this version of the extendability thesis. Perhaps it will suffice to point out one, which is the fact that people sometimes *forget* things that they once knew. For example, I once knew the name of my third-grade teacher but I have now utterly forgotten it. Moreover, I should like to think that the sum of my information about the world has increased since the third grade, and that it has increased because of the many true things I have learned since then. If all these things are true, then it will follow from (ET2) that I never did know the name of my third-grade teacher. This is not a satisfactory result.

From a structural point of view, this example shows that (ET2) is too strong, for it fails to specify any epistemic connection between the supposed increase in (true) information and the question whether S would still know that h were such an increase to occur. My forgetting something and my also learning a number of new things may be totally unrelated from the epistemic point of view. It seems clear that the intent of the extendability thesis is to specify that if a person knows something, then coming to have more information about the world would not result, on epistemic grounds, in that person's losing the previous knowledge. One's loss of previous knowledge (through mere forgetting, for example) will be for other reasons. Perhaps we can capture this idea in the following way:

(ET3) If S knows that h, then for any true proposition, q, if the sum of S's information about the world were to increase as a result of S's coming to know that q, then S would not lose the knowledge that h as an epistemic result of coming to know that q.

The condition formulated here is close to what Hilpinen had in mind. But, like some of the defeasibility conditions considered earlier, this formulation of the extendability thesis places restrictions on an analysis of knowing that are too strong.

To see that (ET3) is too strong, consider the following. Suppose S has just thrown a rock at a window. It is a large rock, an ordinary window, and S can see that the rock is going to hit the window. Moreover, when the rock hits it, the window will break as a result. It seems clear that we would say S knows that the window will break. S's belief is epistemically justified, and there does not appear to be any true defeating counterevidence available. We can, however, imagine some additional bizarre circumstances such that there would be defeating counterevidence in accordance with the account of defeasibility that corresponds to (ET3). First, we may note that because S is epistemically justified in believing that the window will break, he is also justified, under the circumstances, in believing that he will see the window break and in believing that he will hear it break. Now suppose S has a peculiar nervous disease hitherto unknown to the human race. This disease has never before manifested any symptoms in S, but he is about to be afflicted with some symptoms, namely, total visual and auditory blackout. Let us also suppose S will be afflicted with these symptoms at the moment the window breaks, and so will neither see nor hear the window break; let this last fact be the defeating counterevidence.[42] It seems clear that if S came to *know* that he would neither see nor hear the window break (but did not also come to know why), then his belief that the window will break would no longer be epistemically justified

---

42. I am supposing that these characteristics of S will not render his belief epistemically unjustified in accordance with the definition given in Chapter Four.

and he would no longer have knowledge. Hence, by (ET3), S does not know to begin with that the window will break, contrary to the assumption of our example.

Assuming that (ET3) or something like it is the intended interpretation of the extendability thesis, this example shows that we are under no constraints to limit our analysis of defeasibility to one that satisfies the extendability thesis. It is not surprising that the explication of defeasibility proposed by Hilpinen turns out to be too strong. The condition proposed by Hilpinen may be expressed in the following way:

(5.11) S's belief that h is indefeasibly justified if and only if for any true proposition, q, S would be completely justified in believing that h even if S justifiably believed that q.

The example of the rock thrower shows that an analysis of knowing incorporating (5.11) would be too strong, just as it shows that the extendability thesis (ET3) is too strong.

9. *Weak versus Strong Knowledge*

It might be objected that my criticisms of the extendability thesis in the previous section are unfair to both Hilpinen and Hintikka on the grounds that they are concerned with a different kind of knowledge than is illustrated in my examples. Some philosophers have distinguished between weak and strong knowledge, and there are some grounds for thinking that Hintikka, and perhaps Hilpinen as well, are concerned with knowledge of the strong variety. Strong knowledge is associated with the view that a person can have knowledge only if it is not possible for that person to be mistaken.[43] This is sometimes expressed by saying that knowledge requires certainty. Weak knowledge is associated with the view that a person can sometimes have knowledge even though this certainty is lacking. A number of philosophers have held that knowledge in the primary sense is strong knowledge; this is a view with which Hintikka, at least, appears to have some sympathy. He says, for example, that

43. See section 2 above on conclusive reasons and note 16 above.

one can be justified in saying that "I know" only if one's grounds are "conclusive" or "adequate" in some sense. I am not in a position to say "I know" unless my grounds for saying so are such that they give me the right to disregard any further evidence or information. We must realize, however, that having this right need not mean that one's grounds are so strong that they logically imply that what one claims to know is true.[44]

A few sentences later, Hintikka puts forth the general principle, quoted in the previous section, which is Hilpinen's extendability thesis. It appears, then, that for Hintikka the extendability thesis is closely connected with the general view that knowledge is strong knowledge. The examples I have been using seem to be examples of weak knowledge, and so perhaps my criticisms are unfair. But let us consider the distinction between strong and weak knowledge.

After the passage just quoted, Hintikka refers to a paper by Norman Malcolm.[45] In this paper Malcolm attempts to draw the distinction between weak and strong knowledge. Malcolm's paper is probably the most detailed, and certainly the best-known, attempt to make this distinction precise. Malcolm centers discussion of this distinction on a claim made by H. A. Prichard to the effect that when we know something, we know that we know it. According to Prichard, "When we know something we either do, or by reflecting, can know that our condition is one of knowing that thing. . . ."[46] It may not be immediately obvious how this controversial claim is related to the distinction between strong and weak knowledge. For Malcolm, the connection apparently is established in the following way. He says, of Prichard's remark, that it is "worthy of investigation. Can I discover *in myself* whether I know something or merely believe it?"[47] It is clear from this remark that Malcolm is interpreting Prichard's claim as a claim about what we can discover through introspec-

---

44. Hintikka, *Knowledge and Belief,* p. 20. In "Knowledge and Justification," Hilpinen also appears to endorse this distinction and suggests that strong knowledge is relevant to the analysis of 'know' in ordinary usage.

45. Norman Malcolm, "Knowledge and Belief," in *Knowledge and Certainty* (Englewood Cliffs, N.J.: Prentice-Hall, 1963), pp. 58–72.

46. H. A. Prichard, *Knowledge and Perception* (Oxford: Oxford University Press, 1950), p. 88.

47. Malcolm, "Knowledge and Belief," p. 58.

tion ("in myself"). I doubt whether Prichard's remarks should be interpreted in this way, but let us assume, for the sake of argument, that this is Prichard's intention. We then need to specify some characteristic of knowledge such that a person can discover that characteristic by introspection and such that discovery of that characteristic will enable that person to tell whether he has knowledge.

According to Prichard, when we know that h, the reason we also know that we know that h consists in the fact that "we also know that nothing can exist which is incompatible with this fact."[48] According to Malcolm, Prichard is "asserting that nothing that the future might bring could ever count as evidence against the proposition. He is implying that [if a man knows, then] he would not *call* anything 'evidence' against it. He is using 'know' in what I shall call its 'strong' sense. 'Know' is used in this sense when a person's statement 'I know that h is true' implies that the person who makes the statement would look upon nothing whatever as evidence that h is false."[49]

In contrast with this strong sense of 'knowledge', Malcolm characterizes the weak sense as follows: If a man says 'I know that p', then "he did not absolutely exclude the possibility that something could prove it to be false. I shall say that he used 'know' in the 'weak' sense."[50] The distinction between strong and weak knowledge, as Malcolm characterizes it, depends upon what sort of attitude the man has toward his evidence. Whether he has this attitude or not is, presumably, something he can discover by introspection. We can capture this way of making the distinction in the following definitions:

(5.12) S has strong knowledge that h if and only if S has knowledge that h and S is not prepared, at the time, to admit that any future evidence could provide reason to think that h is false.

(5.13) S has weak knowledge that h if and only if S has knowledge that h and S is prepared, at the time, to admit that some future evidence could provide reason to think that h is false.

48. Prichard, *Knowledge and Perception*, p. 90.
49. Malcolm, "Knowledge and Belief," p. 62.
50. Ibid., p. 62.

Defined in this way, the distinction between strong and weak knowledge is not a very interesting one. In both (5.12) and (5.13) it is required that S have *knowledge* that h; the only real distinction drawn is in terms of S's attitude toward future evidence. It hardly seems that this constitutes a genuine distinction between two kinds of *knowledge*. Whether we have strong or weak knowledge will depend upon our idiosyncracies, and that dependence does not seem very important so long as it is always *knowledge* that we can be said to have. Moreover, having knowledge in the strong sense defined by (5.12) has little or nothing to do with whether strong knowledge requires *certainty,* where certainty means that it is not possible that we are mistaken. Nothing follows about the possibility of our being mistaken from the fact that we may not be prepared to admit that any future evidence could provide reason to think that h is false. The only merit that (5.12) appears to have is that it allows us to tell by introspection whether we have the kind of attitude required by strong knowledge or not.

But even an ability to tell by introspection whether we have the kind of attitude required by the definitions of strong and weak knowledge does not guarantee what Prichard wants, namely, that we can tell by introspection whether we have strong *knowledge* or not. We would have to be able to tell whether we have *knowledge,* in addition to telling whether we have the appropriate attitude. Malcolm is aware of this problem, for he remarks: "Reflection can make me realize that I am using 'know" in the strong sense; but can reflection show me that I *know* something in the strong sense (or in the weak)?" He goes on to conclude that "reflection on what I should say if... cannot show me that I *know* something."[51] Given these and other remarks, it appears that Malcolm has in mind a different pair of definitions for strong and weak knowledge. These are:

(5.14) S has strong knowledge that h if and only if S has knowledge that h and it is not possible that any future evidence could provide reason to think that h is false.

(5.15) S has weak knowledge that h if and only if S has knowledge that h and it is possible that some future evidence could provide reason to think that h is false.[52]

51. Ibid., p. 72.
52. This pair of definitions is like the first pair in that the word 'knowledge'

The distinction defined in (5.14) and (5.15) is of interest. If these definitions are adopted, however, there is not much support for Prichard's claim that we can tell, by reflection, whether we have knowledge. There is no reason whatever to think that S can tell by introspection whether it is possible that the future will produce evidence that could provide reason to think h false. Leaving aside Prichard's claim, let us consider the distinction between strong and weak knowledge defined by (5.14) and (5.15). Is this a distinction that we want to recognize? I argue that it is not.

Why might one think that some instances of knowledge are strong and some weak? Malcolm gives several examples of situations in which we would say that S has knowledge, and argues that in some of these we would say that S has knowledge in the weak sense and in the others knowledge in the strong sense. As an example of knowledge in the weak sense, we are given the following.[53] Suppose the question arises whether the creek in Cascadilla Gorge has water flowing in it on a certain day. You claim to know that there is water flowing there, and give as your reasons for belief your knowledge (or belief) that it has just rained heavily and your recollection that you were in the gorge just the other day when there was water flowing in the creek. If we suppose that there is in fact water flowing in the gorge, then it would seem you know that there is. It is certainly *possible,* however, that some further evidence could provide reason to think that there is no water flowing in the creek. Malcolm puts the matter in an unfortunate way by saying, "It certainly *could* have turned out that the gorge was quite dry when you went there, even though you saw it flowing only a few hours before."[54] This further evidence would give reason to think that your claim is mistaken; but it would also show that you did not know to begin with that there was water in the creek. We need an example of some further evidence that would give reason to think the creek is dry but does not entail that the creek is in fact dry. For example, it is possible that on the way to the creek you meet a friend who has just come

occurs on both sides of the equation in each case. There is another way of making the distinction which may be closer to what Malcolm had in mind. This would involve substituting 'justified true belief' for 'knowledge' on the right-hand side of each definition. This change would not greatly affect the points I want to raise in the remainder of this section.

53. Malcolm, "Knowledge and Belief," pp. 59–60.
54. Ibid., pp. 60–61.

from the creek and who tells you mistakenly that it is dry. Assuming that your friend is normally reliable, this testimony would provide reason to think that the creek is not flowing, no matter what your evidence is. Even though you know that the creek is flowing, it is possible you might meet someone who tells you something like this. Hence, your knowledge is weak knowledge.

As an example of strong knowledge Malcolm cites our knowledge that 2 plus 2 equals 4. He argues that our justification for this belief is so impeccable that nothing could *possibly* count as evidence against it. At this point, however, Malcolm's remarks are confused, for he appears to switch from definition (5.14) to definition (5.12) in defense of the claim that our knowledge that 2 plus 2 equals 4 is strong knowledge. Here is what he says about the possibility of further evidence providing reason to think that 2 plus 2 does not equal 4.

> Let us try to suppose, however, that someone whose intelligence I respect argues that certain developments have shown that 2 plus 2 does not equal 4. He writes out a proof of this in which I can find no flaw. Suppose that his demeanor showed me that he was in earnest.... What would be my reaction? I should say "I can't see what is wrong with your proof, but it *is* wrong, because I *know* that 2 plus 2 equals 4." Here I should be using 'know' in its strong sense. I should not admit that any argument or any future development in mathematics could show that it is false that 2 plus 2 equals 4.[55]

The contention that we very well might react in this way to a proof that 2 plus 2 does not equal 4 is irrelevant to the question whether the production of such a proof would provide reasons for thinking 2 plus 2 does not equal 4. We might not take it as providing such reasons, but that does not matter very much. Rather than providing support for the claim that knowledge of simple arithmetic truths is strong knowledge, Malcolm's example appears to provide support for the contrary claim. If someone were to produce the proof that is envisioned, then it is clear that we would have *some* reason to think 2 plus 2 does not equal 4. It is very difficult to imagine what such a proof could look like and perhaps equally difficult to imagine what our reaction would be. But diffi-

55. Ibid., p. 63.

culty in imagining these things does not mean they could not happen. Unless we could find a flaw in the proof or in our proof technique, or some such thing, the situation Malcolm envisions would represent an unresolved quandary and we could not, in such a case, be said to know, or to believe justifiably, that 2 plus 2 equals 4.

If we can imagine such a situation with respect to a hallowed truth of simple arithmetic, then in general, for almost anything we claim to know, we can imagine some set of circumstances that would provide reason for thinking we are wrong in our claim to knowledge. Consequently, the distinction between weak and strong knowledge does not seem to be a fruitful one. Moreover, the general claim that knowledge is, properly speaking, strong knowledge, seems to be false if, as I have suggested, Malcolm's example of strong knowledge turns out not to satisfy his definition. We can, if we wish, retain the distinction between weak and strong knowledge. We can also agree that the extendability thesis is satisfied in cases of strong knowledge. My view is that we have practically no strong knowledge; what we call knowledge in practice is weak knowledge. It is this kind of knowledge that I am concerned to analyze.

10. *An Explication of Indefeasible Justification*

I have construed the intuitive idea behind the defeasibility approach to the analysis of knowledge in terms of approaching an ideally situated state with respect to the reasons one has for believing something. From a given epistemic position, a person might approach such an ideal state to any of a variety of degrees. A person might pick up a bit of information here and a bit there in piecemeal fashion. Ironically, a person will sometimes wind up in a position worse than the one from which he began, even though he has acquired some new information. It is a common fact of experience that a little information often hurts more than it helps, from the point of view of epistemically justified belief. Think, for example, of a man who is fully justified in believing his wife to be faithful until one day he discovers a letter in her desk drawer. The letter begins "My dearest Abigail," proceeds to describe how long it has been since they have seen each other and how the

writer cannot wait until they meet once more, then concludes
"With my deepest love, Alphonse." This bit of information does
serious damage to the husband's justification; but it would be no
damage at all if he only knew that Alphonse is his wife's long-lost
brother, presumed killed in the war, never mentioned in the family, and recently emerged from the jungles of Africa.

Thus, when considering defeasibility in terms of the possible
ways in which a person might move toward a more nearly ideal
epistemic position, we must be wary of restricting attention to
those possibilities that represent piecemeal accumulation of new
information. Hilpinen's proposal fails because it allows for the
possibility that a person's justification might be defeated by acquisition of some arbitrary limited portion of the unpossessed
information. Given such examples as the one involving a rock
thrower, this leniency proves undesirable. The acquisition of
such a limited portion of available new evidence is, we might say,
one extreme on a continuum of ways in which a person could
move toward a more nearly ideal position. The other extreme is
the acquisition of all the additional information available, but this
extreme is, as noted before, only an epistemologist's pipe dream.
We need something in between. Our examples have shown that
only *some* of the possible ways in which a person might move
toward a better epistemic position are relevant to the question
whether a belief is defeasibly justified.

To see what kinds of possible epistemic improvements are relevant to defeasibility, let us consider why it is that the subject's
belief is indefeasibly justified in the example of the rock thrower
but defeasibly justified in the type of case proposed by Gettier. In
Section 3 we considered some proposals by Gilbert Harman. He
points out that in cases like that of the rock thrower, the unpossessed evidence is not evidence that undermines the person's
reasons, but he despairs of accounting for this. We can account
for it by noting an important fact about defeasibility, namely, that
the defeating effect of a bit of counterevidence is itself subject to
defeasibility. This can be made clearer by recalling the analogy
suggested by Chisholm (see Section 5) between defeasibility in
epistemic situations and defeasibility in ethical situations. It is a
common fact of experience that the overriding effect of some
unknown feature of a person's situation with respect to a prima

facie obligation can in turn be overridden by yet another unknown feature. For example, suppose S has a prima facie obligation to pay a debt. Unknown to S, however, the family financial condition has just reached a point at which S is bankrupt and hence no longer able to pay any debts out of the money that was once in the bank. S's prima facie obligation to pay the debt is overridden by this as yet unknown aspect of the situation. But now suppose a wealthy uncle has just died and left the family a whole new fortune. Then, the overriding aspect of the bankruptcy is itself overridden by this new, but as yet unknown, aspect of the situation.

By analogy with this ethical case, let us say that the defeating effect of counterevidence upon a person's reasons is itself subject to defeat.[56] We can then say that a person's belief is defeasibly justified if there is defeating counterevidence such that the defeating effect of this counterevidence is not itself overridden by other aspects of the situation. In the example of the rock-thrower, the subject's justification is not defeasible because, even though there is some counterevidence available (namely, that S will neither see nor hear the window break), its defeating effect is overridden by other aspects of the situation. In the typical Gettier example this is not so. Putting the matter in this way does not yet help us to understand defeasibility, however, for we have simply noted that a prima facie defeat of a justified belief can in turn be defeated.

In the ethical case just considered, the person's prima facie obligation to pay a debt was overridden by the fact that the family had just gone bankrupt, but the overriding effect of the bankruptcy was in turn overridden by the fact that the family had just come into an inheritance. Now imagine that this is in turn overridden. For example, suppose S's spouse has just made some very expensive purchases that eat up the new inheritance. Thus, S's prima facie obligation to pay the debt is once again overridden. This can go on more or less indefinitely, although in any actual situation the unknown features relevant to defeasibility will most likely be few, or at any rate finite. It seems intuitively clear that whether S's prima facie obligation to pay the debt is in fact defeasible or not is dependent upon the final balance of un-

---

56. This idea was suggested to me some time ago by Ralph Slaght.

knowns. It will not do to consider merely the fact that the family has gone bankrupt, nor will it do to consider merely this plus the fact that there has been a new inheritance. If we take the unknowns in this piecemeal fashion, we may be overlooking some further unknown aspect of the situation which nullifies the effect of these unknowns.

In epistemic situations the same considerations hold. If there is counterevidence that overrides a person's reasons, its defeating effect may be overridden by some further unknown evidence whose overriding effect is in turn overridden by yet another unknown body of evidence, and so on indefinitely. As in the ethical case, we must take into account all the unknowns if we are to determine whether a person's belief that h on the basis of a set of reasons, R, is defeasibly justified. The proposal made by Hilpinen fails precisely because he has overlooked this important aspect of defeasibility. Having noted the importance of this aspect, we must now find a way of precisely defining the notion of defeasible justification which will guarantee that all the relevant unknowns are taken into account.

In Section 7 we considered the proposal that defeating counterevidence must be such that S would be justified in believing it to be false. We rejected the analysis of defeasibility incorporating this proposal on the grounds that the conditions given are not sufficient for defeasibly justified belief. We found no reason to think, however, that this proposal does not express a necessary condition for unpossessed evidence to qualify as defeating. Moreover, the wedding example in Sections 5 and 7, in which the cardinal insanely denounces the bishop, would be difficult to account for if we did not impose this requirement. The same is true for unpossessed evidence that might serve to override the defeating effect of another body of evidence. Consequently, it seems that in considering the unknowns with respect to defeasibility we must limit ourselves throughout to true propositions that are unknowns in the sense that the subject has reasons on the basis of which he or she would be justified in believing them false. If q is such a proposition, then it is also the case that there is some *false* proposition, namely not-q, is such that S would be justified in believing it to be *true*.

In most cognitive situations, there are a number of false propositions that we would be justified in believing to be true in addition to whatever true propositions we are or would be justified in believing. A person's epistemic position might improve if all false propositions of this sort were deleted from the corpus of propositions that the person justifiably believes or could believe. Further improvement would result if S came to be in a position such that, for these false propositions, S would be justified in believing their denials. These improvements would require a number of other changes in S's epistemic situation. Suppose, for example, there is some false proposition, q, such that S would be justified in believing q to be true. Then we might imagine that S comes to justifiably believe the denial of q rather than q. For this to happen, S's epistemic situation would have to change in the following ways: S would no longer have reasons such that S would be justified in believing that q, but would instead have reasons such that S justifiably believes not-q; S would no longer believe that q (if S believed q to begin with), but would instead believe not-q; if S's justifiably believing some further proposition r were essentially dependent upon justifiably believing that q, then (unless S acquires some new reasons for believing that r) S would no longer justifiably believe that r; and so forth. There are many different ways in which one's epistemic situation might thus have been different. Some would involve radical changes, whereas others would involve only small changes in the actual world. We can imagine a class of ways in which a person's epistemic situation might change with respect to believing that q such that each member of this class involves only a minimum of changes in S's total epistemic situation. We can say that a *minimal* way of changing a person's epistemic situation with respect to believing that q is one that makes the fewest changes required, under the circumstances, given that S's belief that q is to lose its justificatory status and its denial is to come to be a proposition that S would be justified in believing true. An example will make this clearer.

Suppose Sam justifiably believes that his birthdate is July 16, 1940, but his birthdate is in fact July 6, 1940. His reasons for believing this false proposition include the justified belief that his mother and father told him that his birthdate was July 16, 1940, the justified belief that this date appears on all his school records, and so forth. There are several ways in which Sam's belief might lose its justified status: he might have a look at the hospital records, or his grandmother might remember and tell him the correct date, or the correct date might be discovered during a government security check, or any of a number of other things. For each of these ways in which his epistemic situation might change, there are radical versions and minimal versions. A minimal version for each possible way in which his situation might change would be one that requires the fewest changes in order to preserve his total epistemic situation. Suppose Sam has a look at the actual hospital records. This might be such a shock to him that he becomes a skeptic with respect to everything, in which case we would have a radical change in his epistemic situation. On the other hand, suppose when he looks at the hospital records he simply comes to believe that he has been mistaken all this time about his birthdate and that his parents also were mistaken; in this case his epistemic situation changes only to the point required to bring everything into line with this new information. This would be a minimal change in his epistemic situation.

Let us now extend this to a case in which a person's epistemic position changes with respect to every false proposition that is in fact justifiably believed to be true. Once again there are many ways in which such a change in a person's epistemic situation could come about, although each of these ways would be enormously more complicated than in the simple example above. And once again, for each of these ways there are also minimal versions. By considering such possible changes in a person's epistemic situation we can define the notion of defeasibility. We can say that S's belief that h is indefeasibly justified just in case every minimal way in which S's epistemic position could change with respect to false propositions that S justifiably believes true would leave S's belief that h justified. Instead of considering how a person's epistemic situation might change, we should instead consider how that person's situation might have been different, in order to avoid problems about the passage of time. To begin, we might propose the following definition of indefeasible justification:

(5.16) S's belief that h is indefeasibly justified iff:

(1) S's belief that h is epistemically justified; and
(2) S's belief that h would have been epistemically justified if
   (a) for every false proposition, q, such that S would be epistemically justified in believing q to be true, S had instead justifiably believed q to be false; and
   (b) S's epistemic situation had otherwise been the same except for some minimal set of changes given (a).

This conception of defeasibility lies between the proposal suggested in (5.11) and the extreme situation in which S would have had all the available unknown evidence. By this definition, S's belief that h is indefeasible just in case S's epistemic situation could have been better with respect to false propositions that S would be justified in believing true without S's losing the justified belief that h. This way of explicating defeasibility is close to being correct, as can be seen by reconsidering some of our examples.

In the Gettier example in which a man looks at a clock that is broken and happens to have stopped on the correct time, the man justifiably believes that the clock is working properly, for it has always worked properly in the past. He therefore justifiably believes that the time is what the clock indicates. But he does not know what time it is, for his justification is defective. According to our definition of defeasibility, we can see that his belief is defeasibly justified by first isolating those false propositions that he would be justified in believing true. We do not need to consider all of them, for the following will illustrate the point:

   (a) the clock is working properly.

Now imagine that the subject's epistemic situation had been different in some way such that he justifiably believed the denial of this proposition. We might suppose, for example, that he had inspected the clock and had discovered that it is not working. Then, if his situation had been otherwise different in a way that represents a minimal change relative to what we have just imagined, it is not difficult to see that believing that the time is what the clock indicates would not then have been epistemically justified. In addition, there do not appear to be any other false propositions that our subject would be justified in believing to be true and that would, if his situation had been different in the way prescribed by (5.16), override the defeating effect of the proposition (a). If there were, then in the alternative situation the man would still justifiably believe that the time is what the clock indicates. Hence, his justification is defeasible in accordance with our definition, and we get the correct result, in accordance with our projected revision of (IDK), that this man does not know what time it is.

Now consider a variation in which we would say the man knows what time it is. In this case the subject not only looks at a clock that is not working, but also looks at his wristwatch, which is working properly. We suppose that he justifiably believes of each of these timepieces that it is working properly, and that each indicates the correct time. Then suppose his situation had been different in the same way as in the previous version of the example; that is, he has inspected the broken clock and has found that it is broken. Even so, he would still be justified in believing that the time is what the clock indicates, for we must also imagine that he retains his justified belief that his wristwatch is working properly. If we did not imagine this, we would be in violation of the injunction to imagine only some minimal set of changes required to maintain the epistemic state of affairs, given that false propositions are deleted from the ranks of the justifiably believed. Once again our definition gives the correct result.

Now consider the example of the rock thrower used against Hilpinen's proposal (5.11) above, a case in which we would say S knows that h, but in which (5.11) gives the wrong result. I argue that, according to our definition (5.16), S's justification is indefeasible in this example. As in the previous example, there are a number of false propositions that S would be justified in believing to be true. The important ones are the following:

(b) S will see the window break.
(c) S will hear the window break.
(d) S's sensory mechanisms will continue to function properly.

Because each of these propositions is false, we are to imagine that *S* has instead justifiably believed their denials:

(b′)   *S* will not see the window break.
(c′)   *S* will not hear the window break.
(d′)   *S*'s sensory mechanisms will not continue to function properly.

We then imagine that *S*'s epistemic situation had been different in some minimal way relative to these changes. On any such minimal change, *S*'s belief that the rock will hit the window and *S*'s belief that the window is a normal window would still have been epistemically justified. It is clear that in this alternative situation, it would still be the case that *S* justifiably believes that the window will break: even though *S*'s reasons would include the counterevidence (b′) and (c′), *S* would also have reasons for justifiably believing (d′), and this justified belief nullifies the defeating effect of the counterevidence. If we suppose there are no other false propositions that *S* would be justified in believing to be true which are relevant here, then we may conclude that *S*'s justification is indefeasible and that *S* has knowledge. Once again we get the desired result by incorporating our defined notion of defeasibility into the conditions for factual knowledge.

Perhaps these representative examples will suffice to show that an analysis of knowing which incorporates this conception of defeasibility is adequate to handle the various cases considered so far. Nevertheless, our definition of defeasibility still fails to take into account an important aspect of the notion of defeasibility. To see this, let us recall that the difference between the Gettier cases and the case of the rock thrower is that in the latter the defeating effect of the available counterevidence is in turn overridden, whereas in the Russell-Gettier cases this is not so. There are, however, variations on the Gettier cases wherein, according to our definition, the defeating effect of the available counterevidence is also overridden even though *S* does not have knowledge. All our definition (5.16) requires for indefeasibility is that in the imagined alternative situation *S* would be justified in believing that *h*. There is, however, no stipulation that the reasons upon which *S*'s belief would be based in the alternative world would be the same as those upon which S's belief is based in the actual world. But clearly, it is essential that this be so.

To see this, let us reconsider the case proposed by Gettier, in which Jones justifiably believes that the man who will be the next vice-president has ten coins in his pocket.[57] Now let us consider a variation on this Gettier case. Suppose everything is as before, except that for some reason Jones happens to know that Smith (the man who is really going to get the job) has ten coins in his pocket. In the epistemically improved alternative situation, Jones will justifiably believe that Smith will get the job (for he in fact would be justified in believing that Smith will not get the job) and will also justifiably believe that Smith has ten coins in his pocket. These facts guarantee that Jones would, in the alternative situation, justifiably believe that h (the man who will get the job has ten coins in his pocket). According to our definition, Jones's justification for believing that h would thus be indefeasible, and he would have knowledge. But neither of these things is so.

This argument against the definition (5.16) brings out the fact that a belief is defeasibly or indefeasibly justified only relative to a *particular* set of reasons upon which that belief is based. The fact that a person might become more ideally situated by coming to have new reasons upon which the belief that h would be justified is irrelevant to the question whether the belief is indefeasibly justified. We must require that the subject's actual reasons would continue to hold in the more ideal situation if a belief that is based upon those reasons is to be indefeasibly justified. In the case of the rock thrower it is clear that even if the subject had been more ideally situated the reasons for which he would justifiably believe that the window will break would have been essentially the same as those that actually obtain. But in the revised Gettier case just considered, Jones's reasons would have been replaced by others in the imagined alternative situation.

We must be cautious about the manner in which we express the indicated requirement. It will not do to require that the subject's reasons be exactly preserved in the alternative situation if a belief is to be indefeasibly justified. We must allow for certain differences. First, as noted earlier, a person's belief can be justified even though it is based upon a set of reasons which includes some

57. This example was quoted on pp. 142–143 above.

false beliefs, provided that these false beliefs are not essential to the justificatory status of the belief in question. The notion of essentiality involved here was characterized in Chapter Four on page 120. There is no prima facie reason why such a belief cannot also be indefeasibly justified. When we move to the alternative situation required for determining defeasibility, however, any false beliefs will no longer be among the subject's reasons. Second, in many cognitive situations, particularly those in which a person's belief is indefeasibly justified, the reasons for which the belief is justified will be augmented, but not wholly replaced, by some new reasons in the alternative situation.

In order to rule out the revised Gettier counterexample but allow for the facts just discussed, I introduce the notion of one set of reasons being essentially the same as another with respect to the justification of a specific belief:

(ESR) The set of reasons R' is essentially the same as the set of reasons R with respect to justified belief that h (by person S with relevant characteristics C) iff: some subset of R' is identical with that subset of R which results from the deletion from R of all members that are inessential to justifiably believing that h (for person S with relevant characteristics C).

Given this, I propose the following definition of indefeasibly justified belief:

(DIJ) S's believing that h on the basis of R is indefeasibly justified at t iff:
   (1) S's believing that h on the basis of R is epistemically justified at t; and
   (2) S's belief that h would have been epistemically justified and would have been based upon essentially the same set of reasons as in the actual world if
      (a) for every false proposition, q, such that S would be epistemically justified in believing q to be true, S had instead justifiably believed q to be false; and
      (b) S's epistemic situation had otherwise been the same except for some minimal set of changes given (a).

In the revised Gettier case above, even though Jones's belief that
h would be epistemically justified if clauses (a) and (b) of (2) were
satisfied, this belief would not be based upon essentially the same
set of reasons as in the actual world. Hence, we get the correct
result in that example.

The definition allows, however, for the kinds of changes in the
subject's set of reasons which were mentioned above. It is compatible with the definition that any false beliefs upon which the
belief that h is based would be missing in the alternative situation,
for the resulting set of reasons may remain essentially the same. It
is also compatible with the definition that S's set of reasons
would be augmented by some new ones in the alternative situation, for S's belief that h can still be based upon the old set of
reasons even though it is *also* based upon some new ones.

This completes my account of defective justification. Given the
definition (DIJ) of indefeasible justification, we may say that a
belief is defectively justified just in case it is defeasibly justified,
and nondefectively justified just in case it is indefeasibly justified.
Moreover, we are now in a position to complete the incomplete
definition (IDK) of factual knowledge.

(DKD) A person, S, has factual knowledge that h at a time, t, iff:
there is some set of reasons, R, such that
  (1) S's belief that h is based upon R at t; and
  (2) S's believing that h on the basis of R is indefeasibly
       justified at t; and
  (3) if, at t, S has any other reasons, R', that are relevant
       to justifiably believing that h, then S would be epis-
       temically justified in believing that h on the basis of R
       $\cup$ R' at t.

I call this the *defeasibility analysis* of knowledge. The conditions
presented in (DKD) differ somewhat from those in the earlier
definition (IDK) in that conditions (1), (2), and (3b) of (IDK) have
been deleted. This is only a move toward economy of expression,
however, for satisfaction of the requirements imposed by those
earlier conditions is guaranteed by the conditions of (DKD). Condition (1) of (IDK) requires that it be the case that h if S is to
know that h. Condtion (2) of (DKD) guarantees this to be so, for if
h is not the case, then it is clear that S's believing that h on the

basis of some set of reasons, R, would be defeasibly justified. Condition (2) of (IDK) requires that S believe that h if S is to know that h. This is guaranteed by condition (1) of (DKD), for a person's belief cannot be based upon a set of reasons if that person does not have the belief in question. Finally, condition (3b) of (IDK) requires that S's belief that h on the basis of R be epistemically justified if S is to have knowledge that h. Given the definition (DIJ) of indefeasible justification, this condition is also guaranteed by condition (2) of (DKD).

11. *Summary and Concluding Remarks*

In this chapter I have developed the defeasibility analysis of knowledge. This analysis emerges as a response to the problem of defective justification, which I have developed in early sections of the chapter along with a number of other lines of solution.[58] I believe the defeasibility account is both superior to these other solutions and adequate as an account of knowledge. If so, then we could consider the main task of this book to be completed. One of my purposes, however, is to provide an account of knowledge in terms of the causal ancestry of a person's beliefs and reasons. Part of this causal account has already been provided in the discussion of reasons and the basing relation. Moreover, as I noted at the end of the preceding chapter, my account of epistemic justification is based upon assumptions about the place of human beings in the causal order of things. In the next chapter I return to causal themes and introduce another account of knowledge, one that emphasizes causal ancestries, and is integrated with the extant account of reasons, reason-based belief, and justification. This causal account of knowledge is not suggested as a competitor of the defeasibility view; rather, it is suggested as a refinement of the defeasibility analysis, and the insights in this chapter into defective justification will help with the tasks ahead.

58. There are still other proposed solutions that I have not discussed. Many of these are variations on themes already discussed, and some may themselves be adequate solutions to the problem. I recommend especially Roderick Chisholm, *Theory of Knowledge,* 2d ed. (Englewood Cliffs, N.J.: Prentice-Hall, 1977), chapter 6; Peter Klein, "Knowledge, Causality, and Defeasibility," *Journal of Philosophy* 73 (1976): 792–812; Keith Lehrer, *Knowledge* (Oxford: Oxford University Press, 1974), chapter 9; and Sosa, "How Do You Know?"

REASONS, CAUSES, AND KNOWLEDGE

Although the account of knowledge and justification suggested in the preceding chapters is adequate as an analysis, it remains silent with respect to at least two important considerations. First, our analysis does not tell us much about the origins of human factual knowledge. Second, it does not indicate the dependency relations that hold among various instances of knowledge. In this chapter I shall develop a different account of knowledge, an account that emphasizes both the origins and the structural dependency of knowledge. This new account does not conflict with the one developed thus far; it is only a more precise formulation of the defeasibility view. The account does, however, introduce a consideration not previously employed in our discussion, namely, consideration of the causal ancestry of the reasons upon which a belief is based. Chapter Three presented a causal theory of the basing relation. According to that theory, a belief is based upon a set of reasons if and only if each member of that set of reasons bears some appropriate causal connection to the belief in question. This chapter introduces consideration of the causal origins of reason states themselves. It is my contention that all factual knowledge is ultimately dependent upon the character and quality of the causal ancestries of some of the reason states upon which some of our beliefs are based. The purpose of this chapter is to provide an account of knowledge that makes the structure of this dependency clear.

1. *Primary versus Secondary Knowledge*

According to the account I shall develop in this chapter, all factual knowledge lies within one of two major types of knowledge, *primary* and *secondary*. This section provides examples of each kind and a rough (but unsatisfactory) characterization of the distinction. Succeeding sections will provide precise definitions of each kind of knowledge; these definitions will, among other things, exhibit the ways in which instances of knowledge are dependent upon one another.

One pillar of the traditional empiricist orientation is the claim that all human knowledge arises ultimately from experience. Our experience both of the world around us and of our introspectively available states is a crucial ingredient in our coming to know anything. The primary mechanism of experience is perception, and perception is a causal process. By perceiving various events and states of affairs we sometimes come to know that those events are occurring (have occurred) or that those states of affairs obtain (have obtained). In such a case, the event or state of affairs of which we come to have knowledge is itself an ingredient in the causal ancestry of our coming to know. There is, for example, a yellow cup on my desk while I am writing these words. I am perceiving the cup, and I know that there is a cup on my desk. The event or state of affairs of there being a yellow cup on my desk is itself a member of a causal chain that is now resulting in my believing, and hence in my knowing, that there is a yellow cup there. My knowing that there is a yellow cup on my desk is an instance of what I call *primary* knowledge. Such knowledge may be roughly characterized as knowledge of propositions that designate specific events or states of affairs. In this instance the proposition known is the proposition that there is a yellow cup on my desk, and the state of affairs designated by this proposition is the state of affairs of there being a yellow cup on my desk. This is, as we have noted, also an example in which I am *perceiving* the yellow cup to be on my desk. Not all instances of primary knowledge are of this sort. For example, suppose I come to believe that this cup on my desk was made on a potter's wheel, and suppose this belief is an instance of knowledge. Then the known proposition is the proposition that this cup was made on a potter's wheel, and the event designated by this proposition is the event of the cup's having been made on a potter's wheel. This event, however, is not one that I am perceiving. It is an event that occurred some time ago, and I am now perceiving one of its effects, namely, the cup's being on my desk at this time.

In contrast to instances of primary knowledge are instances of what I call *secondary* knowledge. Simply put, secondary knowledge is knowledge of propositions that do not designate specific events or states of affairs. For example, many people know that all whales are mammals. The proposition that all whales are mammals does not, however, designate a specific event or state of affairs. Similarly, some people know that, necessarily, 2 plus 2 equals 4, but the proposition known does not designate a specific event or state of affairs. Other examples include knowledge that it is possible it will rain tomorrow, knowledge that the frequency of female births within the class of human births is slightly greater than the frequency of male births, and the knowledge that knowledge is hard to come by.

Given this rough characterization of the distinction between primary and secondary knowledge, I can now formulate a few general claims that partially characterize the account of knowledge to be developed in this chapter. One claim is:

(6.1) Every instance of human factual knowledge is either an instance of primary knowledge or an instance of secondary knowledge.

Another, more controversial, claim is:

(6.2) Every instance of secondary knowledge is ultimately dependent upon some instance or instances of primary knowledge.

What I mean by 'dependent upon' and 'ultimately' will become clear when the details of the account have been presented. On an intuitive level, the claim made in (6.2) can be illustrated by considering an instance of general knowledge, such as the knowledge that all whales are mammals. According to (6.2), and given the rough characterization of primary and secondary knowledge, a person can know that all whales are mammals only if that person has *some* knowledge of specific events and states of affairs. This requirement might be satisfied, for example, if a person has perceived various whales and has perceived them to have characteristics that the person knows to be mammalian. The primary knowledge involved would include, for example, the knowledge that whale W has characteristics M. There are other ways in which this requirement might be satisfied: a person might never have perceived a single whale but might have seen detailed pictures of whales, might have read about whales in a book written by someone who has perceived whales, or might have heard that all whales are mammals from some authoritative teacher. In all these cases there is *some* primary knowledge involved (for example, the knowledge that a picture is a picture of a whale).

A third general claim that characterizes my view may be expressed in this way:

(6.3)   Every instance of primary knowledge is dependent upon the character and quality of the causal ancestry of some of the reasons upon which it is based.

The greater portion of this chapter will be devoted to elucidating and defending this general claim. A related claim is:

(6.4)   Every instance of secondary knowledge is ultimately dependent upon the character and quality of the causal ancestries of some instances of primary knowledge.

(6.3) and (6.4) together constitute my version of the traditional empiricist view that all human knowledge ultimately arises from experience. A defense of this claim can be provided only after the details of my view have been presented.

I have roughly characterized the distinction between primary and secondary knowledge in terms of propositions that designate specific events or states of affairs in contrast to those that do not. Various considerations, however, suggest that this rough characterization is unsatisfactory. First, I have claimed without argument that the known propositions involved in my examples of secondary knowledge are not propositions that designate specific events or states of affairs. Someone might object to this claim on the grounds that, for example, the proposition that all whales are mammals designates the specific state of affairs of all whales' being mammals. Rather than argue the point, which seems dubious to me, I shall simply point out that what I have in mind when I speak of primary knowledge is knowledge of propositions that designate *causally efficacious, spatiotemporally located,* specific events or states of affairs. Let us say that an event is causally efficacious just in case it is, or could be, a cause or an effect in some causal chain. I shall assume, as in Chapter Two, that such events are spatiotemporally located individuals. If there is such a specific state of affairs as the state of all whales' being mammals, it surely is neither causally efficacious nor is it spatiotemporally located.

Second, a proposition might designate a causally efficacious, spatiotemporally located event or state of affairs yet not be an object of primary knowledge. This can happen because some propositions have multiple designation. Suppose, for example, I know that there is a yellow cup on my desk, and suppose I also know that all whales are mammals. Then I may also know the conjunctive proposition that there is a yellow cup on my desk *and* all whales are mammals.[1] This conjunctive proposition designates whatever is designated by either of its conjuncts. Via its first conjunct, it designates a causally efficacious, spatiotemporally located specific event or state of affairs; but it also designates whatever is designated by its second conjunct, which is not a causally efficacious, spatiotemporally located specific event or state of affairs. According to the rough characterization of primary knowledge, my knowledge of this conjunctive proposition would be an instance of primary knowledge. For reasons that will become clear later, this result does not suit my purposes. What I have in mind when I speak of primary knowledge is knowledge of propositions that designate *only* causally efficacious, spatiotemporally located specific events or states of affairs.

Shall I say, then, that primary knowledge is knowledge of *nonconjunctive* propositions that designate only causally efficacious, spatiotemporally located events or states of affairs? Unfortunately, not even this cumbersome characterization of primary knowledge will serve. Most of the known propositions that are objects of what I call primary knowledge are not such that they designate only causally efficacious, spatiotemporally located events or states of affairs. Consider the proposition that there is a yellow cup on my desk. In addition to designating the appropriate

1. Some philosophers would make a stronger claim than this, for they believe that a conjunction principle holds for knowledge. According to this principle, if S knows that p and also knows that q, then S knows that p & q. Because a person may simply fail to make a connection among the things he knows, I find this principle suspect. See the discussion of the conjunction principle for justification on page 123 of Chapter Four.

kind of state of affairs (the yellow cup's being on my desk), this proposition also designates the cup and the desk. These are individuals, not events or states.[2] This problem could be dealt with by changing the requirement so that a nonconjunctive proposition is an object of primary knowledge only if the only events or states of affairs designated by that proposition are causally efficacious, spatiotemporally located ones. Even thus modified, however, this characterization of primary knowledge will not suffice. Given the definitions of primary and secondary knowledge to be introduced in later sections, it is possible that a conjunctive proposition can be an object of primary knowledge. Moreover, in accordance with those definitions, some nonconjunctive compound propositions (such as disjunctions, negations, and conditionals) that otherwise satisfy this characterization of primary knowledge turn out to be instances of secondary knowledge.

The essential problem with the rough distinction between primary and secondary knowledge is its attempt to formulate the distinction both in terms of the kinds of propositions known and in terms of what they do or do not designate. The distinction does not ultimately rest on such considerations. Rather, the distinction rests on considerations of the conditions under which a belief is epistemically justified and on considerations of the dependencies that hold among instances of knowledge. Once the definitions of primary and secondary knowledge have been introduced, then the extensions of the terms 'primary knowledge' and 'secondary knowledge' will simply be the classes of instances of knowledge that satisfy the respective definitions. As far as I can determine, the extensions of these terms, as defined, are not necessarily the same as the extensions of any philosophically interesting pair of descriptions of the propositions known in terms of form or designation. Thus, the rough characterization of primary and secondary knowledge should be taken only as an initial attempt at pointing to a distinction that is otherwise probably unfamiliar to the reader. Some additional general claims that characterize my view may be brought forth at this time. One is this:

2. In Chapter Two I adopted the view that events and states of affairs are spatiotemporally located particulars; so I am not suggesting that events and states of affairs are not themselves individuals.

(6.5)   A proposition, *P,* is an object of primary knowledge *only if* *P* designates some event or state of affairs and every event or state of affairs designated by *P* is a causally efficacious, spatiotemporally located specific event or state of affairs.

Although I cannot formulate a characterization of primary and secondary knowledge solely in terms of kinds of proposition and what they designate, my definition of primary knowledge entails the necessary condition expressed in (6.5). Primary knowledge is restricted to knowledge of propositions of the appropriate sort. The following general claim is also true of the view that I shall present:

(6.6)   Some propositions which are such that every event or state of affairs designated by that proposition is a causally efficacious, spatiotemporally located specific event or state of affairs may be objects of secondary knowledge.

Although primary knowledge is restricted to knowledge of propositions of a certain sort, knowledge of propositions of that sort is not restricted (by definition at least) to primary knowledge. Given (6.2), however, any such knowledge will ultimately be dependent upon some instance, or instances, of primary knowledge. Finally, let us note this general claim:

(6.7)   Every known proposition, *P,* such that either *P* does not designate any event or state of affairs or it is false that every event or state of affairs designated by *P* is a causally efficacious, spatiotemporally located specific event or state of affairs, is an object of secondary knowledge.

The claim expressed in (6.7) follows from those expressed in (6.1) and (6.5). I have displayed this claim primarily to help the reader locate the realms of primary and secondary knowledge prior to the actual definition of these notions.

With these preliminary considerations out of the way, I turn to the task of defining primary knowledge, which will occupy the next few sections. Once primary knowledge has been defined, I shall turn to a consideration of secondary knowledge and to a defense of the general claims above.

2. *Primary Knowledge and Causal Connections*

In Chapter One I introduced a version of the traditional analysis of knowledge and have maintained that the conditions contained in that analysis are necessary for factual knowledge. In developing a definition of primary knowledge I again take the conditions of the traditional analysis as necessary. This yields the following incomplete definition of primary knowledge:

(IDPK) A person, S, has primary factual knowledge that h at t iff:

    (1) h; and

    (2) S believes that h at t; and

    (3)   there is some set of reasons, R, such that

        (a) S's belief that h is based upon R at t; and

        (b) S's believing that h on the basis of R is epistemically justified at t; and

        (c)   if, at t, S has any other reasons, R', that are relevant to whether S is epistemically justified in believing that h, then S would be epistemically justified in believing that h on the basis of $R \cup R'$ at t.

The conditions expressed here are the same as those in (IDK) of Chapter One. The analyses, suggested in Chapters Three and Four, of the crucial concepts of basing and of epistemic justification should be assumed in the present effort to define primary knowledge. In Chapter Five, I argued for a set of conditions consisting of a subset of those in (IDPK) with the addition of an indefeasibility requirement. The main difference between the account of knowledge suggested in Chapter Five and the account of primary knowledge to be developed here consists in the replacement of the defeasibility condition with another condition having to do with the causal ancestries of the subject's reason states. Of course, the definition of primary knowledge also has a considerably narrower scope than the general definition suggested in Chapter Five, for not all instances of knowledge are instances of primary knowledge. With these considerations noted, I turn to some preliminary concerns about causation and primary knowledge.

When a person justifiably believes that h on the basis of a set of reasons, R, this set of reasons will typically consist of *local* and *background* reasons. Background reasons consist of general beliefs arrived at on the basis of past experience, beliefs concerning the reliability of any witnesses involved, and other beliefs that tend to remain invariant from case to case. Local reasons are those that are peculiar to the specific proposition, h, in question. For example, if I am observing a dynamite explosion, my local reasons for believing that this explosion is occurring will consist in part of certain visual and auditory perceptual states. My background reasons will consist of general beliefs concerning explosions, some of which may be based upon my own experiences of prior explosions, and others on spoken or written testimony about explosions. Both types of reasons are essential to my being justified.

In many cases, such as the one just considered, our local reasons consist of perceptual states that result from direct observation of the event or state of affairs known. In such cases, there is a straightforward causal chain between the event, H, and the states that constitute the local reasons for which we believe that h.[3] Typically, however, there is no causal chain between the event, H, and our background reasons for believing that h. The latter are typically the causal result of past experience.

Similarly, we often come to know of an event, H, by observing an effect of H, even though we have not observed H itself. I might, for example, come to know that the fuse has been ignited by observing the explosion even though I did not observe the igniting of the fuse. In both cases there is a causal chain between the event, H, and the states that constitute our local reasons. Moreover, in both cases, it is necessary for primary knowledge that there be such a causal chain. I might, for example, hallucinate in such a way that I seem to see the explosion at the very time when it is occurring. Then, even though I would have the same or very similar reasons for believing as when I am actually observing the explosion, I do not know that the explosion is occurring because there is no causal chain.

The type of causal connection illustrated in these examples is

---

3. See definition (DCC) on page 55 of Chapter Two for a definition of the concept of a causal chain.

not the only type relevant to primary knowledge. Often we come to know of some event, H, by observing another event that is part of a causal chain leading to H. A typical example is our knowledge of events that have not yet occurred. Similarly, we often come to know of some event, H, by observing another event, Q, which is an effect of some event that is a common cause of H and Q. Examples involving barometers and rainstorms are typical illustrations of this kind of situation.

Still another type of causal connection is relevant to primary knowledge. We sometimes observe an event or state of affairs which is not actually a cause of H but a pseudo overdeterminant instead.[4] For example, if I observe a person taking a dose of a powerful poison, then I may know that this person will die even if the death is actually the result of some other causal chain.

These kinds of causal connections exhaust the possibilities. A crucial part of my causal account of primary knowledge is the claim that it is a *necessary* condition for such knowledge that at least one such causal connection obtain between the event, H, and the reason states that constitute the *local* reasons upon which the belief that h is based. This causal connection requirement does not hold, however, for any background reasons upon which the belief that h may also be based. As we have noted above, one's background reasons normally will be based upon past experiences. There are, nevertheless, some built-in constraints upon background reasons, for background reasons are beliefs. Given the account of epistemically justified belief in Chapter Four, if S's belief that h on the basis of the set of reasons R is to be epistemically justified, then any belief states in R must also be epistemically justified. Hence, background reasons (beliefs) must be epistemically justified. The same constraint holds for any belief states that might be among S's *local* reasons for believing that h.

Assuming the conditions already specified in (IDPK), we may express the causal connection requirement by adding another condition, (d), to clause (3). I state (d) provisionally as follows:

(3d) For that subset, L, of R which consists of the local reasons upon which S's belief that h is based, each member, r_j, of L is such that *either*

4. See definition (DPO) on page 70 of Chapter Two for a definition of the relation of pseudo overdetermination.

(A)   there is a causal chain from H to r_j;

or (B)   there is some event or state of affairs Q such that
       (i)   there is a causal chain from Q to r_j; and
      (ii)   there is a causal chain from Q to H;

or (C)   there is some event or state of affairs, P, such that
       (i)   there is a causal chain from P to r_j; and
      (ii) P is a pseudo overdeterminant of H.

According to (3d), it is a necessary condition of primary knowledge that at least one of the kinds of causal connections referred to in (A), (B), or (C) obtain between the event, H, and one's local reason states. As we shall soon see, the addition of (3d) to the conditions in (IDPK) does not yield a set of conditions sufficient for primary knowledge, and it will be a considerable task to generate a set of conditions that are sufficient. Before turning to those considerations, however, I want to dispel two objections that may arise at this point.

First, some will object even to the necessity of the conditions in (3d). According to this kind of objection, only a person's reason states and relevant characteristics at a time, t, are important in determining whether that person has knowledge at the time t. It does not matter how a person has come to have the reasons upon which the belief is based. Causal connections of the sort referred to in (3d) are irrelevant to knowledge. Various fanciful examples may be devised in support of this objection. One such example involves what we might call a causally insulated being. Imagine a being that is in many respects just like a human being, having arms, legs, eyes, a body, the ability to speak, and so forth. If you were to see this being walking down the street, you would take it for a human. Moreover, this being has a mental life very much like that of an average human; it seems to see, hear, taste, and smell various things; feels pain; has beliefs, emotions, and the ability to reason; and has dreams during sleep. This being is radically unlike any human being, however, in that it is perceptually insulated from the world around it. Although this being has eyes, ears, and so forth, and although it has what appears to be an ordinary afferent-efferent nervous system, these pieces of equipment are in fact totally inactive causally. But through a remarkable total coincidence, the mental life of this being mirrors the world around it in such a way that it seems to see, hear, etc., just what a causally receptive human being would seem to hear, see, etc., under similar circumstances. Thus, if a yellow cup is on the desk in front of this being, it will seem to see a yellow cup; if this being were to reach out and "touch" the cup, it would seem to feel the cup; and so forth. Moreover, if you were to speak to this being, it would seem to hear you and would in fact respond in such a way that you would have no reason to suppose that you are dealing with a causally insulated entity. Now the question is, would we ascribe any knowledge to such an entity? In some respects this entity is epistemically similar to a human being. For example, it comes to have beliefs on the *basis* of reason states in the same causal ways as human beings. Moreover, some of its beliefs may be epistemically justified. Indeed, such an entity would be entitled to the status of knower with respect to *some* propositions, such as the proposition that it seems to see something yellow, and perhaps also certain mathematical and logical truths. The crucial question is, does such an entity have primary knowledge of external events or states of affairs? Would we say of this entity that it knows that there is a yellow cup on the desk? I assume that those who would argue against the relevance of causal connections of the sort referred to in condition (3d) would allow that this entity has such knowledge. With the exception of the fact that this entity is causally insulated from the external world, its mental life is just like the mental life of those human beings to whom we would ascribe knowledge that there is a yellow cup on the table. What other difference is there that would make a difference? And yet it seems obvious to me that this causally insulated entity does not have knowledge that there is a yellow cup on the table. Despite the remarkable coincidence between this entity's mental life and the events of the external world, it is, after all, just a coincidence. The fact that it is altogether accidental that this entity is correct in any of its beliefs about external events or states of affairs is sufficient to show that there is no knowledge. Moreover, because the only relevant difference between this entity and normal human beings involves the assumption of causal insulation, I take it that the example shows that some appropriate causal connection is necessary for primary knowledge. Strictly speaking, the example does not show that the kinds of causal connections referred to in condition (3d) are necessary for primary knowledge. I claim, however, that these are the relevant kinds of connections; if someone thinks that some other connections are the relevant ones, I invite that person to show what they are.

The example above is, of course, totally incredible. The other example is only somewhat less bizarre, but it is a kind that has been introduced in discussions of causal accounts of knowledge. Let us again suppose an entity whose mental life accurately reflects the events of the external world in much the way that a normal human being's typically does, but, like our causally insulated entity, there is no causal connection of the usual sort between reason states and external events. Rather, there exists a supreme being who has (for some reason) brought it about that this entity will seem to see a yellow cup if there is one on the desk before it, will seem to hear your voice if you speak to it, and so forth.[5] Moreover, this entity will go about forming beliefs and behaving just as a normal human would. Must we then grant that this being has whatever knowledge a normal human being has concerning the external world? If a supreme being has guaranteed that this entity will come to have all the right beliefs, it is not accidental or coincidental that this entity is right about there being a yellow cup on the desk. The case for knowledge is more convincing in this example than in the previous one. However, because it also seems that the causal connection requirement is satisfied, this is no counterexample to (3d). There are several possibilities to consider. Is this supreme being such that it is causally responsible (perhaps in some ultimate ancestral fashion) for the yellow cup's being on the desk and also causally responsible for the entity's seeming to see a yellow cup? If so, condition (B) of (3d) is satisfied. If this supreme being is not causally responsible (even ancestrally) for the yellow cup's being on the desk, then how does it *know* that the yellow cup is on the desk, and thus know to coordinate our entity's mental life with this fact? Presumably this knowledge will be the result of some sort of causal connection; if it is, then one of the conditions in (3d) will be satisfied, and if not, I would again deny that our peculiar entity

5. Such a bizarre being would be somewhat like a Leibnizian monad, in that its internal states would be preestablished to harmonize with events around it.

has knowledge. No matter which incredible consideration we choose, I see no convincing reason to abandon the causal connection requirement formulated in (3d).

These fanciful efforts to devise counterexamples to the causal connection requirement constitute the first kind of objection. The second kind of objection to the necessity of a causal connection requirement is less fanciful and goes like this. Some of our knowledge of causally efficacious, temporally located specific events and states of affairs may be such that there is no causal connection of any of the types specified in (3d) between those events or states and the local reasons upon which the appropriate belief is based. Suppose there are two comets that orbit the sun in such a manner that they always pass within sight of the earth five years apart. Whenever the first comet, comet A, passes within sight of the earth, then five years later the second comet, comet B, passes within sight of the earth. Now suppose S comes to have a justified background belief (perhaps on the basis of authority) that this constant regularity holds. On a given day, S observes comet A and comes to have primary knowledge that comet A is within sight of the earth. Given his background belief and his knowledge that comet A is within sight of the earth, he comes to believe correctly that comet B will be within sight of the earth five years hence. We may grant that S knows that this specific, causally efficacious, spatiotemporally located event will occur. There is, however, no causal connection of any of the kinds specified in condition (3d) between this event and S's having his local reasons for believing that it will occur. Because this seems to be knowledge of the sort that I call primary knowledge, and because the causal connection requirement is not satisfied, we may conclude that satisfaction of the causal connection requirement is not necessary for this kind of knowledge.

I will grant that S has knowledge in this example and that the causal connection requirement is not satisfied. Moreover, I will grant that the proposition known is a proposition that designates only a causally efficacious, spatiotemporally located specific event. I do not, however, take this to present a problem for my account of primary knowledge, for this example is an illustration of the claim (6.6) made in Section 1:

(6.6) Some propositions which are such that every event or state of affairs designated by that proposition is a causally efficacious, spatiotemporally located specific event or state of affairs may be objects of secondary knowledge.

We may note also that *S*'s knowledge that comet B will be within sight of the earth five years hence is clearly *dependent* upon *S*'s knowledge that comet A is presently within sight of the earth; hence, this example also illustrates the claim made in (6.2) of Section 1:

(6.2) Every instance of secondary knowledge is ultimately dependent upon some instance or instances of primary knowledge.

These various objections to the necessity of the causal connection requirement are representative of the strongest kinds of objections I know of. I conclude, therefore, that this requirement is a reasonable one. Unfortunately, the requirement formulates only a necessary condition, as we shall see when we consider examples involving peculiar causal chains.

3. *Defective versus Nondefective Causal Chains*

Suppose Milton is in a museum looking at a glass box that contains a valuable vase. Although he does not know it, the surface of the glass box is actually a cleverly constructed television screen. For someone looking at the box, the visual appearances are precisely what they would be if the surface of the box were clear glass and the vase were being directly observed. Moreover, suppose the vase whose image is being televised is the vase that is actually in the box. Milton comes to believe that the vase is in the box on the basis of reasons *R*, and his believing for these reasons is epistemically justified. But he does not know that the vase is in there. The (necessary) conditions presented in (IDPK) above are met, for there is a causal chain from the vase's being in the box to the reason states that constitute Milton's local reasons for believing that the vase is in the box. In this example, even though a required causal connection obtains, it consists of a very unusual causal chain, for even though Milton's belief that there is a vase in the box is epistemically justified, it is *defeasibly* justified from the point of view of knowledge.

Consider another example.[6] Suppose a medical researcher has been studying the causes of a certain nervous disorder. He has examined a large number of persons who have this disorder and has, through judicious testing and application of experimental methods, isolated the presence of a certain chemical C in the brain as the cause of this disorder. Moreover, he is right about his conclusion with respect to each of the patients whom he has examined; in each of them the disorder was caused by the presence of the chemical. Through monumental bad luck, however, the sample consisting of the patients whom he has examined is seriously biased with respect to the total population of those who have the disorder. Indeed, the disorder is commonly caused, not by the presence of chemical C in the brain, but by a virtually undetectable genetic defect—a defect no one knows about. Now suppose the researcher is visited by a new patient who has the disorder. He concludes that the chemical C is present in this patient's brain. Once again, he is correct; in this patient, as in the others he has examined, chemical C is the cause of the disorder. Yet we may not say of the researcher that he knows that this new patient has chemical C in the brain, for his evidence for this conclusion is seriously biased. Unfortunatey, as in the vase example above, the necessary conditions for knowledge suggested in (IDPK) are satisfied. Because the patient does have chemical C in the brain, there is a causal chain from the presence of chemical C to the researcher's local reason states. As in the vase example, even though the researcher's belief is epistemically justified, this belief is defeasibly justified.

These two examples show that the conditions suggested in (IDPK) are not sufficient for primary factual knowledge. In both cases there is a causal connection, as required, but the subject's belief is defeasibly justified. The leading idea in my causal account of primary knowledge is that in such cases the subject's

6. This example is similar to one proposed by J. T. Tolliver in "On Swain's Causal Analysis of Knowledge," in George S. Pappas and Marshall Swain, eds., *Essays on Knowledge and Justification* (Ithaca: Cornell University Press, 1978), pp. 106–108.

belief is rendered defeasible by characteristics of the causal chains involved. These are the causal chains referred to in condition (3d). To handle such cases I shall introduce a distinction between *defective* and *nondefective* causal chains. Before defining this distinction, however, I introduce the following condition, which is intended as a replacement for the provisional condition (d) to be added to our definition of primary knowledge:

(3d)   For that subset, L, of R which consists of the local reasons upon which S's belief that h is based, each member, r_j, of L is such that *either*

       (A)   there is a *nondefective* causal chain from H to r_j;

or   (B)   there is some event or state of affairs, Q, such that
          (i)   there is a *nondefective* causal chain from Q to r_j; and
         (ii)   there is a *nondefective* causal chain from Q to H;

or   (C)   there is some event or state of affairs, P, such that
          (i)   there is a *nondefective* causal chain from P to r_j; and
         (ii) P is a *nondefective* pseudo overdeterminant of H.

In the following pages I shall define the general distinction between defective and nondefective causal chains. I shall then define the notion of a nondefective pseudo overdeterminant, which is utilized in condition (C) above. These properties, as defined, will apply to any causal chains whatever, even to those not involved in the ancestry of a person's reason states. It should be noted, however, that condition (3d) requires only that the causal chains that are involved in the ancestry of one's reasons need be nondefective if one is to have primary knowledge. By considering examples I shall argue that the addition of (3d) to the original conditions in (IDPK) yields a fully adequate definition of primary knowledge.

Consider the vase example, one of the type covered by clause (A) of condition (3d). Where H is the state of affairs of there being a vase in the box, it is clear that there is a causal chain from H to Milton's local reason states. Because this causal chain is defective, Milton does not know that there is a vase in the box. In what respect is this causal chain defective? We may note that there are events in the causal chain from H to Milton's local reasons such that Milton would be epistemically justified in believing that these events had not occurred (or are not occurring). For example, there is the event of the televised image appearing on the screen. We can see, however, that this consideration could not be generalized to a sufficient condition for defectiveness by considering the following example.

Suppose the president of Harvard writes a letter to an old friend. The president has only recently learned how to type, and so she types the letter herself instead of having her secretary type it for her. Her friend receives the letter, reads it, and as a result comes to know all sorts of things about the president of Harvard. The president's friend does not know, however, that she has just learned how to type, and assumes justifiably that the letter was typed by the secretary. Then, there is an event in the causal chain leading to the friends having his reasons such that his believing that this event did not occur would be epistemically justified. But there is nothing defective about this causal chain with respect to his justification for believing what is said in the letter. It is, moreover, clear why this causal chain is not defective: the fact that the president's friend justifiably believes that the president did not type the letter is not at all *essential* to his justifiably believing what is said in the letter. In the vase example, however, the fact that Milton would be justified in believing that it is not a televised image he sees does seem essential to his justifiably believing that there is a vase in the box.

The previous chapter introduced a definition of defeasible justification. The difference between Milton's situation and that of the president's friend may be characterized in terms of this notion. Milton's belief is defeasibly justified, whereas the president's friend is indefeasibly justified in his belief. These cases also represent the distinction between defective and nondefective causal chains. Combining these considerations yields a partial definition of defectiveness for causal chains. In this formulation 'X' and 'Y' are variables for event names, and a solid arrow, '→', designates a causal chain. Thus, 'X → Y' will take as substituends names of causal chains from X to Y.

[213]

(IDDC) Where S justifiably believes that h on the basis of R, causal chain $X \rightarrow Y$ is defective with respect to this justified belief if: There is some occurrent event, U, in $X \rightarrow Y$ such that

    (i) S would be epistemically justified in believing (the false proposition) that U did not occur; and

    (ii) if (a) S had instead justifiably believed that U did occur and (b) for every other false proposition, q, such that S would be epistemically justified in believing q to be true, S had instead justifiably believed q to be false, and (c) S's epistemic situation had otherwise been the same except for some minimal set of changes given (a) and (b), *then* it is false that h would have been both epistemically justified and based upon essentially the same set of reasons as in R.[7]

These conditions constitute a partial definition because they represent only one way in which a causal chain can be defective. Let us see how this partial definition distinguishes the vase example from that involving the president of Harvard. In the vase example, the causal chain under consideration is the chain from the vase's being in the box to Milton's local reason states. As noted above, there is an event in this chain which satisfies condition (i) of (IDDC). According to the antecedent of condition (ii), we should ask what would have been the case if Milton had instead justifiably believed that there is a televised image of a vase on the surface of the box and had also believed to be false every other false proposition he would in fact be justified in believing to be true, assuming some minimal set of changes to bring that about. Presumably, another of the false propositions that Milton would (in actuality) be justified in believing to be true is the false proposition that the image of the vase which is in the box is not

7. Condition (ii) is adopted from the definition (DIJ) of indefeasible justification proposed on page 193 of Chapter Five. The concept that one set of reasons is essentially the same as another was defined thus:

(ESR) The set of reasons R' is essentially the same as the set of reason R with respect to a justified belief that h (by person S with relevant characteristics C) iff: some subset of R' is identical with the subset of R which results from the deletion from R of all members that are inessential to justifiably believing that h (for person S with relevant characteristics C).

being televised on the front of the box. Now suppose Milton had instead believed this to be false; this would be the same as his believing it to be true that the image of the vase in the box is being televised on the front of the box. If he had justifiably believed this to be true, and had also justifiably believed that the event of there being a televised image of a vase on the box was occurring, then it seems, Milton would have been epistemically justified in believing that there is a vase in the box. However, the set of reasons upon which this belief would have been justifiably based would not be essentially the same as those upon which his belief in this proposition is actually based (that is, the set R).[8] Hence, the consequent of condition (ii) would be satisfied along with the antecedent, and the causal chain involved in this example would qualify as defective.

In the example concerning the president of Harvard, however, (IDDC) does not yield the result that the causal chain involved is defective. Where U is the event of the president's typing the letter herself, even if the president's friend had justifiably believed that this event did not occur and also had justifiably believed to be false every other false proposition that he is in fact justified in believing to be true, he would still have essentially the same reasons for justifiably believing what is said in the letter. Hence, this causal chain does not qualify as defective in accordance with (IDDC). Our partial definition thus provides a way of distinguishing between these two kinds of examples.

(IDDC) does not, however, yield the desired result in the researcher example. Like the vase example, the researcher example is of the type covered by clause (A) of condition (3d). Where H is the state of affairs of chemical C's being present in the patient's brain, there is a causal chain from H to the researcher's having his local reasons for believing that this chemical is present. In this example, however, there is no specific event or state of affairs, U, in the causal chain $H \rightarrow L$ which renders it defective in accordance with the (sufficient) conditions suggested in (IDDC). Even taken as a single event, the entire chain $H \rightarrow L$ is not defective in accordance with (IDDC). Indeed, the causal

---

8. This example is similar in some respects to the revised Gettier case considered on pages 191–192 of Chapter Five.

chain is precisely what the researcher believes it to be (unlike the causal chain in the vase example). I want to say that the causal chain $H \rightarrow L$ in the researcher example is, nevertheless, a defective one, and so I shall need to expand my account of defectiveness.

In what respect is the causal chain leading to the researcher's local reasons defective? The account I shall give can be motivated as follows. If we consider all the actual and possible situations that are relevantly similar to the situation being considered, we can see that within that class of cases the proportion of cases in which a causal chain relevantly similar to $H \rightarrow L$ would obtain is exceedingly small. There are different ways in which a person relevantly similar to the researcher could be caused to have reasons relevantly similar to L; the two most salient ones are cases in which chemical C is present in the brain of the patient (the actual case) and cases in which the genetic defect is present (the usual case), but there are others as well. If one case were selected at random from among this total class of cases (actual and possible), it is unlikely that a case would be chosen in which chemical C is present in the patient's brain. Hence, even though $H \rightarrow L$ did occur, and even though the researcher's actual sample from among the total class of relevant cases has always consisted of similar cases, we may say that it is significantly unlikely that $H \rightarrow L$ should have occurred. These considerations will help us to characterize the defectiveness of $H \rightarrow L$.

Generally, when a causal chain occurs, alternative causal chains will be possible for some specific events or state of affairs in that causal chain. More precisely,

(CA) C^* is an alternative to causal chain $X \rightarrow Y$ with respect to Y if and only if

   (i) C^* is exactly like $X \rightarrow Y$ except that, for some event Z or set of events $\{Z_1, Z_2, \ldots, Z_n\}$, which is in $X \rightarrow Y$, there is instead some event Z^* or set of events $\{Z^*_1, Z^*_2, \ldots, Z^*_m\}$ in C^*; and

   (ii)   had C^* occurred instead of $X \rightarrow Y$, Y would still have occurred and would have been an effect in C^*.

In our example, if the patient had had the genetic defect instead of chemical C in his brain, then there would have occurred an alternative to the actual causal chain $H \rightarrow L$ which would still have resulted in the researcher's having his local reasons. The idea I want to develop is that *one* way in which a causal chain can be defective with respect to a justified belief's being an instance of knowledge is for there to be some significant alternative of this sort to that causal chain. Now we must ask, when is an alternative a significant one?

Not every alternative to a causal chain is significant with respect to a particular justified belief. For example, in the case in which the president of Harvard writes a letter to a friend, the actual causal chain from H to L contains the event of the president's typing the letter herself. One alternative to that causal chain is a causal chain in which the president has her secretary type the letter instead. But the mere fact that there is this alternative does not render $H \rightarrow L$ defective in that case. Another, more important consideration is this: in almost any situation in which there is a causal chain from some H to a person's local reasons, L, it will be possible that the person is hallucinating instead. To hallucinate, however, would mean merely that there is some causal chain occurring which is an alternative to the actual causal chain that results in L. Surely we do not want the mere possibility of hallucination to provide a significant alternative to a causal chain, thereby rendering that causal chain defective.

One consideration that is relevant to the distinction between significant and insignificant alternatives involves the conditions for defectiveness already proposed in (IDDC). In the researcher example, an obvious alternative to causal chain $H \rightarrow L$ is a causal chain in which H is replaced by the state of affairs of the patient's having the genetic defect. If this alternative had occurred, then although the researcher would have had the same local reasons, L, the causal chain leading to those reasons would have been defective in accordance with (IDDC); for there would then have been an event or state of affairs, U, in that causal chain (namely, the state of affairs of the presence of the genetic defect) such that conditions (i) and (ii) of (IDDC) would be satisfied. In the example involving the president of Harvard, however, this is not the case. Even if the alternative had occurred in which the secretary types the letter, the causal chain leading to the subject's reasons would not have been defective in accordance with (IDDC). Thus, the following expresses at least a necessary condition for significance of an alternative:

(IDS) C^* is a significant alternative to $X \to Y$ with respect to S's justifiably believing that h on the basis of R only if:
  (i) if C^* had occurred, then C^* would have been defective in accordance with conditions (i) and (ii) of (IDDC).

Although this necessary condition rules out the Harvard president example, it does not distinguish between the researcher example and examples involving the mere possibility of hallucination. In a case in which a person is hallucinating but not aware of doing so, it is clear that the causal chain leading to that person's local reasons is defective in accordance with (IDDC). Hence, in a normal case the possible alternative involving hallucination would satisfy the necessary condition (IDS) for significance.

We can attempt to distinguish between the researcher example and the hallucination example by referring to the *likelihood* of occurrence of the alternative in question.[9] In the researcher example, it seems likely that the researcher should have been examining a patient who has the genetic defect, and in the normal case it seems unlikely that a person is hallucinating. This might lead us to suppose that an alternative is a significant one provided that it satisfies the necessary condition in (IDS) and is also such that it is likely to have occurred. This suggestion has some merit, for it would allow us to distinguish between the researcher example and the hallucination example. But the demerits of this proposal outweigh its merits. For one thing, it is not clear how we are to understand the notion of likelihood. For another, even given the notion of likelihood it is not clear that the resulting account of significance would be adequate. To see this, we may consider yet another example, based upon one suggested by Alvin Goldman.[10] Henry is driving through the countryside and comes across a barn, which he sees from the front. He comes to believe that h,

9. The result would be a proposal I made in "Reasons, Causes, and Knowledge," *Journal of Philosophy*, 75 (1978): 229–249.

10. Alvin Goldman, "Discrimination and Perceptual Knowledge," *Journal of Philosophy* 73 (1976): 771–791, reprinted in Pappas and Swain, *Essays on Knowledge and Justification*.

there is a barn there, on the basis of his local and background reasons, and there is a straightforward causal chain from the barn's being there (*H*) to Henry's having his local reasons. So far this would appear to be a case of knowledge, assuming that Henry has appropriately justified background beliefs. But suppose someone has, unknown to Henry, constructed some barn facsimiles in the area. These are papier-mâché constructions that from the front look like the other barns in the area, but consist only of that facade propped up by sticks behind. If Henry had seen one of these facsimiles from the front, he would have come to believe that it is a barn and his reasons would have been the same. Hence, there are alternatives to the causal chain $H \rightarrow L$. Are these alternatives likely to have occurred? Is it likely that Henry should have seen a facsimile instead of a real barn? The answer depends upon more facts about the situation. If there are many barn facsimiles in the area through which Henry is driving, then it is likely that an alternative should have occurred. But if there are only a few facsimiles in the area, it seems unlikely that Henry should have been viewing a facsimile. In either case, however, the presence of facsimiles in the area renders it doubtful whether Henry's belief is an instance of knowledge. Consequently, it is doubtful whether likelihood of occurrence is a necessary (although it may be a sufficient) condition for significance of an alternative.

A more fruitful approach to defining the notion of significance involves consideration of what the subject is, or would be, epistemically justified in believing about the alternatives in question. In cases like the researcher example and the barn example, the subject is in a position to believe justifiably that a certain causal chain is occurring (has occurred, will occur).[11] Moreover, the subject is in a position to believe justifiably that this causal chain is occurring rather than one of the causal chains that would count as an alternative to it. In such cases, however, the circumstances are such that if the subject were to believe these things, then this belief would be defeasibly justified. Consider the researcher. As the example has been presented, there is no reason to suppose

11. The expression 'in a position' is intended to be understood in accordance with the notion introduced in Chapter Four with the expression '*S*'s believing that *h* on the basis of *R* *would be* epistemically justified'.

[219]

that the researcher actually has any beliefs about alternatives to the causal chain $H \to L$ which is resulting in his local reasons. For that matter, there is no reason to suppose that the researcher has any very precise belief about $H \to L$: in all probability the researcher would simply have inferred the presence of chemical C from the visible symptoms displayed by the patient. The researcher is surely in a position, however, to believe justifiably that $H \to L$ has occurred (is occurring). The researcher has reasons (including background reasons) such that this belief would be epistemically justified on the basis of those reasons. Similarly, the researcher would be epistemically justified in believing that $H \to L$ is occurring rather than some alternative to $H \to L$. But these possible beliefs would be defeasibly justified, because the researcher is also epistemically justified in believing the false proposition that the sample of patients whom he has examined is representative.

With this consideration in mind, I propose the following definition of a significant alternative:

(DS) C^* is a significant alternative to $X \to Y$ with respect to S's justifiably believing that h on the basis of R iff:
  (i) if C^* had occurred instead of $X \to Y$, then C^* would have been defective in accordance with conditions (i) and (ii) of (IDDC); and
  (ii) if S had believed that $X \to Y$ is occurring (did occur, will occur) rather than C^*, then this belief, if justified, would be defeasibly justified.

Taking the conditions in (IDDC) as one way in which a causal chain can be defective, I propose the following disjunctive set of conditions as a definition of defectiveness:

(DDC)Where S justifiably believes that h on the basis of R, causal chain $X \to Y$ is defective with respect to this justified belief iff:
  either (a) there is some event or state of affairs, U, in $X \to Y$ such that
      (i) S would be epistemically justified in believing that U did not occur; and

(ii)   it is essential to S's justifiably believing that h on the basis of R that S would be epistemically justified in believing that U did not occur;

or (b)   there is some significant alternative, C^*, to X → Y with respect to S's justifiably believing that h on the basis of R.

In the researcher example we get the result that the causal chain $H \rightarrow L$ is a defective causal chain by clause (b) of (DDC). As we have seen, there is an alternative to $H \rightarrow L$ (namely, a causal chain in which the patient has the genetic defect rather than chemical C in the brain) which is a significant one in accordance with (DS). Hence, $H \rightarrow L$ is defective, and by clause (3d) of (IDPK) we get the result that the researcher does not know that the patient has chemical C in the brain.

Our account does not, however, allow the mere possibility of hallucination to render a causal chain defective. In a normal situation, clause (i) of (DS) will be satisfied with respect to hallucinatory alternatives to the causal chain resulting in one's local reasons, but clause (ii) will not be satisfied. Sometimes, however, there is more than a mere possibility that one is hallucinating. If a person is under the influence of a hallucinatory drug, or if a person has an illness whose symptoms include hallucinations, then the person's belief that he or she is not hallucinating may, if justified, be defeasibly justified. If so, the person's epistemic situation is questionable and the appropriate result is the conclusion that he or she does not have knowledge.

The examples considered in this section are of the type covered by clause (A) of (3d), and all of them yield the appropriate result by (3d) that S does not know that h. I shall not provide examples illustrating the type of situation covered by clause (B) of (3d), for such examples can easily be supplied by the interested reader. We must now consider the situations covered by clause (C) of (3d), for that clause contains the as yet unexplicated notion of a nondefective pseudo overdeterminant.

Situations of the type covered by clause (C) of (3d) are those in which there is an event, P, that is a member of a causal chain resulting in S's having his local reasons, L, such that P is a pseudo overdeterminant instead of an actual cause of H. As in the situations covered by clauses (A) and (B), the causal chain beginning with P and ending with L must be nondefective. Our considerations here are more complicated because there is no actual causal chain occurring between P and H. To say that P is a pseudo overdeterminant of H is to say, roughly, that P would have been a cause of H had the causal chain that actually results in H not occurred.[12] Had the causal chain that results in H not occurred, then some other specific causal chain involving P would have occurred. Let us call this latter chain H^*. H^*, then, is an alternative to the actual causal chain, in the sense defined earlier. Generally, when one event, X, is a pseudo overdeterminant of another event, Y, there will be a nonactual causal chain from X to Y which is an alternative to the actual causal chain $Z \rightarrow Y$, where Z is an actual cause of Y. I shall designate this nonactual causal chain with a broken arrow, as in '$X - - \rightarrow Y$'. Then I shall introduce the following definition of defectiveness for pseudo overdeterminants:

(DDPO) For any events or states of affairs, X and Y, X is a defective pseudo overdeterminant of Y with respect to S's justifiably believing that h on the basis of R iff: if $X - - \rightarrow Y$ had occurred, then the causal chain $X \rightarrow Y$ would have been defective with respect to S's justifiably believing that h on the basis of R.

An example will show why, in cases of the sort covered by clause (C), we must require that P be a nondefective pseudo overdeterminant of H. Suppose I observe Mr. Dunfor taking what is clearly a fatal dose of a poison for which there is no known antidote. On the basis of this and my background reasons I come to believe that (h) he will soon die. Moreover, he soon does die, but unknown to me this is a result of his being run over by a truck. Normally we would say that I know he will die, even though he will not die of poisoning; had he not been run over by the truck, it is certain that he would have died as a result of taking the poison. It might be, however, that the taking of the poison is a

---

12. See definition (DPO) on page 70 of Chapter Two for a more precise characterization of this notion.

pseudo overdeterminant of his death in a way that has nothing to do with the fact that it is a poison. Thus, we might suppose that had Dunfor not been run over by a truck, then the poison would have been a cause of his death, but *not* by poisoning him in the usual fashion. Suppose an unusual chemical reaction between the poison and something Dunfor had eaten for lunch would have nullified the normal effect of the poison and would instead have caused Dunfor to go insane and commit suicide had he not been run over by the truck. Now, if *that* is what actually would have happened, I cannot be said to know that Dunfor will die, for my being justified in believing this depends essentially on my observation that it is a fatal dose of poison that Dunfor has imbibed. Even though the imbibing of this poison is in fact a pseudo overdeterminant of his death, my belief is defeasibly justified. Letting P be the event of Dunfor's taking the poison, and H be the event of his death, we can see that P is a defective pseudo overdeterminant of H in accordance with (DDPO). Given (C) of (3d), we get the correct result concerning knowledge.

This completes my causal account of primary knowledge. For convenience I shall display the entire definition at this point:

(DPK) A person, S, has primary factual knowledge that h at t iff:

    (1) h; and

    (2) S believes that h at t; and

    (3)   there is some set of reasons, R, such that

        (a) S's belief that h is based upon R at t; and

        (b) S's believing that h on the basis of R is epistemically justified at t; and

        (c)   if, at t, S has any other reasons, R', that are relevant to whether S is epistemically justified in believing that h, then S would be epistemically justified in believing that h on the basis of $R \cup R'$ at t; and

        (d)   for that subset, L, of R which consists of the local reasons upon which S's belief that h is based, each member, r_j, of L is such that

either

        (A)   there is a nondefective causal chain from H to r_j;

[223]

or (B) there is some event or state of affairs, Q, such that

    (i) there is a nondefective causal chain from Q to r_j; and

    (ii) there is a nondefective causal chain from Q to H;

or (C) there is some event or state of affairs, P, such that

    (i) there is a nondefective causal chain from P to r_j; and

    (ii) P is a nondefective pseudo overdeterminant of H.

The major remaining task is to give an account of secondary knowledge. Before turning to that, however, I want to discuss a particular kind of primary knowledge that has been of considerable interest to epistemologists.

4. Basic Knowledge

Suppose Sally is in pain and believes that she is in pain. Can we say Sally knows that she is in pain? Most of us would certainly allow that this is something Sally can know. Indeed, many philosophers have accorded knowledge of this sort a special status; they have said that knowledge of first-person reports of one's own phenomenal and other mental states is *basic* in some sense.[13] At a minimum, those who hold that such knowledge is basic seem to be claiming two distinct things.[14] First, there is a claim about the justificatory status of beliefs concerning one's current mental states. A strong version of this claim is that one cannot be mistaken about such states, and that beliefs about one's current mental states are therefore *incorrigibly* justified. But,

13. For a useful discussion of this notion, see Mark Pastin, "Modest Foundationalism and Self-Warrant," *American Philosophical Quarterly,* Monograph Series 9 (1975), pp. 141–149, reprinted in Pappas and Swain, *Essays on Knowledge and Justification.*

14. These two theses are distinguished clearly by David Annis in "Epistemic Foundationalism," *Philosophical Studies* 31 (1976): 345–352.

there are weaker versions as well. For example, one might claim that beliefs about one's current mental states are initially justified independently of whatever else one justifiably believes; this version is compatible with the additional claim that such a belief *can* be defectively justified, whereas the strong version is not. Second, the claim that such knowledge is basic usually involves a claim about dependence among knowledge states. A strong version of this claim would be that all knowledge is either basic or ultimately dependent only upon basic knowledge. There are weaker versions of this claim as well, such as that all knowledge either is basic or is dependent upon at least some basic knowledge (but not *only* upon basic knowledge).

The view that I suggest combines a fairly strong version of the justificatory status claim with a very weak version of the dependency claim. I suggest that *some* of our beliefs about our current mental states are nondefectively justified in a very strong sense, but that not all of our nonbasic knowledge, whether primary or secondary, is dependent upon basic knowledge. I shall discuss the first of these claims in this section; in the next section I shall introduce some considerations relevant to the second claim.

Returning to Sally and her pain, let us grant that Sally justifiably believes that she is in pain. Section 8 of Chapter Four introduced a distinction between beliefs that are belief-independently justified and beliefs that are belief-dependently justified. This distinction was suggested as the PR model version of the traditional distinction between beliefs that are evidentially basic and those that are evidentially nonbasic, but we noted that the traditional class of evidentially basic beliefs is considerably narrower than the class of beliefs which is belief-independently justified. The example involving Sally was used there as an example of belief-independently justified belief. I now want to suggest that Sally's belief that she is in pain may have a much stronger justificatory status as well, and that if it does, then her *knowledge* that she is in pain will qualify as basic.

It is clear that Sally's being in pain is a specific event or state of affairs and that if Sally is to know she is in pain her knowledge will be an instance of primary knowledge. If so, then in accordance with my definition there must be some set of reasons upon which Sally's belief that she is in pain is based, and there must be an appropriate nondefective causal ancestry of her local reasons for this belief. The causal situation is of the type covered by clause (B) of (3d). I submit that the local reason for which Sally believes that she is in pain is the very state of her being in pain. Where h is the proposition that she is in pain, and L is her local reason for believing that h, L and H are *one and the same state of affairs.* Clause (B) of (3d) tells us that there must be an event or state of affairs, Q, such that there is a nondefective causal chain from Q to H and also a nondefective causal chain from Q to L. Let Q be whatever is causing Sally to be in pain (Sally need not know what Q is). Then, in this situation, the causal chain from Q to H and the causal chain from Q to L are one and the same. Moreover, this causal chain is nondefective with respect to Sally's justifiably believing that she is in pain. Furthermore, I want to make the stronger claim that this causal chain *could not be* defective, and that in this sense Sally's believing that she is in pain is incorrigibly justified. Let me expand on this controversial suggestion.

Suppose Sally is in pain because there is a pin stuck in her leg (Q). There is a causal chain from Q to her being in pain. Could this causal chain be defective? I suggest that it could not be defective, because as long as Sally is in pain and justifiably believes that she is in pain, it does not really matter how she *came to be* in pain. Even if the causal chain from Q to her being in pain is incredibly bizarre, she still knows she is in pain. And no matter what alternative causal chains might have resulted in her being in pain, she still knows that she is in pain. With respect to Sally's knowing that she is in pain, every possible causal chain (including the actual one) leading to her local reasons is nondefective. Whenever the situation is as it is with Sally in this example, I shall say that we have an instance of *basic primary knowledge*.

When I say that some of our primary knowledge is basic and that these are instances of incorrigibly justified belief (in the sense above), I do not mean to say that any given person is always or even ever incorrigibly justified in believing propositions about current mental states. Suppose Sally gets easily confused between pain and tickling; then, Sally might *not* know she is in pain. Suppose her belief is more complicated, and she believes her pain to be pin-stab pain. Then, even if her belief is justified, the causal chain involved might very well be defective. I am claining only that *some* of our justified beliefs about *some* of our current mental states *can* be instances of basic primary knowledge.

5. *Secondary Knowledge*

For heuristic purposes, I opened this chapter by suggesting a rough distinction between primary and secondary knowledge in terms of the kinds of propositions known and what those propositions designate. I also noted that this way of drawing the distinction is ultimately hopeless. The terms 'primary' and 'secondary' are intended to suggest that some instances of knowledge (the secondary ones) are dependent upon others (the primary ones). The total body of of a person's knowledge at a given time forms a structure that is ordered by these dependency relations. In suggesting that knowledge forms a structure based upon dependency relations, I am in the company of most other epistemologists. The dependency relations that hold among instances of primary knowledge and secondary knowledge yield a structure that is reminiscent of the foundational view. Indeed, some readers of this essay will perhaps classify my account as a foundational one. I have no objection to that, so long as it is clear that there are significant differences between my view and those that traditionally have been defended by foundationalists.

According to the account of primary knowledge presented in earlier sections of this chapter, primary knowledge is dependent upon the existence of a direct causal connection of an appropriate sort between the event or state of affairs designated by the known proposition and the reasons upon which the belief in question is justifiably based. According to the traditional empiricist versions of foundationalism, a given corpus of knowledge has a foundation consisting in known propositions that are located at the experiential level. This foundation may be restricted to basic knowledge of the sort characterized in the preceding section, or it may encompass a broader class of experiential knowledge, depending upon the form of foundationalism involved. On the view that I suggest, if knowledge can be said to have a foundation, this foundation consists of propositions that are primarily known. As is evident from the examples considered in my discussion of primary knowledge, the scope of primary knowledge is considerably broader than the realm of the experiential, at least as conceived by most traditional foundationalists. One can have primary knowledge not only that one is in pain or is appeared to in a certain fashion, but also that there is a vase in a certain box or that a particular event happened ten years ago. The traditional foundationalists would argue that the latter instances of knowledge lie outside the foundation of knowledge. It might be suggested that within the realm of what I call primary knowledge there is a discernible structure based upon dependency relations. Perhaps, for example, some instances of primary knowledge (such as the knowledge that there is a yellow cup on my desk) are dependent upon other instances of primary knowledge (such as the knowledge that I seem to see a cup on my desk). I do not want to argue that no instances of primary knowledge are dependent upon others, for in fact it seems that some are. My theory, however, is not committed to the kind of dependency structure traditionally associated with foundationalism. Neither my account of epistemically justified belief nor my account of primary knowledge requires (for example) that one can know that there is a yellow cup on the desk only if one has some even more basic knowledge.

Another respect in which my view differs from many traditional foundational views has to do with the notion of dependency which is involved in the claim that some instances of knowledge are dependent upon others. Many traditional foundationalists employ a very strong but natural notion of dependency. According to this notion, to say that one instance of knowledge is dependent upon another is to say that one would not have the former if one did not have the latter (all else remaining the same). A structural view that is naturally associated with this conception of dependency is the 'building block' view. According to this view, knowledge has a foundation, the items of which do not depend upon other instances of knowledge. Further instances of knowledge are dependent only upon items in the foundation. Still further instances are independent upon items in the foundation along with those that are dependent only upon the foundation, and so forth. Take away the foundation, and the whole structure falls; take away the items on a given level, and all items above that level fall. Although this kind of structural view has an appealing simplicity and clarity, it bears little relation to the one I suggest. The concept of dependency that I employ in claiming that instances of secondary knowledge are (ultimately) dependent upon instances of primary knowledge is considerably weaker than the notion described above. Moreover, the structural view that I defend is not the building block variety; rather, the structure resembles a web (to borrow a familiar metaphor) in which many items are *inter*connected in such a way that no item of knowledge need be essentially dependent upon any other specific item of knowledge. The web metaphor is often used by nonfoundationalists (particularly coherentists). The view that I suggest does have certain affinities with nonfoundational accounts, but I would require that the web of knowledge be firmly pinned to the actual world at the level of primary knowledge. It is time, however, to stop speaking in metaphors and turn to the details of my account.

I have claimed in (6.2) above that instances of secondary knowledge are ultimately dependent upon at least some instances of primary knowledge. The dependency involved is not the strong kind discussed in the preceding paragraph. On my account of knowledge, every instance of knowledge is an instance of belief. Moreover, in accordance with the general defeasibility account given in Chapter Five, every instance of belief which is an instance of knowledge is based upon some set of reason states, R, and the belief is indefeasibly justified on the basis of those reasons. Such a belief may, however, also be based upon some other set of reasons, R^*, and may be indefeasibly justified on the basis of those reasons as well. Indeed, a given belief may be based upon many different sets of reasons; my account of knowledge requires only that at least one of these sets of reasons be such that the definition (DKD) is satisfied. Similarly, the definition (DPK) of primary knowledge presented earlier in this chapter requires only that there be *some* set of reasons, R, which satisfies the conditions given. It is compatible with (DPK) that the belief involved also be based upon any number of other sets of reasons. Moreover, my account of primary knowledge requires that at least one set of reasons upon which a belief that h is based be causally connected in an appropriate fashion with the event or state of affairs designated by 'h' if that belief is to be an instance of primary knowledge. Note, however, that this account does not require that *every* set of reasons upon which the belief that h is based must be so causally connected in order that one have primary knowledge. Nor does this account require, of any specific set of reasons, that it be the set of reasons which is causally connected with the event or state of affairs known. The account requires only that some set of reasons be thus causally connected with H. In this sense and this sense only, primary knowledge is dependent upon the existence of an appropriate causal connection [see (6.3) above]. In this same sense, I suggest, secondary knowledge is dependent upon primary knowledge and ultimately dependent upon the character of the causal ancestry of some primary knowledge.

Suppose S knows that h, and this is an instance of (the as-yet-undefined notion of) secondary knowledge. As with any instance of knowledge, this will be an instance of reason-based belief. In accordance with the general approach to defining knowledge adopted in this book, S's belief that h must be based upon some set of reasons, R, and this set of reasons must be such that S's believing that h on the basis of R is indefeasibly justified. As noted in the previous paragraph, however, this belief may be thus based upon any number of different sets of reasons; as long as one such set satisfies the conditions for knowledge, the subject knows. On the view that I suggest, this instance of knowledge will be an instance of *secondary* knowledge only if at least one such set of reasons is *also* a set of reasons which essentially contains some beliefs that are instances of primary knowledge. I do not require that all sets of reasons upon which the belief may be based contain instances of primary knowledge, nor do I require that any particular instance of primary knowledge be contained in a set of reasons upon which the belief is based. I require only, as a necessary condition for secondary knowledge, that at least one source of indefeasible justification for the belief in question be pinned to the realm of primary knowledge. In this sense and this sense only, secondary knowledge is dependent upon primary knowledge.

Having suggested the sense in which secondary knowledge is dependent upon primary knowledge, I shall introduce a definition of secondary knowledge and then consider a variety of examples in illustration of this definition; this discussion will also illustrate the dependency claims introduced above and in Section 1 of this chapter. The definition of secondary knowledge is this:

(DSK) A person, S, has secondary knowledge that h at t iff:
  (1) h; and
  (2) S believes that h at t; and
  (3) there is some set of reasons, R, such that
    (a) S's belief that h is based upon R at t; and
    (b) S's believing that h on the basis of R is indefeasibly justified at t; and
    (c) if, at t, S has any other reasons, R', that are relevant to whether S is epistemically justified in believing that h, then S would be epistemically justified in believing that h on the basis of $R \cup R'$ at t; and
    (d) some (proper or improper) subset, B, of R is such that:
      (i) every member of B is an instance of primary knowledge; and
      (ii) the set consisting of $R - B$ would not be a set of reasons upon which S's belief that h would be indefeasibly justified; and
  (4) there is no set of reasons, R^*, such that the conditions of (DPK) are satisfied for S, h, and R^* [that is, S does not have primary knowledge that h at t].

Conditions (1), (2), and (3a–c) are essentially the same as the conditions of (DKD) suggested in Chapter Five. The satisfaction of those conditions guarantees that S has knowledge. Condition (4) simply stipulates that S's knowledge is not primary.[15] The pivotal condition is thus (3d); it is this condition that distinguishes *secondary* knowledge from knowledge in general. Let us now consider some examples of secondary knowledge to see how this definition works.

15. It is necessary to include this, for otherwise it is possible that an instance of knowledge could satisfy *both* the definitions of primary and secondary knowledge. Any such instance, therefore, will count only as primary knowledge.

I claim to know that all whales are mammals. This unrestricted universal generalization does not designate a causally efficacious, spatiotemporally located event or state of affairs; thus, my knowledge will have to be secondary [see (6.7) above]. What might be my reasons for believing that all whales are mammals? Different persons will have different reasons, and a given person may have several sets of reasons for believing such a proposition. I might believe that all whales are mammals because my crystal ball says so or simply because I feel like believing it (that *is* a reason). But unless my crystal ball is known by me to be a special one, or unless my internal promptings are special, believing for these sorts of reasons would not be justified. The more standard sorts of reasons for believing that all whales are mammals include beliefs arrived at by observations of many different whales and their mammalian characteristics, or beliefs arrived at by hearing it said by an appropriate authority or by figuring it out from a definition of mammalhood plus a detailed description of whale characteristics. When we believe that all whales are mammals on the basis of these sorts of reasons, we take our beliefs to be epistemically justified. According to definition (DSK), if my belief that all whales are mammals is to be an instance of secondary knowledge, then at least one set of reasons, R, upon which this belief is based and upon which the belief is indefeasibly justified must contain a subset, B, consisting of beliefs that are instances of primary knowledge, and the set $R - B$ must be such that believing that all whales are mammals on the basis of that set would not be indefeasibly justified.

Suppose my belief that all whales are mammals is based upon only the following set of reasons: I have read in a textbook that all whales are mammals, and I know that the author of this textbook is a respected biologist and that textbooks written by authorities are generally reliable. On the basis of my reading the textbook I come to believe that the textbook states that all whales are mammals; let this be the belief b_1. Let the belief that the author of this textbook is a respected authority be the belief b_2, and let the belief that textbooks written by authorities are generally reliable be the belief b_3. On the basis of these beliefs I come to believe that all whales are mammals. My set of reasons, R, thus consists of beliefs b_1, b_2, and b_3, along with whatever reasons these beliefs are in turn based upon. Suppose, moreover, that my characteristics are such that my believing that all whales are mammals on the basis of R is epistemically justified. Now consider belief b_1, the belief that the textbook states that all whales are mammals. This belief either will or will not be an instance of primary knowledge. If it is an instance of primary knowledge, then condition (3d) of (DSK) is satisfied (letting B be the unit set of the belief b_1). Assuming the other conditions of (DSK) to be satisfied, I have secondary knowledge, and this result seems appropriate. On the other hand, if belief b_1 is not an instance of primary knowledge, then we must ask, why not? Some possible explanations are excluded by the set-up. If b_1 is not an instance of primary knowledge, this cannot be due to the fact that b_1 is not epistemically justified on the basis of some reasons, for this supposition would contradict our assumption that my belief that all whales are mammals is epistemically justified on the basis of R [see (DEJ), Chapter Four]. Similarly, the explanation cannot lie in b_1's being false, for we have supposed it to be true. Thus, b_1's not being an instance of primary knowledge will be due either to the fact that the nondefective causal connection requirement is not satisfied or (implausibly) to the fact that b_1 is an instance of *secondary* knowledge. If the former is the explanation, then condition (3b) of (DSK) is not satisfied and I do not know that all whales are mammals, a result that seems appropriate. If the latter is the explanation, then I would argue that b_1 must itself satisfy the conditions of (DSK). If it does, then b_1 will be based upon some set of reasons which satisfies condition (3d) of (DSK), and because my belief that all whales are mammals is in turn based upon b_1, whatever primary knowledge b_1 is based upon will also be primary knowledge upon which my general belief that all whales are mammals is based. Hence, R will satisfy condition (3d), and assuming the other conditions of (DSK) to be satisfied, my belief that all whales are mammals is an instance of secondary knowledge. On the assumption that R is the only set of reasons upon which my belief that all whales are mammals is based, these considerations provide some support for my claim that beliefs that are instances of secondary knowledge must be based upon some instance of primary knowledge.

Suppose, however, my belief that all whales are mammals is

based upon another set of reasons. Suppose I believe correctly that biologists define a mammal as any organism that has characteristics M; let this belief be the belief b_4. I also believe correctly that all whales have the characteristics M; let this be the belief b_5. Then suppose my belief that all whales are mammals is based upon beliefs b_4 and b_5. Even if these beliefs are instances of knowledge, they are not instances of primary knowledge, for the propositions believed do not designate causally efficacious, spatiotemporally located events or states of affairs. And yet I certainly can know that all whales are mammals on the basis of this set of reasons. It might appear that this is a case in which I have secondary knowledge but in which condition (3d) of my definition is not satisfied. Contrary to appearances, however, this case does not present any problems for (DSK). The set of reasons, R, is the set $[b_4, b_5]$. It is true that no subset of this set R satisfies (3d), for neither b_4 nor b_5 is an instance of primary knowledge. But if my belief that all whales are mammals is to be indefeasibly justified on the basis of this set of reasons, as is required by condition (3b), then beliefs b_4 and b_5 must each be epistemically justified. According to our definition of epistemic justification (DEJ) in Chapter Four, these beliefs must be justifiably based upon some additional reasons R_{b4} and R_{b5}. Upon what sorts of reason states could b_4 and b_5 be thus justifiably based? I submit that these beliefs could be epistemically justified only on the basis of further beliefs, and that these beliefs will include some instances of primary knowledge. If so, then, by the definition of the basing relation (DB) presented in Chapter Three, my belief that all whales are mammals will also be based upon these instances of primary knowledge; that is, my belief that all whales are mammals will be based not only upon the set R, but *also* upon the set R', which is $\{b_4, b_5, R_{b4}, R_{b5}\}$. The set R' contains a subset, B, consisting of instances of primary knowledge, and the set $R' - B$ would *not* be a set of reasons upon which my belief that all whales are mammals would be indefeasibly justified. The members of B are the basis for my justifiably believing b_4 and b_5, and these members must be so justified if I am to believe justifiably on their basis that all whales are mammals. Consequently, although the set of reasons R does not satisfy condition (3) of (DSK), there is a set of reasons, R', which does satisfy that condition. This is all that is required for secondary knowledge, assuming, of course, that (1), (2), and (4) of (DSK) are also satisfied. This argument rests upon my assumption that beliefs b_4 and b_5 could be epistemically justified only on the basis of further beliefs, some of which are instances of primary knowledge. Careful consideration of the example leads me to believe that this assumption is correct, but I do not know how to prove that it is correct.

In this example of secondary knowledge wherein the proposition known is an unrestricted universal generalization, I have argued that knowledge of such propositions is ultimately dependent upon some instance or instances of primary knowledge. I chose the example involving the proposition that all whales are mammals because this proposition is of the type that is sometimes said to be true by definition. Some philosophers will say that knowledge of such propositions is, in some sense, independent of the need for justification in experience. It has never been very clear to me what such philosophers have in mind. Perhaps they mean that one can have knowledge of such propositions if one knows the relevant definitions, knows them to be definitions, and that one need not also have engaged in empirical investigation of, say, whales. If this is what is meant, then there is no conflict between my account of the dependency of secondary upon primary knowledge and what these philosophers want to say. I do not require that one must have primary knowledge about any specific whales in order to have secondary knowledge that all whales are mammals. Moreover, my account allows that one can know that all whales are mammals *if* one knows the relevant definitions. It does require, however, that ultimately, somewhere in the structure of one's reason-based justifications, there will be instances of primary knowledge. Perhaps this will be found somewhere in the basis of one's justified belief that a mammal is defined as an organism with characteristics M; or perhaps it will be found somewhere in the basis of one's beliefs that whales are organisms that have those characteristics. Given the multitude of ways in which we can come to have beliefs about general features of the world around us, it would be folly to require any specific kind of primary knowledge to be the basis of general knowledge. I have argued, however, that some primary knowledge is thus required.

From the point of view of the structure of epistemic dependency, I do not draw any sharp distinction between secondary knowledge of propostions such as the one that all whales are mammals and secondary knowledge of propositions such as the one that everything either has or does not have the property *P*. The proposition known in this instance is a logical truth, and many philosophers have wanted to accord a special status to knowledge of such propositions. As with definitional truths, it has been claimed that one can know logical truths independently of the need for justification in experience. I do not want to deny that we have knowledge of logical truths or that we can have this knowledge independently of any need for empirical investigation of instances of the truth in question. Let '*l*' designate our logical truth above. Then, if a person, *S*, is to have knowledge that *l*, *S* must believe that *l* on the basis of some set of reasons, *R*. These reasons may range from the crystal ball variety to something much more sophisticated, such as authoritative testimony or reasoning. In any case in which such a belief is justifiably based upon reasons, these reasons will, I submit, contain essentially some beliefs that are instances of primary knowledge. These instances of primary knowledge need not be beliefs that would count as evidence for *l*; they may be beliefs that form the basis for beliefs about what certain words and phrases mean ('property', 'having a property', 'everything'). These instances of primary knowledge may be beliefs that would be taken as evidence, such as the belief that a proof appears on a certain page in a certain logic book. But whether the primary knowledge involved is evidential or not, my account requires that even knowledge of logical truths is (in my sense) dependent upon primary knowledge.

Some philosophers will object to this on the grounds that at least some persons are sometimes in a position to 'grasp intuitively' the meaning of logical truths or to 'see intuitively' that the proposition in question is true. If so, then the only reason state upon which a belief in a logical truth need be based is the state of intuitively grasping or intuitively seeing that the proposition is true. That is all you need for knowledge. Although I cannot prove that no person is ever in such a position, I find the notions of intuitively grasping the meaning of a logical truth and of intuitively seeing that such a proposition is true to be too vague a metaphor; and I know of no philosophical discussion of such states that goes beyond that level. If those who speak of such states as sufficient for knowledge are speaking of anything at all, they are, I submit, speaking of *belief* states. And if this is what they are speaking of, then what they say can be accommodated in my account of secondary knowledge.

In addition to general knowledge of the sort discussed so far, there are other kinds of general knowledge which fit more obviously into the framework of my account. For example, we have knowledge of various restricted generalizations, such as the generalization that all the buildings in Manhattan were constructed after 1400. We also have knowledge of statistical generalizations, such as the generalization that slightly more than half the human babies born are females. In addition, we have knowledge of unrestricted contingent generalizations that are not definitional truths, such as the generalization that all human beings are larger than electrons or the generalization that no mosquitoes are larger than the planet Jupiter. For each of these, I do not believe it necessary to argue at length that the secondary knowledge we have is dependent upon some instances of primary knowledge.

I turn now from general knowledge to other kinds of secondary knowledge. In the opening section of this chapter I suggested an example involving two comets and suggested that this example illustrates the claim made in (6.6) that some propositions that designate only causally efficacious, spatiotemporally located events or states of affairs may be objects of secondary knowledge. In this example, I have supposed that S's knowledge that comet B will be visible from the earth five years hence does not satisfy the definition of *primary* knowledge. S's belief that comet B will be visible in five years is based upon his belief that comet A is now visible and upon his belief that whenever comet A is visible, then comet B is visible five years later. But, I have supposed, there is no appropriate causal connection between the future event of comet B's being visible from the earth and S's having his local reasons. Assuming this to be correct, we can now see that S's belief that comet B will be visible qualifies as an instance of *secondary* knowledge, for it is justifiably based upon a set of reasons which includes the belief that comet A is now visible and which would not be justified without this belief (all else being equal). Moreover, the belief that comet A is now visible is a clear instance of primary knowledge. Hence, the definition (DSK) gives us the result that S's knowledge that comet B will be visible is an instance of secondary knowledge.

Let us now consider a well-known example suggested by Edmund Gettier.[16] Suppose Smith believes that either Jones owns a Ford or Brown is in Barcelona. This belief is based upon the following reasons: Jones has presented Smith with evidence that he (Jones) owns a Ford, Smith has seen Jones driving a Ford, and Jones is known by Smith to be very reliable. On the basis of the various beliefs involved, Smith believes that Jones owns a Ford. From this Smith deduces that either Jones owns a Ford *or* Brown is in Barcelona, even though he has absolutely no idea where Brown is. It so happens that Brown is in Barcelona but Jones's Ford has just been repossessed. Hence, the disjunctive proposition believed by Smith is true, but even though Smith's belief is epistemically justified, it is clear that he does not know the disjunction in question. This is the result obtained on the general defeasibility analysis of knowledge suggested in Chapter Five. In the present context, however, we must ask whether this kind of example qualifies as primary knowledge or as secondary knowledge. In order to designate this case as an instance of primary knowledge, we would have to say that the disjunctive proposition involved designates some causally efficacious, spatiotemporally located event or state of affairs. If we could say this, then our account of primary knowledge would give us the result that Smith does not have knowledge because the causal connection requirement would not be satisfied. It is at least odd, however, to say that this disjunctive proposition designates some causally efficacious, spatiotemporally located event or state of affairs. Happily, we can avoid having to say this if we assign such examples to the realm of secondary knowledge. For, Smith's belief that either Jones owns a Ford or Brown is in Barcelona is based upon a set of reasons, R, which fails to satisfy condition (3d), and hence condition (3b), of definition (DSK). If we treat this case as one of

16. Edmund Gettier, "Is Justified True Belief Knowledge?", *Analysis* 23 (1963): 121–123, reprinted in Michael Roth and Leon Galis, eds., *Knowing: Essays in the Analysis of Knowledge* (New York: Random House, 1970).

secondary rather than primary knowledge, then we can explain the fact that Smith does *not* know by reference to the fact that the primary knowledge he needs (namely, the knowledge that Jones owns a Ford) is lacking. On the other hand, suppose it were true that Jones does own a Ford. Then, our conditions for secondary knowledge would give us the correct result that Smith does know, for in that case Smith's belief that Jones owns a Ford would be an instance of primary knowledge, and the conditions of (DSK) would be satisfied. Indeed, such a case would be an excellent illustration of the claim that instances of secondary knowledge are dependent upon some instances of primary knowledge.

Finally, I want to consider negative knowledge, or knowledge of negative propositions. I would claim to know, for example, that the chair in my study is not green. Is this an instance of primary knowledge or of secondary knowledge? If we say it is an instance of primary knowledge, then we shall have to say that the state of affairs of the chair's not being green is a causally efficacious, spatiotemporally located state of affairs, and there will have to be an appropriate nondefective causal connection between that state of affairs and my local reasons for believing that the chair is not green. This would present no special problem were it not that this state of affairs is a somewhat dubious candidate for the causal role required of it by our account of primary knowledge. The state of affairs in question is a *negative* state of affairs, and many philosophers have found such states of affairs to be unacceptable additions to our ontology. I shall not argue for a position on this long-standing problem, although I agree with those who find negative states of affairs ontologically peculiar. As in the earlier example, we can avoid having to countenance such states if we treat negative knowledge of this type as secondary. In the case at hand, my belief that the chair is not green is based upon my belief that the chair is black and also upon my general belief (an instance of secondary knowledge) that being black excludes being green. Moreover, my belief that the chair is black is, we may suppose, an instance of primary knowledge. Assuming the other conditions of (DSK) to be satisfied, the example qualifies in an unproblematic fashion as secondary knowledge. If we treat such examples in this fashion, we need not say that the state of affairs of the chair's not being green is a state of affairs that obtains. Rather, we may (if we wish) say that it is a possible state of affairs which fails to obtain and that we know it fails to obtain because we have primary knowledge of some other state of affairs which precludes it.

Other examples of negative knowledge may also be treated as cases of secondary knowledge. For example, I claim to know that there are no elephants in my study at this time. Such knowledge would be accounted for in the way in which restricted generalizations are: my negative knowledge may be taken to be knowledge that all the items in my study are nonelephants. Presumably this knowledge will be based upon some instances of primary knowledge.

With these examples, I conclude my discussion of secondary knowledge.

6. *Summary and Concluding Remarks*

In this chapter I have attempted to distinguish between primary knowledge and secondary knowledge. I have argued that primary knowledge is dependent upon the character and quality of the causal ancestries of various of our reason states, and that secondary knowledge is dependent upon primary knowledge. The account presented is therefore a causal account of knowledge, an account in which the causal origins of reasons and beliefs play a prominent role. It is also a defeasibility theory, as presented in the previous chapter. For any purported instance of knowledge we must first ask, is it an instance of indefeasibly justified belief? If it is, then it is knowledge; if not, not. We may then ask, is it an instance of primary knowledge? For the answer we look to our definition of that notion. If it is not an instance of primary knowledge, then it will be an instance of secondary knowledge and will be dependent upon some primary knowledge. This provides a structure for human knowledge which is not artificial or unrealistic. It is my hope that the structural picture that results from my account is also the one that is to be found in our knowledge of the world around us.

INDEX

REASONS AND
KNOWLEDGE

Designed by Richard E. Rosenbaum.
Composed by The Composing Room of Michigan, Inc.
in 10 point Times Roman V.I.P., 2 points leaded.
with display lines in Times Roman.
Printed offset by Thomson/Shore, Inc. on
Warren's Number 66 Antique Offset, 50 pound basis.
Bound by John H. Dekker & Sons, Inc.
in Holliston book cloth.